LINGUISTIC FINGERPRINTS

HOW LANGUAGE CREATES
AND REVEALS IDENTITY

ROGER KREUZ

Prometheus Books
Guilford, Connecticut

Prometheus Books

An imprint of Globe Pequot, the trade division of
The Rowman & Littlefield Publishing Group, Inc.
4501 Forbes Blvd., Ste. 200
Lanham, MD 20706
www.rowman.com

Distributed by NATIONAL BOOK NETWORK

British Library Cataloguing in Publication Information Available

Library of Congress Cataloging-in-Publication Data Available

ISBN 978-1-63388-897-5 (cloth) | ISBN 978-1-63388-898-2 (ebook)

∞™ The paper used in this publication meets the minimum requirements of
American National Standard for Information Sciences—Permanence of Paper for
Printed Library Materials, ANSI/NISO Z39.48-1992

He that has eyes to see and ears to hear may convince himself that no mortal can keep a secret. If his lips are silent, he chatters with his fingertips; betrayal oozes out of him at every pore.

—Sigmund Freud, *Introductory Lectures on Psychoanalysis* (1916–1917)

You know my method. It is founded upon the observation of trifles.

—Arthur Conan Doyle, *The Boscombe Valley Mystery* (1891)

To Phil and Andy, who had faith

Contents

Prologue		ix
Acknowledgments		xiii
1	A Language of One's Own?	1
2	Beginnings	19
3	Who? Anonymous and Concealed Authorship	41
4	Which? Tales of Disputed Authorship	63
5	It's a Crime! A Forensic Linguistics Casebook	89
6	Fake! Forgeries and Misattributions	109
7	Oops! Misses and False Positives	131
8	Ghost Stories: A Voice of One's Own?	153
Epilogue		171
Notes		173
Bibliography		203
Index		231
About the Author		241

Prologue

Have you spent much time thinking about stylometry? The odds are good that you've never heard of this term, even though you've probably engaged in some armchair stylometry without realizing it. Perhaps you've received an email from a foreign prince in desperate need of assistance. You may have been promised a handsome reward if you could help him transfer his large fortune from one country to another. Instead of springing into action to assist, you probably decided the message was spam and consigned it to the trash, as the proposal seemed too good to be true. But perhaps you also noticed misspelled words or odd phrasing—mistakes that a wealthy prince would be unlikely to make. Or perhaps the general tone was overly elaborate or strangely informal. By putting these clues together, you decided that the sender was not who they claimed to be.

Identifying a bogus email pitch is a fairly trivial example of how we make attributions about the authors of texts. There are, however, many other situations in which figuring out who wrote something is more consequential. Consider the glowing product reviews that you might encounter on a website like Amazon. Were they written by satisfied customers, or were they the work of scammers promoting a counterfeit product? Did a student write their own term paper, or was it plagiarized from an online source? And who is the person or people behind the online messages attributed to Q—the figure at the heart of the QAnon movement?[1] Stylometry can provide answers to questions like these.

Stylometric techniques can be used to exonerate as well as to identify. In 2014, for example, *Newsweek* claimed to have unmasked the creator of Bitcoin, a shadowy figure known only by the pseudonym Satoshi Nakamoto. A writer for the magazine claimed that Nakamoto was a computer engineer living in California, although when confronted, the man protested that he had never even heard of this type of cryptocurrency.[2] Matthew Herper, a staffer at *Forbes*, arranged to have a stylometric analysis performed on social media posts by

Newsweek's suspect. The results suggested that the individual who had been hounded by the news magazine was not, in fact, the creator of Bitcoin.[3]

Stylometry can be defined as the quantitative analysis of the features of written texts. This term was first used at the end of the nineteenth century by the Polish philosopher Wincenty Lutosławski (1863–1954). He had set himself the task of arranging Plato's 35 Socratic dialogues in their order of composition. The idea was not a new one: Conrad Ritter had attempted something similar, albeit on a smaller scale, about a decade earlier. Based on his study of these philosophical texts, Ritter proposed that stylistic features could be used to divide the dialogues into early, middle, or late compositions by Plato.

But whereas Ritter made use of 40 such features, Lutosławski identified some 500 textual "peculiarities," as he referred to them.[4] For Lutosławski, a feature might be the use of a particular idiom, metaphor, or distinctive turn of phrase, and he used these "stylistic affinities" to construct a chronology for the dialogues. His procedure, however, has been criticized as arbitrary and unreliable.[5] And Lutosławski didn't attempt to refine or extend it. He conducted the study of Plato early in his career and then moved on to other interests. It was not until the mid-twentieth century that the term "stylometry" began to be used in its modern sense.

The purpose of this book is to provide the reader with an overview of stylometry: where the idea came from, what it has accomplished, and where it is headed. Chapter 1 makes the case that people have distinctive ways of using language. This is most obvious in the way they speak, although the same is true for written language as well. A person's speech and writing tell the story of where they grew up, their age and gender, and even whether their speech is considered "genuine" by others. The rest of the book builds on this idea and addresses whether a person's linguistic idiosyncrasies are distinctive enough to reveal their unique identity.

Chapter 2 presents a history of stylometry in five acts. In the first, we see how idle speculation by a nineteenth-century British mathematician inspired an American polymath to undertake the first comparative stylometric study. The scene then shifts to the 1940s, when a retired British statistician tried to establish the authorship of the most famous anonymous text in Christendom. Research on the books of the New Testament takes us all over the world, witnessing more than a century of scholarship. The fourth act takes place in 1960s America as two statisticians tackle authorship questions in some of the nation's founding documents. And in the final section, the action shifts to Australia in the early 2000s as an English professor creates a technique that would become the gold standard for future stylometric work.

Chapter 3 provides several examples of stylometry being used to identify the authors of anonymous or pseudonymous works. Some of these cases involve well-known writers, such as Joe Klein (of *Primary Colors* fame), J. K. Rowling, and Thomas Pynchon. There is also an analysis of a play that some have attributed to Shakespeare. In chapter 4, the focus is on disputed authorship, and these cases form an eclectic mix. L. Frank Baum (the creator of the Land of Oz), Edgar Alan Poe, C. S. Lewis, the Brontë siblings, Harper Lee, and James Patterson all make appearances.

Chapter 5 provides a sampling of stylometric techniques used by forensic linguists to identify suspects or to solve crimes. The stories include two well-known cases from England as well as two that will be familiar to many Americans: the JonBenét Ramsey ransom note and the Unabomber manifesto. Chapter 6 tackles the issue of fakery, and, once again, the cases are diverse: a bogus decree by a Roman emperor, a spurious philosophical work by Cicero, a forged Shakespearian play, and letters attributed to Mark Twain and General George Pickett.

Chapters 3 through 6 provide several impressive examples of stylometric success. But these techniques aren't perfect, as chapter 7 makes clear. In some cases, author attributions have been made and then retracted, as in the case of a funeral elegy purportedly written by Shakespeare. In others, no author was conclusively identified: these include "the resister" inside the Trump administration, a best-selling Italian novelist, and an anthrax terrorist.

Chapter 8 addresses how the contributions of ghost writers can be detected via stylometry. The cases described include radio addresses given by Ronald Reagan, Thomas Paine's *Rights of Man*, Davy Crockett's autobiography, and John F. Kennedy's *Profiles in Courage*.

Many of the cases appearing here have been reported only in the scientific and technical literature. My purpose in writing this book was to make this fascinating research accessible to a broader audience. I hope that you find these stories as thought provoking and as enlightening as I do.

Acknowledgments

It's a pleasure to thank those who helped make this book a reality.

I'm grateful to Roger Shuy and Patrick Juola for providing both guidance and encouragement as I grappled with the burgeoning research literatures on stylometry, author identification, and forensic linguistics. Thank you for patiently answering my questions.

I'm indebted to Richard Roberts and Katherine Kitzmann, who read sample chapters and provided feedback at the beginning of this project. When the manuscript was fully drafted, Susan Fitzgerald, Rick Marcus, and Katherine Kitzmann (once again!) helped me to exorcise the grammatical and spelling gremlins that had crept—inexplicably—into the text. They also pulled no punches regarding questionable wording and didn't let me get away with half-baked explanations. I'm very fortunate to have such attentive and helpful beta readers.

The interlibrary loan department of the Ned McWherter Library at the University of Memphis was an invaluable resource. It would not have been possible to complete this book without the consummate professionalism of the library's staff.

I'd also like to thank my dean (now provost) Abby Parrill, my department chair Randy Floyd, administrative assistant Tori Tardugno, and the invariably helpful Jessica Abernathy. In different ways, they provided me with the support and the working conditions that I needed to complete this project. My colleagues and friends Bob Cohen, Gina Caucci, Richard Roberts, Rick Marcus, Leah Windsor, and Stephanie Huette all graciously allowed me to bend their ears whenever some new enthusiasm had overtaken me.

Andy Ross, my talented agent, made sure that this book found a good home. And at Prometheus, I'm indebted, once again, to Jon Kurtz for his support and to Bruce Owens and Jessica McCleary for their expert editing of the manuscript.

I'm truly grateful to you all!

CHAPTER ONE

A LANGUAGE OF ONE'S OWN?

METAPHORS FOR LANGUAGE AND IDENTITY

Metaphors, by definition, never match up precisely with the concepts they describe. Comparing the atom to a miniature solar system doesn't do justice to the nature of electron shells, and the war on cancer is far removed from armed conflict between nations. Nevertheless, such metaphors are useful because they capture something important about the two concepts being compared, such as the movement of smaller bodies around a larger one or the seriousness of efforts to eradicate a disease. Inevitably, however, some details are obscured even as other aspects are brought into sharper focus.

In discussions of linguistic identity, two bodily metaphors have frequently been invoked to illuminate this concept: the human voice and fingerprints. Both comparisons are useful, although both have limitations with regard to the specifics. A catalog of their strengths and weaknesses will help flesh out what it means for one's language to be a part of one's identity.

VOICES IN YOUR HEAD?

In many ways, a person's linguistic identity—the characteristic way they speak and write—can be thought of as that person's voice. When we are caught up in a compelling work of fiction, for example, it can seem that we hear the author's voice inside our own head. Our brain creates this illusion, but it is the author's distinctive linguistic identity on the page that triggers this immersive experience.

An author's linguistic identity is an amalgam of many factors: the words and phrases they tend to employ, the grammatical constructions they frequently make use of, and even what they choose to write about. Voice is the reason that no one would confuse the plays of Tennessee Williams with those of William Shakespeare. Whereas Williams employed simple and direct dialogue, Shakespeare's is dense with metaphors and allusions. We don't find rhyming couplets in Williams, but we certainly do in Shakespeare. And there are no battle scenes in the work of Williams—at least not of the military variety.

Voice is sometimes used to refer to the worldview of an author. Voice can also be used synonymously with a term like "style" or "tone," although in some cases, it is useful to make distinctions. Style typically refers to the mechanical aspects of writing, such as the vocabulary and grammar a writer tends to use. Tone, on the other hand, refers to the emotional atmosphere that a writer creates. This might be intimate, as in a love letter, or clinical and objective, as in a financial report. For our purposes, voice can serve as the umbrella term for all of these.

How well does the concept of linguistic identity map onto a person's physical voice? The metaphor captures the idea of change and growth that occurs during childhood and adolescence. Our voices become deeper as the vocal tract lengthens, and our writing becomes more complex as we acquire a larger vocabulary. In addition, the metaphor aptly reflects the relative stability of both throughout the adult life span. Our voices sound much the same at age 30 as they do at 40 and at 50, and our writing does as well. Professional authors may go through stylistic phases as they hone their craft, but that seems to be the exception rather than the rule.

One problem with the voice metaphor is that it doesn't truly capture the distinctiveness of a person's linguistic identity. For example, it is possible to disguise one's voice well enough to fool someone else. A skilled impersonator can make their physical voice sound just like that of a particular celebrity or a politician. However, it turns out to be fairly difficult to pull this off in writing. The idiosyncratic ways that people choose to express themselves are difficult to maintain in written imitations of any length. This is one of the reasons why forgers are often caught: they may be adept at imitating the physical characteristics of another person's handwriting, for example, but they lack knowledge of what that person might write about or how they typically choose to express themselves.

In sum, the correspondence between one's physical and psychological voice is illuminating in many respects, but the term "voice" lacks the distinctiveness that is the hallmark of one's linguistic identity. For that reason, a metaphor that better captures the singular nature of a person's speech and writing may be more appropriate for our purposes.

THE MYTH OF FINGERPRINTS?

If each person's linguistic identity is truly unique, then a comparison to finger-prints might serve as a better analogy. No two people share the exact same set of loops, whorls, and arches on the ridges of their fingertips—not even identical twins.[1] But is it accurate to say that no two people talk or write in exactly the same way? If so, then a recorded conversation or a writing sample would be as valuable to law enforcement as a thumbprint or DNA evidence.

As it happens, one of the best-known authorities in forensic linguistics has taken pains to debunk the notion of linguistic fingerprints. John Olsson is a professor emeritus of Bangor University in Wales. He has worked for many years as a forensic linguist and has published extensively on this subject. In his 2004 book, he claimed that the term "linguistic fingerprint" creates a false im-pression of precision and unfailing accuracy.[2] And on this point, he is certainly correct, as we will see in later chapters.

In a later book, Olsson criticized the fingerprint metaphor for implying an immutability that simply doesn't exist.[3] After all, we are born with our finger-prints but not with our language. And once we acquire our native tongue, our spoken and written voice can still change throughout our lives. Our vocabu-laries increase, and our dialect may shift. Our life experiences can profoundly change us in a variety of ways.

Anyone who has come across some long-forgotten juvenilia tucked away in an attic or basement can probably recall the shock of reading text that is simultaneously them and not them. Even successful authors, such as W. H. Auden and Nathaniel Hawthorne, have disowned some of their earlier work.[4] This can happen when writers distance themselves from a work's content, but it can also occur when they no longer recognize their own voice in their initial, more tentative work.

Olsson also points out that we are not monolithic language users. We speak and write in different ways with different people: fairly formally, perhaps, with our supervisor at work and more casually with our friends and family.

Sociolinguists refer to such changes as shifts in register. As Shakespeare put it in *As You Like It*, "One man in his time plays many parts." In a similar way, we find ourselves shifting in register depending on whom we're speaking to or what we're speaking about. This linguistic fluidity is effortless—and utterly unlike the unchanging ridges on our fingertips.

Another problem with the fingerprint metaphor is that it implies a certain comprehensiveness. Law enforcement officers can record a person's prints and file them away in a database. These exemplars can then be compared to prints left at a crime scene years or even decades later. In other words, a recorded set of fingerprints is informationally complete. A forensic linguist, however, is almost always working with the equivalent of partial prints: suicide notes, threatening letters, and the like are typically less than 200 words long.[5]

The fingerprint metaphor also implies that we know how to characterize such distinctive linguistic patterns. Whereas researchers have created classification systems for the arrangements of ridges on the fingers and palms, linguists are nowhere near reaching a consensus about which aspects of a person's speaking or writing are the most diagnostic. Is it the length of the words that a person uses? The length of their sentences? A proclivity to use certain terms or phrases? All of these? Or none of them? A host of such characteristics has been proposed, studied, and debated. Some, as we will see, have been employed with great success to identify the authors of texts. But a comprehensive approach to classifying linguistic identity remains a distant and perhaps unachievable goal.

Finally, unlike fingerprints, which are difficult or impossible to fake, it may be possible for someone to counterfeit another person's linguistic identity— that is, to take on their verbal mannerisms and characteristic modes of expression to such a convincing degree that others are fooled by the imitation. And as we will see, it is indeed possible to fool some people, at least some of the time.

Despite its imperfections, the notion of linguistic fingerprints appears frequently in popular discussions of linguistic identity.[6] And for that reason, I have also used it in the title of this book and throughout its contents. It is a convenient shorthand that is easily understood—even if it is less than a perfect metaphor.

SIGNATURES AND IDIOLECTS

Might there be a better metaphor? Some researchers make use of the term "signature" to refer to a person's linguistic identity.[7] In many respects, this is a useful comparison, as it captures the idea of relative uniqueness while retaining the possibility of refinement. Fingerprints don't change over time, but the characteristic way a person signs their name may well evolve as they move from adolescence through adulthood and into old age. In a similar way, someone who grew up in one linguistic community and relocates to another may develop a very different way of expressing themselves.

Signatures, however, are much more easily forged than someone's complete linguistic identity, and here the metaphor falls flat. To summarize, we find ourselves in possession of three partially defective metaphors: "voice" is too broad, "fingerprint" is too narrow, and "signature" is too simplistic.

Academicians, however, have no qualms about inventing new terms if older ones are found to be inadequate. In 1948, the American linguist Bernard Bloch coined the term "idiolect" to refer to language use that is "peculiar to one speaker."[8] Since then, researchers have tended to use this term when referring to a person's unique linguistic identity.[9] Idiolect is a combination of the prefix "idio," which means "personal" or "private," and "dialect," which describes the characteristic speech of a group of people.

Unlike many other terms that have escaped from the ivory tower, "idiolect" hasn't yet crossed over into general usage. Its insularity can clearly be seen in *Manhunt*, a television program that aired on the Discovery channel in 2017. This series recounts the Unabomber investigation, a triumph of forensic linguistics that will be discussed in chapter 5. In several episodes, investigator James Fitzgerald makes use of the term, and it is always greeted with suspicion by his superiors. Fitzgerald's obsession with dissecting the language used by the Unabomber was ultimately vindicated, but he did himself no favors by employing a term that sounded like mysterious technobabble.

It should already be clear that linguistic identity is a complex construct and one that encompasses a variety of distinct features. In the following sections of this chapter, we explore some of the elements of linguistic identity that make up one's idiolect. And in the chapters that follow, we will see how such factors can be employed by those who practice the stylometric art of author identification and forensic linguistics.

WHERE ARE YOU FROM?

In April 1940, a new radio program began to air on WOR in New York City. Titled "Where Are You From?," it featured an unlikely host: a 27-year-old lecturer of English at Brown University. Each Wednesday evening, Dr. Henry Lee Smith Jr. would converse with members of his studio audience. Based on how they said certain words, he would try to guess their place of origin. And he was right more often than not, with an overall accuracy of about 80 percent.[10]

At first blush, this may not seem all that remarkable since most English speakers can differentiate between various accents, such as British, Australian, or U.S. Southern English. Henry Smith's abilities, however, were much more impressive than this. He was able to differentiate speakers of the various boroughs of New York City and could pinpoint the Manhattanites to within "a few blocks of their homes."[11]

For some readers, this may bring to mind the phonetician Henry Higgins in George Bernard Shaw's *Pygmalion*, who claimed the ability to place anyone in London within two miles and "sometimes within two streets."[12] But Higgins was a fictional character, whereas Smith was performing on live radio. For most of his audience, it seemed like a magic trick, akin to pulling a rabbit out of a hat. How did he do it?

Smith was born in Morristown, New Jersey, in 1913 and grew up in Baltimore. He studied at Princeton and earned his doctorate in Oriental languages and literature in 1938.[13] While working as a lecturer at Barnard College in New York City, he enlivened his lectures on linguistics—and honed his skills—by predicting the place of origin of his students. Undoubtedly, Smith had a good ear and a good memory for dialect differences. But he accomplished his linguistic legerdemain by zeroing in on words that are spoken differently in different geographic regions of the United States. His stock in trade was a small set of words that functioned as linguistic tells. These would reliably betray the origin of his program's guests.

One of Smith's go-to questions involved asking people to pronounce the triplet "Mary," "marry," and "merry." Depending on where someone grew up, the three words might be pronounced the same or differently. He might also inquire whether fried foods were "greasy," like the country, or like "sleazy." Other questions involved regional vocabulary. For example, he might ask whether a black and white animal that emits a strong odor is called a "skunk" or a "polecat." And based on these and other responses, he was able to pin a speaker to a place with a high degree of accuracy.

It may come as a surprise to learn that this sort of detective work can be automated. In December 2013, the *New York Times* ran a regional dialect quiz that mimicked Henry Smith's modus operandi. The feature would go on to become one of the most viewed articles in that paper's long history. Respondents were asked 25 simple questions about the words they use. On completion of the survey, they were rewarded with a personalized dialect map showing which parts of the United States matched their responses most closely.[14]

For many who took the quiz, the accuracy of the results was uncanny. Typically, the state where someone had grown up could be predicted. Some of the questions asked about pronunciation differences of the "Mary," "marry," and "merry" variety. But three-quarters of the questions zeroed in on regional vocabulary.

For example, what do you call the shoes that you wear to gym class? They are called "tennis shoes" throughout much of the country but not in New England, the mid-Atlantic states, or southern Florida, where "sneakers" reigns supreme.

The word for a public convenience that supplies a jet of water to quench one's thirst? Most Americans would call it a "water fountain" or a "drinking fountain." But if you're from Rhode Island or eastern Wisconsin, it's a "bubbler."

If you have a hankering for "crawfish," odds are that you hail from Louisiana or eastern Texas. "Crayfish" can be found in New England and the upper Midwest. "Crawdads" will be encountered in western Missouri and eastern Kansas, while other terms for these creatures include "mudbugs" and "freshwater" or "mountain lobsters."

And an elongated sandwich with a variety of meats and vegetables might be called a "sub," a "hero," a "grinder," a "poor boy," an "Italian sandwich," a "hoagie," or a "bomber"—based, once again, on geographic region.[15]

Why do these dialect differences exist? In the United States, distinctive patterns are strongest in the eastern and southern parts of the country. As one travels from east to west, these differences become less pronounced, with the far West being relatively homogeneous. Speakers chosen at random from the streets of Boston and Baltimore—separated by 400 miles—will probably sound somewhat different, whereas the inhabitants of Seattle and San Francisco will sound more alike, even though those cities are twice as far apart as Boston and Baltimore.

The reasons for this are complex and multifaceted but primarily have to do with historical settlement patterns.[16] Areas settled by colonists early in the nation's history tend to have distinctive accents, whereas regions settled later, by more heterogeneous groups, are typically more similar in speech.

Here's another example that's linked to geography. Before reading further, think about how you pronounce the word "horrible." Close your eyes and say the word to yourself: "horrible." Now think about how you pronounced the first syllable. Did you say it so that the vowel sounds like the one in "hard" or like the one in "more"? If you grew up on the East Coast, you probably said "HAR-ible." But if you spent your childhood west of the Appalachians, there's a good chance you said "HORE-able" instead. And this is true for other, similar words, such as "orange," "Florida," and "correlation."[17]

Once you become aware of such differences, it is difficult not to notice them. The author of this book, who grew up in the Midwest, learned about "horrible" in a dialect class in college. Ever since then, he has noticed unlikely pronunciations cropping up on television shows. Many programs are set (and filmed) in Southern California, but many of the actors are from the eastern United States. As a result, it's not uncommon to hear an actor playing a native Californian referring to things that are "HAR-ible" or to California's citrus crop and its "AR-anges." It's a small thing, but it bugs him.

The same is true for how people pronounce the triplet "Mary," "merry," and "marry" that we encountered earlier. According to the Harvard Dialect Survey, which asked more than 11,000 people this question, a majority of U.S. speakers—57 percent—pronounce all three exactly the same. However, for about one respondent in six, all three are pronounced differently. The survey participants in this smaller group live all over the country, but they are concentrated in lower New England, the New York City area, and New Jersey.[18]

Linguists sometimes refer to such tells as "shibboleths," after the Bible account related in chapter 12 of the Book of Judges. In that story, the inhabitants of Gilead identified members of an invading tribe of Ephramites by asking them to pronounce the Hebrew word *shibbólet* (which means the grain-containing part of a plant). The first sound of that word is pronounced like the "sh" in "shield," which did not exist in the Ephamites' language. When challenged, they could only produce an "s" at the beginning of the word. They were slaughtered as a result.

A similar shibboleth was used during World War II in the Pacific. Japanese soldiers disguised as Americans or Filipinos would be challenged to utter words containing several "l" sounds, like "lollapalooza." If an "r" sound was heard instead, the soldiers "would open fire without waiting to hear the remainder."[19]

Another question raised by this discussion is how linguists mapped such differences in the first place. Consider, for example, "bucket" versus "pail." Do they refer to the same thing? Either term can be used to refer to a cylindrical container with a handle over the top, and most people would agree that the words are essentially synonymous. However, a given person might show a marked preference for using one member of the pair as opposed to the other. And if one person has a preference, it's likely that others in their town or city share that predilection. And zooming out even further, it's likely that most of the speakers in the same geographic region refer to such a container in the same way. But is it possible to demarcate where the domain of "bucket" ends and the empire of "pail" begins?

If you were so inclined, you could answer this question by visiting cities, towns, and villages within a given region and asking native inhabitants to indicate their preference for these two terms. You could then create a map showing in which places "bucket" reigns supreme and, conversely, where "pail" rules the roost. And if you suspect that such word choices aren't random, then you would hope that some sort of pattern would emerge from these data.

This isn't just a thought experiment—this procedure was carried out during the Great Depression. Between 1931 and 1933, an intrepid band of fieldworkers fanned out across New England, interviewing 416 speakers in 213 different communities. And the researchers didn't ask only about buckets and pails: their informants were subjected to questionnaires that were 750 items in length.

The project was led by an Austrian American linguist named Hans Kurath. His team eventually produced the magisterial *Linguistic Atlas of New England*, published in three volumes between 1939 and 1943. Known as LANE, the volumes contain 734 maps of New England, with tiny symbols showing the preferences in both pronunciation and word choice that the project had documented.[20]

The researchers discovered a complex pattern of preferences and also some distinct boundaries between word choices. Kurath and his colleagues proposed that these divisions reflected settlement patterns from several centuries earlier when New England was first populated by immigrants during colonial times. The work of Kurath's team was extended into the mid-Atlantic as well as the southern Atlantic states, and the results were the same: the vocabulary preferences of today provide us with fossilized evidence of previous generations who tamed the wilderness and brought their dialects with them.

Getting back to "bucket" and "pail," these studies showed that while New Englanders had a strong preference for "pail," speakers in southern Pennsylvania were more likely to refer to "buckets." The researchers found they could draw a wavy line across northern Pennsylvania and New Jersey to separate the "pail" and "bucket" communities. Such a boundary line is referred to as an *isogloss* and functions like the isobar on a weather map to separate regions with different atmospheric pressure.

From this discussion, it should be clear that when it comes to one's speech, geography is destiny. And this is only one factor out of many that influences how people speak. The subtle—and sometimes not subtle—effects that our speech has on how others see us are described in the final two sections of this chapter.

IT'S HOW YOU SAY IT

How does the way you speak affect how others perceive you? And how does your speech affect how you perceive yourself? Research by social scientists and linguists has shown that the effects of accent and dialect on one's identity are both large and pervasive.

Consider the way in which language is first acquired. It's been shown that children tend to pick up the dialect of their peers instead of that spoken by their mothers and fathers.[21] Although this may seem strange, it squares with the experience of many parents. Couples who have relocated for employment or other reasons are often surprised when their children begin to speak differently than they do. Kids want to fit in with their peers and may begin to change their speech away from what they hear at home to the vernacular of their friends. In some cases, this may be an overt and deliberate choice, but in many others, the change may occur without conscious awareness.

And as people get older, they develop their own linguistic identity. To cite one example, they show an in-group bias for those who speak as they do and become largely unable to differentiate the various accents of out-group members. Most Americans can identify an accent as "British" but are unable to differentiate the many different varieties spoken in the United Kingdom. An American might be able to recognize Cockney, spoken in the East End of London, because of several well-known examples in films and television programs. However, few would be able to differentiate between Geordie (the dialect of Newcastle), Brummie (Birmingham), and Scouse (Liverpool).

This in-group bias manifests itself in a variety of ways. For example, we believe that people we like sound more similar to us than other people do.[22] Unfortunately, however, the reverse is also true. Several studies have shown that speakers whose dialects differ from our own are evaluated more negatively. Nonnative speakers, for example, are perceived as being less credible than native speakers.[23] And one of the truly insidious aspects of such negative evaluations is that we may not be consciously aware of such prejudices.[24]

The tight linkage between identity and how one speaks is seen in a phenomenon called foreign accent syndrome (FAS). After suffering a brain injury, some people have experienced a change in how they speak. In other cases, FAS is caused by reconstructive jaw surgery. A slight change in how someone pronounces their vowels can be sufficient for others to perceive the affected speaker as "foreign sounding."

In one documented case of FAS, a midwestern American woman in her forties had surgery to shorten an abnormally large mandible. The procedure changed her speech in such a way that others perceived her as speaking with a British accent. People would encourage her to talk so that others might hear her "funny" accent, and she felt as if she was being asked to perform tricks like a circus animal. Distressed by such episodes, she eventually traveled to England to find others who sounded like her. To her chagrin, she discovered that the Brits thought she hailed from South Africa![25]

Unless people make a conscious decision to alter their speech, perhaps by taking an accent reduction class, their way of speaking will mark them, for good or ill, for the rest of their lives. This can be a problem because some accents are relatively prestigious and tend to be spoken by more affluent or highly educated individuals, whereas others are stereotypically associated with lower socioeconomic status or less educational opportunity. Americans like to believe that U.S. society lacks the rigid social hierarchies that exist in other parts of the world, but people often make social and class judgments based on how others speak.

The consequences of such perceived differences are sobering and rather frightening. Speakers with lower-status accents are perceived less positively than those with higher-status speech patterns.[26] And these attitudes can engender feelings of linguistic insecurity. This is the self-consciousness experienced by individuals who speak a less prestigious dialect than others.[27] In the United States, for example, the Southern dialect is stereotypically associated with unsophisticated attitudes and low intelligence. The college student who moves from Mobile to Manhattan to attend college will likely have to contend with the negative attributions that others automatically make about her.

Many people believe that as geographic regions become more interconnected, the distinctive accents of old will fade away and that everyone will end up speaking in the same, relatively homogeneous way. In some places, this does seem to be true. Consider the Research Triangle of North Carolina. Its name refers to the three research universities that anchor its corners: in Raleigh (North Carolina State), Durham (Duke), and Chapel Hill (the University of North Carolina). For several decades, these institutions and affiliated high-tech industries have drawn highly educated academicians and researchers to the Piedmont region of the state. And through processes referred to as dialect mixing and leveling, the speech of the Triangle has lost much of its former distinctiveness.

But mixing and leveling can't be the whole story. If it were, then the language spoken in the British Isles over the past millennium should have evolved into a uniform standard—something that clearly has not happened. It's been estimated that across England, there is a change in accent every 25 miles.[28] And in some regions, like the so-called Hoosier apex of southern Illinois and Indiana, speakers have continued to speak a more Southern dialect of English that seems out of place in the Midwest.[29] But unlike the Research Triangle, this area hasn't received a large influx of people from other regions, and this lessens the likelihood of dialect mixing and leveling.

Finally, research by linguists suggests that, if anything, regional accents are becoming even more pronounced across large swathes of North America. A good example of this continuing evolution is the Northern Cities Vowel Shift. This is a change in pronunciation by Americans living in communities near the Great Lakes (think Buffalo, Cleveland, Detroit, and Chicago). In these places, the word "block" sounds more like "black" as the vowel is fronted (i.e., produced with the tongue toward the front of the mouth). In addition, these speakers tend to produce other vowels toward the back, with "busses" sounding more like "bosses."[30]

Social class and geographic region, however, aren't the only factors that influence a speaker's dialect. Men and women speak differently as well. One example of this is the use of upspeak, or high rising terminal as it's more formally known. Speakers who employ upspeak tend to end every statement as if it were a question? You know, instead of a statement of fact? Another example would be vocal fry, which produces a characteristic creaky or popping sound in one's speech.[31] Because these ways of speaking are associated with younger women, they tend to be perceived relatively negatively by others: unserious at best or annoying at worst.[32]

How about one's age? Researchers have found characteristic differences in language use based on how old someone is. And this isn't simply a matter of using old-fashioned terminology, like referring to a refrigerator as an "icebox" or a backpack as a "rucksack." The psychologist James Pennebaker and his colleagues have analyzed data from thousands of research participants who were asked to write about their personal experiences. They found a number of striking differences related to age. For example, until about the age of 40, people use positive emotion words, such as "happy" and "love," and negative emotion words, such as "sad" and "hate," at relatively equal rates. After that age, however, the use of negative emotion words declines somewhat, while the use of positive emotion words increases significantly.[33]

And there are other social and perceptual factors encoded in one's speech. For example, one's race can be associated with differences in pronunciation. A form of the language referred to as African American Vernacular English (AAVE) exhibits characteristic patterns in the production of many speech sounds that make it distinct from other dialects of English.[34] In addition, men tend to have lower voices than women and children because of their longer vocal tracts and the effects of puberty.[35] And if English is someone's second language, their pronunciation will be influenced, to some degree, by their native tongue.

Attributions that are triggered by a person's accent can have a variety of deleterious effects. Consider the 2013 prosecution of George Zimmerman for the killing of Trayvon Martin, which included the testimony of Rachel Jeantel. She was talking on the phone with Martin when the altercation with Zimmerman began, and her account was of considerable interest to the court. But because she spoke AAVE, her testimony was hard for the judge and jury to understand. It appears likely that the jury discounted her account of the incident as a result.[36] After one day of deliberation, the jury found Zimmerman not guilty of second-degree murder.

In sum, the way that a person speaks can reveal much about their identity, including their geographic origin, gender, age, and race. And these cues can activate a variety of stereotypes in the minds of others. To put it simply, the perceptions that others form about us can begin as soon as we open our mouths.

MANUFACTURING AUTHENTICITY

On September 24, 2011, President Barack Obama gave a speech at the Congressional Black Caucus Foundation Phoenix Awards Dinner. It was a fiery call to action and notable not only for the words he used but also for how he chose to articulate them. At the end of the address, he exhorted his audience with the following: "Put on your marchin' shoes! Shake it off! Stop complainin'! Stop grumblin'! Stop cryin'! We are gonna press on! We got work to do."

Videos of his address, which can be easily found online, are at odds with the transcript released by the White House's Office of the Press Secretary, as well as news outlets like National Public Radio, C-SPAN, and the *Washington Post*. In all these accounts, the president is quoted as having said, "Put on your marching shoes. Shake it off. Stop complaining, stop grumbling, stop crying. We are going to press on. We've got work to do."

In contrast, the White House correspondent for the Associated Press, Mark Smith, chose to transcribe Obama's words faithfully. He claimed that he was respecting the president's intent by producing an accurate rendition of his words as they were delivered to his audience. Nevertheless, Smith was criticized for having created an "inherently racist" version of the speech, in the words of author and talk show host Karen Hunter during an interview with Chris Hayes of MSNBC. Linguist John McWhorter, however, disagreed and claimed that Smith's version was "actually the correct one."[37]

This dispute raises a number of questions. Why did the president choose to express himself in vernacular English ("gonna," "we got work") and drop his "g"s at the end of words ("marchin'," "complainin'," "grumblin'," "cryin'")? And why was its transcription seen as controversial?

Disputes about how to depict nonstandard English in print have a long history. Mark Twain caused a stir in the literary world when he published *The Adventures of Huckleberry Finn* in 1884. Its use of a particular racial slur—which appears more than 200 times[38]—would make it a lightning rod of controversy in the twentieth and twenty-first centuries. In Twain's day, however, the more remarkable—and, for many, the more objectionable—aspect of the text was his attempt to represent the speech of Jim, the formerly enslaved man whom Huck befriends.[39]

Twain warns his reader in an introductory note that the book includes speech from a number of dialects, including the "Missouri Negro dialect." He assures the reader that he is basing his characterizations on "personal familiarity with these several forms of speech."[40] This didn't stop detractors from characterizing the book as coarse and vulgar, however.

The particular linguistic sin that Obama was accused of has a history as well. In the late 1960s, linguist William Labov documented that "g"-dropping varied by social class. White residents of New York City whom he categorized as "lower class" dropped their "g"s in words like "working" and "living" about 80 percent of the time, whereas those he labeled as "upper middle class" dropped them at a rate of only 5 percent. However, he also found that this behavior varied by formality: all the participants dropped "g"s in casual speech, but the rates were lower for "careful speech" and lower still when he asked his informants to read isolated words.[41]

Should a chief executive engage in such behavior on the national stage, and does it matter if he is Black? This question would come to the fore a number of times during Obama's tenure from both ends of the political spectrum. The actor Samuel L. Jackson, a supporter of the president, took Obama to task for "g"-dropping in an October 2013 interview in *Playboy*, claiming that it was unpresidential.[42] And on the political right, Peggy Noonan, in a July 2014 *Wall Street Journal* editorial, also opined that the chief executive shouldn't drop his "g"s.[43]

But if "g"-dropping is a sin, then it's a failing shared by many other politicians. Mitt Romney, for example, was accused of this verbal transgression while campaigning in the Deep South during the 2012 Republican primaries along with professing a fondness for catfish and cheesy grits. Grace Wyler, the reporter who noted this behavior, characterized it as pandering.[44]

George W. Bush, on the other hand, frequently dropped his "g"s both as a presidential candidate and in the White House. But could it be characterized as pandering when he did it? Bush was born in Connecticut in 1947 while his father was attending Yale. The following year, the family moved to West Texas, where George Sr. began work as an oil field equipment salesman. His son attended public schools in Midland and then in Houston before going on to Phillips Academy in Massachusetts and undergraduate studies at Yale. As a result, even though the younger Bush is the scion of a patrician family, his manner of speech developed in western and southeastern Texas. It's also worth noting that in his formal televised addresses, President Bush seemed to take care not to drop his "g"s.

Sarah Palin is also thought to have come by her "g"-dropping honestly. Her unique way of speaking became a topic of discussion during the fall of

2008 while she campaigned as the running mate of John McCain. Although Palin had been born in Sandpoint, Idaho, her family moved when she was an infant to Skagway, Alaska, and then to Anchorage and Wasilla. After the 2008 campaign, linguists determined that she had "g"-dropped about 12 percent of the time, a rate high enough for it to be noticeable.[45] But was it an affectation? Palin had been a TV sports reporter in Anchorage during the 1980s, and recordings of her linguistic stylings from that time are similar to her speech on the 2008 campaign trail.[46]

So who is allowed to drop their "g"s, and who isn't? For politicians in particular, the main issue is whether they present themselves as being who they really are. In contrast, those who simply mimic their audiences to win their favor—and their votes—may be perceived fairly negatively. Put simply, to be successful in politics, one must be authentic—or at least appear to be.[47] And according to this way of thinking, politicians like George W. Bush and Sarah Palin pass the test for genuineness. Both speak in ways that are characteristic of their early environments, and even if they sometimes accentuated certain aspects of their speech to increase their appeal, neither was pretending to be someone they were not.

By the same logic, however, Mitt Romney fails the test of authenticity. He was born the same year as Bush, in 1947, but in Detroit, Michigan. When he was six, the family, headed by his auto executive father, moved to Bloomfield Hills, a tony suburb of the Motor City. Like Bush, he attended public elementary schools but then moved on to an exclusive prep school not far from his home. After graduation, he enrolled at Stanford before spending two and a half years as a Mormon missionary in France. He would eventually earn an undergraduate degree from Brigham Young and a joint JD/MBA from Harvard. He served as the CEO of a private equity company and as governor of Massachusetts before seeking the presidency. Nothing about his history, in terms of race, social class, or geographic origin, would seem to qualify him as a genuine "g"-dropper.

But what of Obama? As with much else about the forty-fourth president, it's complicated. Born in Hawaii to a mother from Kansas and a father from Kenya, Obama lived in Indonesia from the age of six to ten, then with his grandparents in Honolulu while attending a prep school. He moved on to Los Angeles and Occidental College, then across the country to Columbia to finish his undergraduate studies. After three years working as a community organizer in Chicago, he earned a law degree at Harvard. Back in Chicago, he taught constitutional law at the University of Chicago for 12 years before entering politics.

Given his peripatetic early life, it is difficult to make claims about what Obama's dialect *should* be. Was it influenced by his early exposure to Indonesian, a language in which he became fluent? Was his speech affected by Hawaiian Pidgin, a co-official creole with its own diverse set of influences, including Portuguese, Japanese, and Cantonese? Given his identity, it is likely that Obama's ties to the Black community trump any other linguistic influence. And "g"-dropping is a characteristic of vernacular Black English although not necessarily a defining one.[48]

The problem for Obama, however, is that "g"-dropping is also characteristic of other dialects, such as southern and rural speech. These are linguistic communities that he has never been a part of. And, as mentioned earlier, "g"-dropping is also typical in informal speech, which doesn't truly fit with Obama's dispassionate and professorial demeanor. For many Americans whose dialect does include "g"-dropping, they see in Obama someone who doesn't look like or act like them. As a result, his use of a characteristic found in their own speech may not seem genuine.

In terms of authenticity, the crux of the issue for Obama may be whether he engages in strategic shifts in his way of speaking. After all, it's not unusual to have the language of others unconsciously influence one's own. A homesick freshman, for example, talking on the phone with her parents back home may find the twang of her birthplace creeping into her voice. In a similar way, Obama's speech at the Phoenix Awards Dinner—to a largely Black audience—may have spontaneously caused him to adopt a manner of speaking that is more reflective of vernacular Black English than his usual speaking style. Such shifts, however, aren't necessarily strategic or deliberate.

Linguists even have a name for such shifts: they refer to it as code-switching.[49] It can happen without the speaker even realizing it. In other cases, however, the effect may be calculated. Elizabeth Holmes, the young female founder of Theranos, is thought to have consciously deepened her voice in order to project an air of maturity and authority as she navigated the power structure of Silicon Valley.[50] And some older adults deliberately appropriate the slang of a younger generation in order to be seen as in vogue—much to the embarrassment of their children or grandchildren.

The case of "g"-dropping illustrates how issues of race, class, age, and region can create a tangled skein with regard to perceptions of linguistic identity. And a verbal mannerism that comes across as folksy in the speech of an elderly white man may be perceived quite differently when it comes out of the mouth of a younger Black man—especially if he is the nation's leader.

Now that we have considered how spoken language creates identity, we can turn to how written language reveals it. The next chapter presents some of the landmark developments in the study of author identification and the beginnings of modern stylometry.

CHAPTER TWO

BEGINNINGS

THE PROGENITOR

Questions about authorship have probably existed for as long as people have been writing things down. As a result, the historical record is replete with scholarly disputes about who wrote what. Did Moses write the first five books of the Old Testament? Did Abelard and Heloise, the infamous twelfth-century lovers, pen the letters that are ascribed to them? Did a commoner from Stratford-upon-Avon write the plays attributed to Shakespeare, or should the credit go to someone else?[1] And more broadly, when a work's authorship is in some doubt, how can such questions be resolved? At the end of the nineteenth century, a technique for answering such disputes was proposed by a self-taught physicist from Ohio.

Thomas Corwin Mendenhall was born in 1841 in Hanoverton, a small village in the Mahoning Valley not far from Canton. The town experienced a burst of economic activity when the Sandy and Beaver Canal was constructed, but by the time Mendenhall was growing up there, the canal was no longer profitable, and the town was in decline. In the 1850s, his family moved on to Marlboro, a Quaker community near Akron. The home of his abolitionist parents functioned as a stop on the Underground Railroad for enslaved people fleeing the South.

Mendenhall apparently displayed pedagogical gifts early in life. At the tender age of 17, he was already the head of the local elementary school. He would go on to earn an instructor's credential at a teacher's college, but that was the extent of his formal education. Mendenhall then moved on to Columbus, married, and had a son. By 1873, he had gotten himself appointed as a professor of physics and mechanics at the newly established Ohio Agricultural and Mechanical College. This institution would become better known as Ohio State University. He accomplished this feat even though he lacked a college degree of any kind, although the school bestowed an honorary doctorate on him two years later.[2]

He would go on to spend three years in Japan on a mission to modernize that country's educational system. He became interested in meteorology and earthquakes and helped to establish the study of those phenomena in his host country. He brought these interests back to Columbus and established a meteorological service at Ohio State.

Mendenhall also served as president of the Rose Polytechnic Institute in Indiana, the Worcester Polytechnic Institute in Massachusetts, and the American Association for the Advancement of Science. He studied lightning and championed the adoption of the metric system. Later, as head of the U.S. Geodetic Survey, he established the precise boundary line between the United States and Canada. He even had a valley and a glacier named after him.

Not all of his varied enterprises would meet with success, as we will see. But one of his major triumphs was the invention of a device for measuring local gravitational fields. The Mendenhall Gravimeter was the most accurate instrument of its time and was used by field stations worldwide. The device would be employed by Albert Michelson to measure the speed of light, a feat that would earn Michelson a Nobel Prize in 1907.

Given Mendenhall's fecund, restless, and scientifically inclined mind, it should come as little surprise that he became interested in a topic like the quantification of texts and the attribution of authorship. Archimedes had once said, "Give me a place to stand, and I shall move the earth." In a revealing twist on the Greek mathematician's words, Mendenhall was quoted as saying, "If I could find the place to stand, I could measure the weight of the world."[3] His faith in counting and calculation appeared limitless. But could a quantitative approach provide scholars with a way of determining the authorship of disputed or fraudulent works?

The germ of this idea was planted in Mendenhall when he read a book about the British mathematician Augustus de Morgan.[4] In an 1851 letter to a friend, de Morgan wondered whether an author's average word length might serve as a unique marker for that writer's style. This letter was included in a memoir published by his wife in 1882.[5]

De Morgan never followed up on the implications that his insight might have for later work on author attribution. In the letter, he had speculated that the same author, writing about two different topics, would compose texts that were more similar to one another in terms of the average length of words than two authors writing about the same subject (his example was Herodotus and Thucydides, writing about history). However, de Morgan described this as an idle thought experiment: he never got around to rolling up his sleeves to attempt a proof of his notion. The question was left unanswered, and Mendenhall set out to find a solution.

His first essay on this topic appeared in the journal *Science* in 1887. In it, Mendenhall credits de Morgan as the inspiration for his own work and reports several tests of the mathematician's hypotheses. De Morgan's first assertion had been that an author's average word length could serve as a unique index of his or her style—their linguistic fingerprint, in other words. To test this, Mendenhall chose to examine the works of nineteenth-century British authors.

In one analysis, Mendenhall counted the letters in the first 1,000 words of Dickens's *Oliver Twist* and graphed the results. He plotted word length, from one to 12 letters, on the horizontal axis and used the vertical dimension to indicate the number of words for each word length. Dickens's writing creates a fairly characteristic curve: as one moves from left to right on the *x*-axis, the number of words ascends steeply, peaking at an average length of three letters. After that, it declines fairly rapidly. His count included a small number of 11- and 12-letter words before trailing off completely. The resulting curve could be thought of as the overall "shape" of Dickens's vocabulary. Mendenhall's graph provided the results for the first 1,000 words of the novel. But would other passages from Dickens's book display this same shape?

To find out, Mendenhall counted the words and letters in five different 1,000-word passages from *Oliver Twist* and overlaid the resulting curves on the same graph. Although there are some differences, particularly among the longer words, the curves are pretty much identical. But was this pattern truly characteristic of Dickens's style? Mendenhall also compared 10,000 words from *Oliver Twist* to *A Christmas Carol*, which had been written five years later. Once again, the curves were virtually the same.

But Dickens himself could be an outlier. That is, his consistent writing style might not be representative of the population as a whole, which would be, in this case, all authors writing in English. Would another author display a similar degree of regularity?

Mendenhall's paper also includes a graph depicting the word lengths for two consecutive 1,000-word passages found in William Makepeace Thackeray's *Vanity Fair*. And the two are almost identical, or "sensibly the same," as Mendenhall described it.[6] It may be that Dickens and Thackeray are atypical, but the odds that both men are outliers are relatively low.

Mendenhall then turned his attention to John Stuart Mill's *Principles of Political Economy* and his *On Liberty* and created curves of 5,000 words from each work. The results from the essays by Mill are similar to one another but look different than the results from the novelists Dickens and Thackeray.

Finally, he analyzed two addresses given by the American economist Edward Atkinson. Both speeches were on the topic of labor, but they were given to distinctly different audiences: one was a group of laborers, and the other was the alumni of a theological seminary. Despite that difference, Atkinson's word-length curves for the two addresses are remarkably similar.

Mendenhall concluded his paper by explicitly stating that his method could be used "to solve questions of disputed authorship"[7] but claimed that as many as 100,000 words from a given author might be necessary to make meaningful comparisons.

He returned to this subject in 1901. Perhaps inevitably, Mendenhall chose to wade into the almost impenetrable thicket of debate about Shakespeare. Questions about the Bard's identity had begun to be asked in earnest in 1848, when the American author Joseph Hart claimed that the plays were the work of several individuals.[8] By the turn of the century, the notion that Francis Bacon had written Shakespeare's plays was popular, and a number of people encouraged Mendenhall to apply his methods to see if the curve of Shakespeare's plays aligned with a curve derived from Bacon's oeuvre.

Mendenhall had learned an important lesson from his earlier foray in studying authors: counting their words and letters is tedious and exhausting. Fortunately for him, a benefactor offered to pay a couple of women to perform the necessary labor. These indefatigable assistants, working as a team, made use of a specialized counting machine. They toiled for three to five hours a day at the mind-numbing task and after several months had counted the letters in about 400,000 words of Shakespeare. (This is a bit less than half of the words in the plays traditionally attributed to him.) They also counted the letters in nearly 200,000 of Bacon's words. These included the texts of *Henry VII*, *The Advancement of Learning*, and a number of his essays.

And the result? The curve generated by Shakespeare's plays didn't look much like the curve derived from Bacon's works. However, Mendenhall's assistants had also counted smaller numbers of words from the works of other playwrights and novelists. Much to his surprise, he found that the curve for Christopher Marlowe agreed with Shakespeare "about as well as Shakespeare agrees with himself."[9]

So, case closed? The problem with Marlowe is that he was inconveniently dead by 1593, and most of Shakespeare's plays seem to have been composed after that date. Die-hard Marlovians, however, point to the fact that their man had died under mysterious circumstances and that his death may have been faked. Over a century later, Marlowe's supporters are still citing Mendenhall to buttress their claims.[10]

Time has not been particularly kind to Mendenhall's memory. His author profiling was taken to task by statisticians for reasons having to do with his method of sampling and the way he reported his results[11] as well as some of his basic assumptions.[12] He's also been criticized for comparing Shakespeare's verse with Bacon's prose, which is a bit like comparing linguistic apples and oranges.[13]

Despite such criticism, Mendenhall deserves to be better known than he is today. As the progenitor of a more objective, quantifiable approach to author profiling, he laid the groundwork for later work on attribution and stylometric analyses. The quantitative edifice he constructed may not have aged well, but later work nevertheless rests on this foundation.

THE ENTHUSIAST

What is the most widely read Christian text of all time? The answer would have to be the Bible. But what book would be second? It is probably *The Imitation of Christ*, a text that was written in the early fifteenth century and was extremely popular for many years afterward. Hundreds of hand-copied manuscripts survive, and once mechanical printing was established, about 50 years after *The Imitation's* composition, hundreds of editions were produced, both in its original 42,000-word Latin version and in scores of translations. In recent history, figures as diverse as the Trappist monk Thomas Merton and former president Bill Clinton have placed it on their lists of all-time favorite books.

The appeal of *The Imitation* is easy to understand since it is full of practical guidance for those seeking to live as upright people of faith. The first of the four books that make up the work is titled "Useful Reminders for the Spiritual Life" and contains sections with headings like "Of Thinking before You Act," "Of Avoiding Hasty Judgments," and "Of Putting Up with Others' Faults."[14] Written at a time when people lived crowded together and with few creature comforts, meditations on patience and forbearance would have been consoling for many.

The Imitation is also full of adages that have entered the English vernacular. "Choose the lesser of two evils," "out of sight, out of mind," and "man proposes, but God disposes" are but a few well-known examples. Given the popularity and influence of this work, it may be surprising to learn that it was released anonymously. This is, however, in keeping with the text's philosophy, which places a premium on self-abnegation and the seeking of inner fulfillment as opposed to worldly recognition.

That's not to say, however, that there isn't a leading candidate with regard to its authorship. Soon after *The Imitation* became popular, it was attributed to Thomas à Kempis, a German Dutch clergyman who was born near Köln and led a monastic life in the present-day Netherlands. It is believed that he wrote the books that make up *The Imitation* to provide instruction to the novices of his order. A hand-copied manuscript from 1441, which survives in Brussels, has his name on it, although it is unclear from the inscription whether he wrote the work or merely produced a copy of it.[15] Over time, a number of other possible authors for *The Imitation* have been proposed.

Some of these contenders for authorship can be dismissed fairly easily. Early on, for example, there was a belief that Bernard degli Uberti, a bishop of Parma who would become better known as St. Bernard, had produced it. There are clear similarities in tone between the writings of the Catholic saint and *The Imitation*—but also a major problem. *The Imitation* includes quotations from St. Francis of Assisi, who was born about 1181, or nearly 50 years after St. Bernard's death in 1133.[16] Unless Bernard possessed a time machine or a really good Ouija board, he is not a viable candidate for the paternity of *The Imitation*.

Other claims about the work's authorship have also been rejected. In 1604, for example, an assertion was made that it was the work of one John Gersen, a prelate who served as abbot at Vercelli. However, this seems to have been an attempt by the Benedictines to lay claim to the book and the prestige associated with having a member of their order as its author.[17] It isn't even clear that such an individual ever existed.

By the early modern period, there were only two serious candidates remaining as the possible authors: Thomas à Kempis and Jean Charlier de Gerson, a French theologian and chancellor of the University of Paris. External evidence favored à Kempis, but in the minds of some scholars, the dispute had not been settled. As recently as 1925, for example, the French historian Alfred Pereire made a forceful argument for Gerson.[18]

This question about the authorship of *The Imitation* would become a major focus in the life of a British mathematician. George Udny Yule was born in Scotland in 1871 and initially trained as an engineer. However, he came under the influence of Karl Pearson, one of the founders of mathematical statistics, and ended up redirecting his talents in that direction. Yule was eventually offered a lectureship in statistics at Cambridge University and taught there for many years.[19] He worked in a variety of areas and is probably best known among his fellow statisticians for contributions to time-series analysis and econometrics.[20] At the age of 60, he suffered a heart attack that left him a semi-invalid and forced him to take an early retirement from teaching. After a career of more traditional statistical work, he turned his attention to applying quantitative techniques to author attribution and the study of literary vocabulary.[21]

Yule's first foray into stylometry was a paper he published in 1939. In it, he explored whether sentence length could be used to identify the author of a given text. He showed that the average number of words per sentence differs consistently when comparing texts written by four randomly chosen authors: Francis Bacon, Samuel Taylor Coleridge, Charles Lamb, and Thomas Babington Macaulay. Of the four, Bacon is the most long-winded: his sentences clock in at an average of 49 words. Macaulay, on the other hand, is the most laconic, employing on average only 22 words per sentence. Yule concluded that sentence length can function as "a characteristic of the author's style."[22]

Because of his choice of sentence length as his unit of analysis, Yule had to contend with defining what constitutes a sentence, which might seem unproblematic at first blush. However, he had to figure out how to deal with embedded quotations from other writers as well as the inconsistent terminal punctuation employed by his candidate authors.

Since à Kempis was a prolific writer, Yule had no difficulty in identifying known texts from which to draw a random sample of sentences to examine. The works of Gerson, on the other hand, are a "rather appalling mass" from which he had to take care to select "normal prose" as opposed to, for example, the lists of curt injunctions that the chancellor had enthusiastically compiled.[23]

In general, Yule found that Gerson composed wordier sentences than à Kempis and that the average sentence length for *The Imitation*—16.2 words— was a better match with à Kempis (17.9) than with Gerson (22.7). This result aligned with Yule's preconceived notions about the true author of *The Imitation*, but it also demonstrates the problem with using sentence length as an authorial yardstick. How closely must sentence lengths match in order to conclude that a given individual is the true author of an anonymous work?

By the early 1940s, Yule turned from sentence length to a consideration of vocabulary richness as a way of differentiating writers. His goal, as before, was to develop quantitative techniques for making attributions about the authors of disputed works. He shifted his focus to word-frequency distributions but continued to explore whether à Kempis or Gerson was the author of *The Imitation*.

Vocabulary richness, also known as lexical diversity, is a measure of how many different words an author employs in a given text. Some writers have a large vocabulary and use many different words in their work, whereas others make use of a more limited pool of terms. In general, texts with high lexical diversity will be more challenging to read. However, lexical diversity might also function as the fingerprint that differentiates two or more authors.

To quantify lexical diversity, Yule created a statistic—characteristic K— that takes into account a variety of factors. These include the number of words in a text, called tokens; the total number of unique words, called types; the number of times a given word repeats within a text; and the text's length. For example, the phrase "I came, I saw, I conquered" contains six tokens but only four types since the word "I" appears three times. The formula for K assigns different weights to these repetitions, and a text with a relatively high K has many repeated words. Texts low in K, on the other hand, contain more lexical diversity.

Taking samples from *The Imitation* and from the texts written by à Kempis and Gerson, Yule calculated K for the disputed text and for its two candidate authors. The value of K for *The Imitation* was 84.2, whereas the statistic for à Kempis was 59.7. Gerson's K was a mere 35.9. Neither author's result is a great match with *The Imitation*, but à Kempis's K is closer than Gerson's, and Yule concluded that it was additional evidence that à Kempis had authored the devotional work.[24]

An important detail concerning Yule's methodology is that he chose to examine only the nouns in his text samples. This was done partly to make all the counting required somewhat easier, but it also reflects a prejudice that is worth noting. Yule wrote that he chose to exclude "words of little or no significance as regards style, such as prepositions, pronouns, etc."[25] His intuitive belief that function words provide no useful stylometric information would prove to be mistaken, and we have already seen some evidence of this in the discussion of idiolects in chapter 1.

In sum, this retired stylometric hobbyist can be seen as an important transitional figure in the history of attributional research. Yule's earlier work on *The Imitation* has much in common with Mendenhall's notions about the defining characteristic of an author's style. For Mendenhall, the focus was word length, and in Yule's initial forays, it was sentence length. In his later work, however, Yule concluded that the actual words employed by authors are even more diagnostic. Later developments in stylometry would prove that he was right—but also that he had chosen the wrong class of words to study.

There was, however, an even more consequential impediment for these pioneers and their search for a telltale linguistic signature. The fundamental problem with metrics such as word length, sentence length, and vocabulary richness is the assumption that the essence of a given author's writing style can be divined from one variable and distilled into one number and that this unitary measure can differentiate one author from another—or from all others. By examining only one variable at a time, these methodologies are simply not sensitive enough to detect the subtleties that underlie an author's linguistic fingerprint.[26]

Yule had performed a valuable service in shifting stylometric attention to particular classes of words, but there was no way to fully exploit this insight by employing a univariate approach. It would take another generation—and the advent of computers—before the multivariate analyses of function words would revolutionize the field. Appropriately enough, the breakthrough would come from the analysis of texts from an earlier revolution.

GOSPEL TRUTH

As part of his stewardship of the early Christian church, Paul the Apostle wrote a series of letters to the far-flung communities of faith throughout the

Roman Empire. They are believed to have been written between 47 and about 68 CE, when he was tried and executed in Rome. These epistles provided encouragement to persecuted communities but also often addressed matters of Christian doctrine. As a result, the dispatches became foundational documents for Christianity and make up 13 of the 27 books of the New Testament. These so-called Pauline epistles were recognized as canon during the fourth century, and their authorship went largely unquestioned until the early nineteenth. And when stylometric techniques for analyzing texts were developed at the end of that century, the authorship of the Pauline epistles became a natural focus for such work.

There is a scholarly consensus concerning seven of the 13 epistles: they are almost universally regarded as letters that Paul himself wrote and also appear on the earliest lists of canonical works. These are First Thessalonians, Galatians, First Corinthians, Philippians, Philemon, Second Corinthians, and Romans. Debate about authorship has been focused largely on the remainder, which includes Ephesians, Colossians, and Second Thessalonians. An additional three of the disputed six are collectively referred to as the pastoral Epistles, or the pastorals for short. These are First Timothy, Second Timothy, and Titus.[27]

The epistles believed to have been composed by Paul are similar in theme and are also alike in their style and vocabulary. The disputed epistles, on the other hand, deviate in a variety of ways from those that are viewed as authentic. In the first decade of the nineteenth century, the biblical scholars Johann Schmidt and Friedrich Schleiermacher came to view the three pastoral Epistles with particular suspicion. They ultimately rejected them as inauthentic, basing their conclusions on the letters' tone, content, and theological considerations.[28] Additional doubts along the same lines were raised in 1880 in an influential analysis by Heinrich Holtzmann, a professor of theology at the University of Strasbourg.[29]

But could a more fine-grained linguistic analysis shed additional light on this authorship issue? One problem with analyzing the 13 Pauline epistles is that several are extremely short. Only two—Romans and First Corinthians—exceed 8,000 words in the original Ancient Greek. Five of the six disputed works contain fewer than 2,000 words each, and one—Titus—is a mere 779 words in length. (The corresponding word counts in English translations are about one-third higher.[30])

As an aid to study, scholars have compiled concordances for the books of the Bible. A concordance can be thought of as an index on steroids: the occurrence of each and every content word is listed alphabetically and keyed to the book, chapter, and verse where it can be found. This is convenient for those who might want to know what, for example, the Bible has to say about a topic like love, a word that appears 310 times in the King James Version: 131 times in the Old Testament and 179 in the New Testament. Concordances of the 5,600 Greek root words in the New Testament had been compiled by the sixteenth century,[31] and these were pressed into service by those looking for clues concerning Paul's authorship.

A concordance allows users to find not only common terms but also those that are mentioned rarely or even only a single time. A word that appears only once in a text or group of texts is referred to by the Greek term *hapax legomenon* (meaning "something that has been said once"), or *hapax* for short.

Why would the presence of unique words be important? In 1921, the British clergyman Percival Harrison suggested that a text with a large number of such hapaxes, relative to similar texts, might be an indication that it was inauthentic. Imagine, for example, that you receive an email every now and then from an elderly aunt who typically writes to you about the weather or her grandchildren's sports activities. Words like "sunny" or "softball" might occur frequently. But if you receive a message from her that refers to things she'd never mentioned before, such as "sequestration" or "chirality," you might well suspect that someone has hacked your aunt's account and written the email instead.

Harrison looked for the hapaxes in the Pauline letters and found more of them in the three pastoral Epistles—about 11 to 13 per page—than in the other 10 letters, which have only three to seven per page. His conclusion was that the three pastorals are likely inauthentic and suggested that they had been composed during the second century instead.[32]

There are, however, a number of problems with using hapaxes as a way of assessing an author's identity. The British scholar Walter Workman counted the hapaxes in eight plays of Shakespeare and found a similar range as in the Pauline letters: about three to 11 unique terms per page. In comparison to *Julius Caesar* and *Comedy of Errors*, both of which had a low number of hapaxes per page—fewer than five each—*Hamlet*, *King Lear*, and *Macbeth* all had 10 or more unique words per page. But clearly, the latter plays are as "Shakespearian" as the former.[33] In addition, a recent reanalysis of the Pauline letters by Jermo van Nes, who controlled for proper nouns, quoted text, and prepositional compounds, failed to find a higher incidence of unique words in the pastoral Epistles when compared to the epistles that are regarded as authentic.[34]

Another issue with tabulating unique words is even more fundamental: what counts as a word? At first blush, the answer may seem obvious, but it turns out to be unexpectedly complex. Let's imagine, for example, that a hapax within a given set of English texts is the word "unhappiness." It should be counted as a unique term if it appears only once. But what if the author also made use of the word "happy"? The use of the former term seems to imply knowledge of the latter. So should "unhappiness" be counted as unique or not?

A solution to this quandary can be found in linguistics. In that field, scholars have decreed that each concept is represented by a single uninflected word form, called a *lemma*. By this logic, "happy" is a lemma, and all of its variant forms—such as happiness, unhappy, and unhappiness—are part of the same concept. (This is why a dictionary will instruct a user seeking the word "broken" to look instead under the headword "break.") But even this solution isn't foolproof. Does the use of the word "selfish," for example, imply that the author knows the word "self"? The two concepts are related but distinctly different. As a result, making decisions about whether hapaxes exist in a given set of texts can be somewhat subjective.

Most disputes over author attribution have been the subject of a study or two. In contrast, the literature on the authorship of the Pauline epistles is vast, with scores of papers and entire books devoted to various aspects of the problem. It undoubtedly ranks as the most studied authorship issue in history. As a result, only a few representative studies will be summarized here.

Andrew Morton, a minister of the Church of Scotland, addressed the Pauline authorship question in the 1960s by following the lead of Yule, whose work was described in the previous section. By examining the distribution of sentence lengths in the epistles attributed to Paul, Morton concluded that only four of them—Romans, Galatians, and First and Second Corinthians—had been written by him.[35]

Of more significance for later stylometric work, however, was Morton's study of the use of common function words. Specifically, he examined Greek texts for the use of conjunctions, such as *kai* ("and"), and particles, such as *de* ("but"). Along with Mosteller and Wallace's work on the *Federalist Papers*, described later in this chapter, the insight that function words could differentiate the writing styles of authors would become one of fundamental importance. It represents a decisive movement away from the more subjective stylistic features that earlier scholars had employed. In a paper with Sidney Michaelson published in 1972, Morton would refer to this approach as "the new stylometry."[36]

A 2011 survey of British New Testament scholars provides a useful snapshot of the state of consensus about the Pauline epistles. Of the 109 respondents, there was virtually universal agreement about the seven letters that have been traditionally attributed to Paul. A bit more than half of the respondents endorsed Second Thessalonians and Colossians as authentically Pauline. Ephesians fared a bit worse at about one-third. And with regard to the three pastoral Epistles, fewer than one-quarter of the scholars were willing to ascribe them to Paul.[37]

A 2019 study by Jacques Savoy sought to apply multivariate techniques to the Pauline authorship problem. (The logic of such methods is described in later sections.) The body of texts he analyzed—called a corpus—consisted of all 21 New Testament epistles, which comprise about 52,000 words in the original Greek. Introductory verses indicating the author and the audience were removed.

Savoy tested three models of authorship. In line with Morton's claim, a Four Letter hypothesis assumes that only Romans, Galatians, and First and Second Corinthians are authentic. A Seven Letter hypothesis adds in Philippians, First Thessalonians, and Philemon. Finally, a Ten Letter hypothesis assumes that all the letters, with the exception of the three pastoral Epistles, are genuine. By employing a variety of techniques, Savoy was able to identify three groups of letters. Although he found some support for the Four and Ten Letter hypotheses, the study failed to unambiguously support either of them. He concluded that the three groups of letters could have been written by the same person or by two or three different people. As mentioned earlier, textual analysis of the epistles is problematic because many of them are short. In addition, there is evidence that Paul employed one or more assistants to write the letters, and this could have affected the results as well.[38]

So where does that leave us? Some scholars have suggested that this authorship problem may be insoluble given current evidence. Others have argued that more sophisticated studies of the letters' vocabulary could provide additional information.[39] Finally, some hold out hope that new types of data could be extracted from the epistles and that new types of statistical analyses might be developed to test the various authorship theories.[40] The problems posed by the Pauline epistles have not been solved, but the methods developed to address them have served as an essential test bed and incubator for the field of authorship attribution.

FOUNDING FATHERS

The American Experiment was in trouble. Although the former colonists had been successful in their war of independence against Britain, they now had to figure out how to govern themselves. The Articles of Confederation, drafted and approved during the war, had been a stopgap measure, and it was clear that something more permanent and comprehensive was needed. During the summer of 1787, the founders gathered in Philadelphia to create a constitution for the United States. This governing document would require ratification by the individual state legislatures. And by the fall of that year, it was far from certain that the proposed framework, with its call for a strong central government, would be approved by them.

Seeing the need to explain their handiwork, three of the founders wrote a series of 77 essays to champion the proposed constitution. Their goal was to encourage New Yorkers to elect Federalists to the state's ratifying convention, scheduled to meet in June 1788. The essays they produced were published in three New York City newspapers over a seven-month period, from the fall of 1787 through the following spring. These 77 essays, along with eight others, were also collected and published in two volumes.[41] The New York delegates met in Poughkeepsie beginning on June 17. Five weeks later, the U.S. Constitution, along with a series of amendments to guarantee personal freedoms and rights, was ratified by the delegates in a vote of 30 to 27. The essayists had carried the day—but by a very narrow margin.[42]

It would be difficult to overstate the historical importance of these documents. Although they were instrumental in securing ratification of the Constitution, they have also been cited hundreds of times in decisions by the Supreme Court.[43] The authorship of some of the essays, however, has been a matter of continuing debate. Anti-Federalist feelings ran high in New York, and since two of the authors had taken part in the Constitutional Convention, all of them were published under the pseudonym "Publius" to conceal that fact. It is now known that the authors were Alexander Hamilton, James Madison, and John Jay. But which man wrote which essays?

Two days before his fatal duel with Aaron Burr in 1804, Hamilton gave his lawyer a list in which he declared authorship of 63 of the essays. Madison, after his presidency in 1818, would lay claim to having written 29 of them.[44] Clearly, one man or the other was misremembering who had written what.

Based on external evidence, such as the existence of handwritten drafts or the topics under discussion, there has long been a consensus about who wrote most of the 77 original essays. Hamilton was thought to have penned 43 of them, Madison had authored 14, and Jay had written five. Three others were thought to have been written jointly by Hamilton and Madison. But that left 12 for which the authorship was in dispute. Madison and Hamilton held similar beliefs and wrote in similar styles. Would it ever be possible to assign authorship to the dozen disputed essays? For a century, there was no real progress on answering this question.

In 1916, S. A. Bailey, identified only as a member of the Salt Lake City Bar, published a short article on the *Federalist* authorship problem and made an observation that would prove to be crucial. He noted that the conjunction "while" tends to be employed in the essays that were indisputably written by Hamilton, whereas in the disputed papers, there was a strong preference for "whilst," which is a synonymous term. As it happens, "whilst" was frequently employed by Madison in the essays that were definitely written by him and also in his other writings.

Based on this difference, Bailey concluded, "One little circumstance, however—the use of one little word—seems to indicate quite clearly that the disputed numbers were the product of the brain and the pen of Madison."[45] Bailey's conjecture was intriguing, but was it definitive? Could authorship be proven by the use—or the avoidance—of only a single term?

In 1941, Fred Mosteller, a mathematics graduate student at Princeton, had his attention drawn to the *Federalist* authorship problem by the political scientist Frederick Williams. They decided to see whether sentence length could serve as a useful metric for differentiating the writings of Hamilton and Madison. As we have seen, Udny Yule used this technique to attribute *The Imitation of Christ* to Thomas à Kempis.

Mosteller and Williams began to patiently count the words in each sentence of the essays, although doing this reliably turned out to be surprisingly difficult. Finding themselves in need of assistance, they recruited their wives into the counting enterprise.[46] All this effort, however, led to a discouraging result: with regard to sentence length, the two founding fathers were identical twins. For the essays with undisputed authorship, the mean length of Hamilton's sentences was 34.55 words, while Madison's was 34.59. Even a measure of variability was virtually the same: the standard deviation for Hamilton's sentences was 19.2, while Madison's was 20.3. Clearly, the approach that Yule had championed would not be sufficient to determine authorship in this case. And the disruptions caused by World War II prevented the two men from continuing work on the problem.

In 1959, Mosteller returned to the *Federalist*. By then, he was a faculty member at Harvard. He joined forces with David Wallace, a statistician at the University of Chicago. The two men had gotten to know each other during a sabbatical that Mosteller had taken there. As they discussed finding a problem to work on together, Mosteller received a letter from the historian Douglass Adair. He had learned of Mosteller's interest in the *Federalist* problem and drew his attention to Bailey's conjecture about "while" and "whilst." Although these two words appear in less than half of the essays, perhaps other terms could be found that would aid in determining the authorship of the disputed papers.

The words that writers employ, however, are highly dependent on the topic under discussion. And since the *Federalist* essays address many different topics, their use is highly context dependent. In other words, the terms an author uses may be more a reflection of their topic than their writing style. Mosteller and Wallace realized that an analysis of common function words, which appear in all the essays, might provide a way around this problem. With the help of many students, they set about creating concordances, or lists of words, that appear in each essay.

In one sense, the researchers were lucky: they had a corpus of 94,000 words known to have been written by Hamilton and 114,000 that were unquestionably penned by Madison. However, this bounty was tempered by the fact that all those words had to be collated and coded. At first, it was all done by hand, but eventually, the task was computerized. It must be kept in mind, however, that making use of computers in the early 1960s was laborious and expensive. The IBM 7090 behemoth they worked with would cost about $20 million today, and programming such machines was still in its infancy. It took months to write and debug the necessary code, and a small army of students was employed to punch the necessary cards.[47]

In the end, however, the search for asymmetries in word use was successful. They were able to validate Bailey's claim regarding Hamilton's and Madison's differential use of "while" and "whilst." In addition, they found that, in the essays with known authors, Hamilton employed "upon" and "enough" more frequently than did Madison. Madison, on the other hand, used "by" and "from" more often than Hamilton. And a computer would allow them to perform a multivariate analysis of these differences in word usage.

They settled on a set of 30 words that provided the greatest discrimination between the two authors. In addition to those already mentioned, the final set included adjectives ("apt," "kind") adverbs ("commonly," "consequently"), conjunctions ("though," "while"), determiners ("both," "this"), and prepositions ("of," "on").

Mosteller and Wallace employed a Bayesian approach to quantify their results. At the outset, they arbitrarily assumed 50-50 prior odds regarding authorship; that is, Hamilton and Madison were viewed as equally likely to have written a particular essay. Then they looked at the frequencies of the 30 words, one by one, and used the result to refine their prior probability estimate. Finally, they quantified their findings in terms of odds ratios.

And the results? Mosteller and Wallace concluded that Madison had written all 12 of the disputed essays. The weakest odds concerning authorship were for essay no. 55: 80 to 1 for Madison. The researchers characterized this as strong but not overwhelming. The next weakest result was for no. 56 (800 to 1 for Madison). All the others gave Madison extremely high odds ratios.[48] With regard to the two essays that historians had been most divided about—nos. 62 and 63—the evidence was overwhelming that Madison had written them.

Mosteller and Wallace reported their findings at a joint meeting of the American Statistical Association, the Biometric Society, and the Institute of Mathematical Sciences, held in Minneapolis in September 1962. It had taken them and their legion of student workers three years to complete the project, even with the help of their mainframe computer.[49]

Reflecting on their accomplishment, Mosteller and Wallace were prescient as they looked to the future. In the preface of their 1964 book on the *Federalist* project, they wrote,

> Methods like ours can be used for other authorship studies, and we anticipate that the cost will become relatively cheap in the future. Preparing text for a high-speed computer is currently responsible for a major part of the cost. Savings should come when an electronic reader becomes available that can read text directly from printed material into the computer.[50]

The benefit of applying statistical techniques to questions of authorship, however, was not immediately recognized. Seven years after the publication of Mosteller and Wallace's book, the statistician Stephen Fienberg published a review to bring their work to the attention of historians.[51]

It took a while for others to catch up, but Mosteller and Wallace's efforts were foundational for contemporary work on author attribution. Their results have also stood the test of time. As researchers devise new stylometric techniques, they often test them on the authorship of the *Federalist* essays. These results have supported their original conclusions again and again.[52] In their study of the founding fathers, Frederick Mosteller and David Wallace would themselves become founding fathers for employing more sophisticated statistics and computers to assist in author attribution.

THE RENEGADE

In the late 1970s, John Burrows was a frustrated man. The 50-year-old professor of English was on sabbatical leave at Oxford University and deeply engrossed in studying the vocabulary of *Mansfield Park*. To create a concordance of words that appeared in Jane Austen's text, Burrows found himself laboriously copying them, one by one, onto index cards. It was a remarkably tedious process, and he was hamstrung by the same technology that had been available to Thomas Mendenhall a century earlier. Given that *Mansfield Park* weighs in at 160,000 words, Burrows's project soon became unmanageable.[53]

Back home in Australia at the University of Newcastle, Burrows borrowed a page from Mosteller and Wallace's playbook and decided to see if his study could be computerized. In 1979, Burrows began work to create machine-readable versions of Austen's novels. Although he was grappling with the same issues as the earlier researchers in their analysis of the *Federalist* essays 20 years before, the tools available to him could now make such tasks much easier. In particular, the development of early markup languages like COCOA greatly simplified the task of creating and analyzing digital versions of analog texts. Burrows was able to create a concordance of all 710,000 words that make up Austen's oeuvre, and he now had the tools he needed to delve into her language use.

Burrows chose to analyze the most common words that appear in Austen's six novels. These include personal pronouns (such as "I" and "you"), prepositions ("in," "of"), and conjunctions ("and," "but"). The conventional wisdom in his field was that such language is inert—the necessary connective tissue for language but uninteresting in and of itself. These common words had traditionally been regarded as unwanted spoil by literary scholars who went digging in the linguistic mines of the authors they studied. Burrows decided to see if the conventional wisdom was correct.

He found that the 30 most frequent words make up about 40 percent of the total verbiage in Austen's works, and these became the grist for his analytical mill. In particular, he zeroed in on the words spoken by 48 of Austen's major characters, whom he defined as those with at least 2,000 words of dialogue. What he found was that the characters' voices were distinctively different from the voice of the narrator as well as from one another: they displayed individual idiolects, just as real people do. Furthermore, the idiolects of Austen's characters were different from those in the works of other authors he analyzed, such as Virginia Woolf and Henry James.

What was the basis for Burrows's claims about Austen? Like Mosteller and Wallace, he made use of multivariate analyses to tackle the problem. The first step was to identify the most frequently used words spoken by Austen's characters and to create correlation matrices of these terms. These matrices can be thought of as big spreadsheets in which each cell represents how many times one of Austen's characters used a particular word.

To impose order on such an unruly set of numbers, these matrices can be reduced to eigenvectors via principal component analysis (PCA). This statistical technique seeks to find underlying dimensions that can account for the most variance in the data. Although there are as many dimensions as there are items in the analysis, the first principal component is the one that accounts for the most variance, the second accounts for as much of the remaining variance as possible, and so on. The data from the first two components, or vectors, can then be plotted. PCA can be thought of as a distance metric: points that are close to one another in a two-dimensional space—be they characters, novels, or authors—have more in common than those that are farther apart.

Such analyses can reveal aspects of language use that would otherwise remain hidden. For example, Burrows discovered that when he analyzed only the purely narrative sections from Austen's six novels via PCA, one of the resulting vectors was a map that aligned the books in the chronological order of their composition. In other words, Austen's own idiolect changed over time, but an analysis of her most used words was sensitive enough to discern this gradual transformation.[54]

Burrows's book on Austen, published in 1987, was a landmark achievement and the beginning of what is now called computational stylistics. It was not, however, a development welcomed by everyone. Students of literature and, in general, scholars of the humanities had traditionally confined themselves to qualitative textual analysis. A movement toward quantification was viewed by many with distaste or dismissed as fundamentally misguided.

To a surprising degree, academicians are an insular and territorial bunch, and they tend to view scholars from other disciplines who encroach on their turf as unwanted interlopers. G. Udny Yule, Fred Mosteller, and David Wallace—the protagonists from the earlier sections of this chapter—were mathematicians and statisticians. They could be easily dismissed by critics of quantification as mere dilettantes who dabbled in textual studies. And Morton was a man of the cloth, not an academician! Burrows, however, was one of their own: a respected colleague and card-carrying member of their tribe. Nevertheless, he was also someone who wanted to bring numbers and calculation into the arts. And for some, this was tantamount to releasing a mathematical serpent into the humanists' Garden of Eden.

Given such attitudes, there were critics who were less than impressed by Burrows's book on Austen and the methods he employed in it. One reviewer, with ill-concealed snark, opined that "most of the conclusions which he [Burrows] reaches are not far from the ordinary reader's natural assumptions."[55] And in a later paper, Burrows himself acknowledged the "special scepticism" that statistical analyses tend to engender.[56] But he didn't let the doubters deter him. If anything, his response was more in line with Patrick Henry's famous quote: if this be treason, make the most of it.

In a paper written with Anthony Hassall and published in 1988, Burrows made his first foray into author attribution. The subject of the article was the narrative *Anna Boleyn*, published by Henry Fielding in 1743. His conclusion was that the beginning of the narrative had been written by Fielding but that it had been continued by his sister Sarah. Furthermore, it seemed that the ending had been either revised or added by her brother.

Burrows made use of the same technique he had employed in his study of Austen: an analysis of the most common words in the text using PCA. He was able to make claims about the narrative's multiple authors by analyzing sections of the work separately and by comparing them to known writing by the two siblings. Although others had speculated that Sarah's linguistic fingerprints could be discerned in the narrative, Burrows was able to provide quantitative evidence in support of this theory.[57]

In 1989, Burrows stepped down as a professor of English at Newcastle to become the founding director of the university's Centre for Literary and

Linguistic Computing.[58] It seemed that his transformation into a different kind of scholar was complete. He continued to publish research on author attribution and literary style, to hone his statistical techniques, and to push back against the critics of computer-assisted literary criticism.[59]

In 2002, Burrows's contributions were honored when he was named a recipient of the Roberto Busa Prize. It was certainly an appropriate recognition: Busa, an Italian Jesuit priest, had spent 30 years creating a massive concordance of some 10 million words penned by the medieval theologian Thomas Aquinas.[60] And in accepting the Busa Prize, Burrows acknowledged the debt he owed to his intellectual forebearers, such as Mendenhall and Yule.

The heart of his address was a proposed refinement of his analytical technique, which he dubbed Delta. Instead of using raw frequency counts in the correlation matrices, Burrows proposed replacing them with z-scores. This is a commonly used statistical technique in which a standardized score is computed by subtracting the mean of a distribution of scores from an observed value and then dividing it by the standard deviation of that distribution.[61] This standardization is desirable because it prevents the most common words in the text, which appear extremely frequently, from swamping and suppressing the effects of words that are slightly less common.[62]

In a follow-up paper that explained his methodology in more detail, Burrows was candid about its limitations. For example, in studies using this technique, it was found that the texts to be analyzed need to be 1,500 words or longer.[63] This requirement makes the Delta procedure ill-suited for forensic purposes, such as determining whether a criminal suspect wrote a ransom note or sent a series of cell phone texts. (For such brief snatches of language, law enforcement makes use of other methods, and some of these will be described in chapter 5.) Burrows would perfect his technique in the following years, as with a metric he dubbed Zeta in a 2007 paper,[64] and others would make refinements of their own.

Over time, it became clear that Burrows's Delta has other limitations. For example, it seems to perform better with some languages than others. A study by Jan Rybicki and Maciej Eder showed that Delta provided good discrimination for texts written in English and German but that it performed somewhat less well for those written in Latin and Polish.[65]

And critiques of the quantitative methods employed in the digital humanities have persisted. Nan Da, for example, has argued that those who use tools like PCA are essentially throwing away any useful data that don't conform to the two most significant vectors in their analyses.[66] But even the critics of so-called nontraditional authorship attribution, who accuse its practitioners of cherry-picking their results, acknowledge that Burrows is "one of the most scientifically rigorous."[67]

Burrows died in 2019 at the age of 90, a few days after the passing of his wife.[68] He lived to see his Delta procedure become the "standard first port-of-call for attributional problems"[69] as well as its inclusion in a number of stylometric software packages. And in the following chapters, we will see examples of how Burrows's Delta has helped to identify the authors of disputed works, expose forgeries, and unmask ghostwriters.

CHAPTER THREE

WHO?

Anonymous and Concealed Authorship

SPARTACUS

On January 16, 1996, Random House published *Primary Colors: A Novel of Politics*.[1] Ostensibly, it was what the subtitle suggests: a work of fiction. It is the story of a starry-eyed staffer serving with a presidential campaign who becomes disillusioned by the trench warfare required for his candidate to emerge victorious. Virtually anyone who followed politics, however, could read it as a thinly veiled description of Bill Clinton's quest for the U.S. presidency in 1992.

Political pundits were delighted to have two puzzles to solve, although the first one would prove easier to crack than the second. Part of the fun in reading such a work is figuring out the real-life equivalents of the dramatis personae. As it happened, the characters in the novel were so transparent that guessing who was who was an almost trivial task. Jack Stanton, the garrulous presidential candidate with an eye for the ladies, is all too obviously Bill Clinton. His long-suffering wife Susan is clearly a stand-in for Hillary Clinton. New York Governor Orlando Ozio closely resembles Mario Cuomo. Cashmere McLeod is a proxy for Gennifer Flowers and so on. Although some of the book's characters are composites of real people, there was little that was left to the reader's imagination.

In penning such a novel, its author was joining a long tradition stretching back more than three centuries. The genre is referred to as roman à clef ("novel with a key") and was invented by the French writer Madeleine de Scudéry. Similar to the author's goal in *Primary Colors*, de Scudéry's novels allowed her to criticize and mock the political figures of her own time. But by changing people's names and some minor details, the authors of such works create a bit of plausible deniability should its less-than-flattered real-life subjects accuse the author of libel or character assassination. Dozens of prominent writers have employed this subterfuge over the years.

The other puzzle in the case of *Primary Colors*, however, was the identity of the author, as it had been published anonymously. During the spring of 1996, the book would be a cause célèbre among the chattering classes, as public guesses were followed by vehement denials. That only deepened the mystery. This second puzzle would take six months to solve and would involve an unlikely duo: a Shakespeare scholar at Vassar College and a handwriting expert in North Carolina.

Speculation about the author's identity began even before the book was released. Two weeks before publication, a review in *Publishers Weekly* noted that the author's credentials had been vetted by a third party. This fact, combined with the author's deep knowledge of Beltway culture, led to speculation that they were a high government official and possibly even a member of the Clinton administration. The quality of the writing suggested that it was the product of a professional author.[2] Conjectures like these narrowed the list of potential suspects considerably.

The book would become a bestseller and was number one on the *New York Times* list for several weeks. Less than a month after publication, the film rights, which sold to Mike Nichols, netted the anonymous author more than a million dollars.[3]

On February 2, the *Washington Post* published a piece on whom they viewed as the top 35 authorial suspects, along with the odds that each person was "Anonymous." All of them were contacted, and all denied having written the novel.[4]

Later that month, *New York Magazine* published its own story about *Primary Colors*. The author of the piece was Donald Foster, a Vassar professor of English who had recently gained notice for identifying an anonymous funeral elegy as an unknown work by Shakespeare. If Foster was capable of settling a centuries-old cold case, it seemed likely that he could identify an unknown political novelist. The editors contacted him to ask for his assistance.

The magazine staff supplied Foster with digital versions of texts written by a number of individuals who might be Anonymous. The eight most likely suspects from the *Post's* list included columnists, political writers, and humorists. The magazine also gave Foster the first 30 pages of *Primary Colors*. He carefully analyzed the novel's opening pages, looking for uncommon words the author had employed. He selected 400 terms that were somewhat unusual, such as "Caucasian," "strut," and "threatening." Foster then had a computer program check the other writers' samples for instances of those words. However, none of the other writers tended to use them.

Foster requested more text from the novel as well as writing samples from their next tier of six suspects, which included columnists and novelists. None of these candidates matched Anonymous in terms of using the same uncommon words, and none had a voice that sounded like the person who wrote *Primary Colors*. Anonymous's writing did have some similarities with the writing of novelist Lisa Grunwald, but the match wasn't strong.

At this point, Foster nearly threw in the towel. He hadn't even gotten halfway through the *Post*'s list but decided to go ahead and check its next candidate: *Newsweek* columnist Joe Klein. Many pundits had dismissed him out of hand as a strong contender because a character in the novel who resembles Klein is described unfavorably. The *Post* had only given him 50-to-1 odds of being Anonymous. Foster decided to look at him anyway. And he immediately began to note similarities.

Both authors used the same adverbs, like "entirely," "precisely," and "wistfully." Both were fond of offbeat adverbs, like "goofily," "eerily," and "spottily." They wrote about states as modes, as in "listening mode," "campaign mode," and "crisis mode." Both loved prefixes like "semi-," "quasi-," and "mega-." Both showed a predilection for words ending in "-ish," such as "smallish," "warmish," and "puckish." Both drew out interjections ("ahh," "naww"). Finally, both Anonymous and Klein used certain words that didn't show up in any other suspect's samples, like "riffle," "gazillion," and "unironic."

Moving on from words, Foster spotted other similarities between Klein's *Newsweek* columns and Anonymous's style. Both used colons in atypical ways ("and: thus"). Both often employed dashes and brackets. There were similar short sentences beginning with "and then" or ending with "sort of." Words were run together ("okayokay"). Phrases were capitalized to emphasize them ("World's Most Obscure Universities"). People were "gutbuckets" or "slimebuckets." "Fella" was preferred over "fellow," and things were "well-oiled" or "well-greased."[5]

Foster was sure that he had his quarry.

Klein certainly had the résumé of someone who could have authored *Primary Colors*. From 1987 to 1992, he was a political columnist for the *New*

York Times. He then moved on to *Newsweek*, where his reporting on the Clinton campaign helped that periodical win a National Magazine Award. And during the period in which the novel was written, he had been providing political commentary for *CBS News*. The means, motive, and opportunity all seemed to be aligned.

Others came forward with similar suspicions. David Kusnet, chief speechwriter for Clinton during the 1992 campaign, noted that the author displayed a deep knowledge of New York politics, which argued against anyone who had spent their career solely in Washington. He publicly called out Klein as the suspected author.[6]

But Klein wouldn't admit it. On February 20, during his coverage of the New Hampshire primary, he was confronted with Foster's just-published exposé. "For God's sake," he exclaimed, "definitely, I didn't write it." He did, however, acknowledge that there were certain similarities between his work for *Newsweek* and the novel.[7]

The *Washington Post*'s own analysis was undertaken by Walter Stewart and Ned Feder. These scientists had created a plagiarism checker for the National Institutes of Health. Designed to sniff out cribbing in the scientific literature, their algorithm looked for exact matches of strings of 20 or more characters. This program suggested that a former *Post* writer and novelist, Sally Quinn, was the author, although she denied the attribution as well.[8]

Four months after publication, Anonymous was heard from again in an article in the *New York Times*. Anonymous claimed to be channeling their inner Dickens and satisfying a desire to write something "light and naughty in the Victorian manner."[9] Unsure about whether they could pull this off and not wanting to embarrass themselves, the author initially wanted to employ a pseudonym but was eventually persuaded to publish anonymously.

Undaunted by its earlier failure, the *Post* acquired, from a secondhand bookseller, a copy of *Primary Colors* that contained notes written by its author on several of its pages.[10] The newspaper had also gotten hold of samples of Klein's handwriting. In early July, *Post* reporter David Streitfeld contacted Maureen Casey Owens, a document examiner who had worked for 25 years with the Chicago Police Department. Streitfeld asked her to make the necessary comparisons.

Under the microscope, Owens spotted several telltale similarities. For example, the writer of both samples displayed a tendency to form lowercase "a"s with a slight serif on the right-hand side. "W" was written wide, with a low center and a curved ending. The "g"s were open and formed with a straight downstroke. After four days of analysis, Owens was able to report that the two samples were close matches.[11]

In hindsight, Joe Klein's denial of authorship in the February *Washington Post* article reads more like a non-denial. Channeling his inner Kirk Douglas, he had said at that time, "I am Spartacus. All of us who are accused of this should stand up and say 'I am Spartacus.' And share the royalties."[12]

On July 17, Klein was confronted with the evidence from the handwriting expert and asked point-blank if he was Anonymous. He replied, "I've said everything I have to say."[13] Later that day, however, Klein came clean at a news conference. He tried to defend his previous denials by using his journalistic profession as a shield. "There were times when I had to lie to protect a source, and I put this in that category," he asserted.[14]

Two years later, Mike Nichols's film *Primary Colors* was released. Its star-studded cast included John Travolta, Emma Thompson, Billy Bob Thornton, and Kathy Bates. The movie would not repeat the book's success, however: box office receipts failed to recoup the film's budget.

And things didn't go so well for Klein, either. He resigned from his gig at CBS nine days after acknowledging he had lied about not being the author of *Primary Colors*.[15] A sequel called *The Running Mate*, published in 2000, failed to attract much of an audience, and his later career at *Time* was not particularly distinguished. His greatest success had come when no one knew who he was.

PEEKING INTO THE CUCKOO'S NEST

On April 4, 2013, a crime fiction novel titled *The Cuckoo's Calling* was released by Mulholland Books, an imprint of Little, Brown. The story is typical for its genre: Cormoran Strike, a disabled army vet turned private eye, investigates the demise of a supermodel who fell from a balcony. Was it suicide, or was it murder? The book's cover identified the author as one Robert Galbraith. In publicity materials released by the publisher, he was described as a first-time author and a retired military policeman—much like his protagonist.

That spring, *Cuckoo's Calling* garnered some decent reviews: *Publishers Weekly*, for example, described Galbraith's novel as a "stellar debut," although others were less kind.[16] Financially, the novel enjoyed only modest success: during its first three months on the market, 1,500 print copies were purchased in Britain,[17] while booksellers in the United States moved only 500.[18] None of this was unusual for a novelist's debut effort in a genre already crowded with similar tales of murder and intrigue.

There was, however, something about the book that was unusual and possibly unique in the annals of publishing. It had been penned not by a first-time author but by one of the best-known and best-selling authors of all time. Robert Galbraith was, in reality, J. K. Rowling, and her publisher had agreed to release *Cuckoo's Calling* under a pen name.

The true story about the novel and its author was revealed in distinctly different ways. One was through old-fashioned gossip, while the other was decidedly more high-tech: a computerized comparison of the contents of the "Galbraith" book against Rowling's oeuvre and those of her fellow crime fiction writers.

Although Rowling had told only a few of her closest associates that she had composed a crime novel, this information came to the attention of Christopher Gossage, a partner at Russell Solicitors, the law firm that represents Rowling. He casually mentioned the book's true authorship to Judith Callegari, a best friend of his wife. Callegari, in turn, saw a Twitter posting by *Sunday Times of London* journalist India Knight in which she praised Galbraith's novel. In response, Callegari tweeted that *The Cuckoo's Calling* was the work of a well-known author. When Knight asked who that might be, Callegari spilled the beans and then, thinking better of it, deleted her account.[19]

Knight, in turn, told Richard Brooks what she had learned from Callegari. Brooks, the *Times'* art editor, decided to see if he could verify Callegari's claim. The circumstantial evidence was intriguing. He learned, for example, that Galbraith and Rowling had the same agent as well as the same editor at Little, Brown. Why would a first-time novelist be working with the editor of one of the world's best-selling authors? Brooks also thought that *Cuckoo's Calling* was simply too well written to have been penned by a retired military man without prior published work.

A close reading of Galbraith's novel revealed some intriguing similarities to Rowling's other books. For example, the purported crime novelist made use of certain Latin phrases, something that is unusual in that genre. But it was something that Rowling had done in the Harry Potter series. There were also descriptions of drug use, and similar scenes appear in Rowling's *The Casual Vacancy*, a book she had published the previous year.[20] In short, there was plenty of smoke, but was there a fire? Brooks decided that he needed independent verification.

And for that, the *Sunday Times* turned to a computer scientist in Pittsburgh, Pennsylvania, and a philosopher at Oxford.

Patrick Juola is a professor at Duquesne University. He is well known for having married textual analysis with software that can automate the process of author attribution. Working with his students, Juola developed software called the Java Graphical Authorship Attribution Program (JGAAP). The software is open source, so anyone can download and experiment with it. And instead of relying on one technique, the software provides a suite of analyses, including Burrows's Delta (described in the previous chapter) and a variety of other distance measures.[21] Put simply, the program allows a text by an unknown author to be compared against two or more known authors.

Imagine that someone used JGAAP to compare a randomly chosen Elizabethan play—one by Christopher Marlowe perhaps—against one of Shakespeare's and one written by Samuel Beckett. The program would dutifully report that the play in question has a much higher match with Shakespeare's play than with Beckett's. That doesn't, of course, mean that Shakespeare was the secret author of Marlowe's plays—or vice versa. It simply means that two English playwrights who were both born in 1564 are a lot more alike in their writing style than with a playwright who was born in Ireland some 340 years later.

Cal Flyn, a freelance writer working with the *Sunday Times*, asked Juola to compare *The Cuckoo's Calling* with Rowling's non–Harry Potter novel, *The Casual Vacancy*. He also compared Galbraith's book to three others penned by contemporary female British crime novelists: Ruth Rendell's *The St. Zita Society*, Val McDermid's *The Wire in the Blood*, and P. D. James's *The Private Patient*.[22]

Juola conducted four different tests. In one, his program generated a distribution of word lengths for each of the novels. He also compiled a list of the 100 most frequent words in each work. A third measure compared "n-gams," or strings of characters that are adjacent to one another. Juola chose to conduct a 4-gram analysis of each text. For example, Cormoran, the first name of Galbraith's protagonist, contains the 4-grams CORM, ORMO, RMOR, and so on. Finally, Juola looked at bigrams, or adjacent word pairs, such as AT BIGRAMS, BIGRAMS OR, and OR ADJACENT, in the first clause of this sentence. These can function as yet another marker of linguistic identity but at the level of phrases as opposed to words.

The next step was to compare the results from *Cuckoo* to those of the other books. Out of the four tests of similarity, all the other authors except for

Rowling were ruled out by at least one test. This strongly suggests—although it can't prove—that Galbraith and Rowling are one and the same.[23] It's also worth noting that such tests can't rule out the possibility that Galbraith is simply a Rowling wannabe who had carefully copied her style and word choice, although such a charade would be extremely difficult to pull off in a book-length work.

The *Sunday Times* and Flyn also reached out to Peter Millican, the Oxford professor of philosophy who also studies author attribution. His program, called the Signature Stylometric System, is conceptually similar to Juola's. In his analysis, Millican included two books from each of the four known authors. (For Rowling, the selected books were *The Casual Vacancy* and *Harry Potter and the Deathly Hallows*.) Not surprisingly, Millican found that the pairs of books written by the same author were judged as most similar to each other. But what of *The Cuckoo's Calling*? It lined up nicely with both *The Casual Vacancy* and the Harry Potter tome.

It's worth noting that Juola's and Millican's programs aren't performing magic—the wizarding kind or otherwise. They're simply counting a very large number of things very, very quickly. It would have taken the indefatigable Thomas Mendenhall years or even decades of mind-numbing labor to perform similar analyses of Shakespeare's plays. But it took Juola only about 30 minutes to make the required comparisons.[24] Millican, analyzing twice as many books as Juola, took five hours to arrive at the same conclusion.[25]

Both Juola and Millican were circumspect in reporting their results to Flyn since they could not state unequivocally that Rowling had written *The Cuckoo's Calling*. All they knew for certain was that *Cuckoo* was closer to Rowling's prose than to that of any of the other authors in their analyses. Armed with these results and the gossip that had reached the *Times* via Twitter, the paper confronted Rowling's publisher with the evidence, and Rowling chose to come clean. On July 14, the *Sunday Times* published an article by Brooks and Flyn in which they described their "unmasking" of Galbraith.[26]

Rowling was said to have been livid when her identity was revealed.[27] But it would be an understatement to say that the revelation was good for *The Cuckoo's Calling*'s sales. Shortly after the *Sunday Times* exposé, the book became a number one bestseller.[28] Not a word of the story between its covers had changed, but they were now viewed in a different—and more magical—light. The book would finish the year as the ninth-best-selling work on *USA Today*'s top fiction list for 2013. By October 2015, *Cuckoo* had gone on to sell a million copies in the United Kingdom across all formats.[29]

Six months after the exposé, the attorney whose loose lips led to Rowling's outing was fined £1,000 for his indiscretion, and his law firm had to pay for the costs associated with Rowling's legal action. The firm also made a donation to the nonprofit of her choice, the Soldier's Charity.[30]

But why had Rowling chosen to publish *Cuckoo's Calling* under a pseudonym in the first place? Using the name of an unknown male author instead of her own seems like a strategy designed to *depress* sales. What author would want that? Perhaps one who has no real need for additional income—and no other way of getting an objective evaluation of her work.

In a statement made after being outed, Rowling said that "it has been wonderful to publish without hype or expectation, and pure pleasure to get feedback under a different name."[31] And the earlier response to her first post–Harry Potter book may have been instructive. When Rowling released *A Casual Vacancy* under her own name in 2012, her comedy of manners garnered some high-profile negative reviews, including pans in the *New York Times* and the *Los Angeles Times*.[32] It seems likely, therefore, that Rowling wanted to test the waters for her foray into the crime genre by using a nom de plume.

Finally, to refute any suspicion that the whole affair had been a publicity stunt to stimulate sales, Rowling declared that she was donating the first three years of the books' profits to the Soldier's Charity. She would go on to write more Cormoran Strike novels under Galbraith's name, even though her army veteran's alter ego had been effectively dispatched by the unlikeliest of foes—a couple of computer programs that count words and letters.

DIARY OF A PUBLIC MAN

In August 1879, the *North American Review* published the first part in a series that appeared to provide new details about the events leading up to the Civil War. Titled *Diary of a Public Man*, the series gave its readers an insider's account of 78 of the most tumultuous days in U.S. history, from late December 1860 to mid-March 1861. Specifically, it chronicles the waning days of the Buchanan presidency and the first 12 days of Lincoln's. The narrative begins a week after the secession of South Carolina and encompasses the withdrawal of six more states from the Union during January and February 1861. The secession crisis would lead to the firing on Fort Sumter in April and then four years of unprecedented violence and bloodshed that would scar both the North and the South.

Even under normal circumstances, an insider's account of presidential politics would have considerable historical value. The events recounted in *A Public Man*, however, provide a unique glimpse into an unparalleled crisis at the highest levels of government. It is rich in details found in no other account from the period. The diary entries contain the words of Stephen Douglas and William Seward and no fewer than three conversations involving Abraham Lincoln.

Seventy years after its publication, the *New York Times* would characterize *A Public Man* as "the most tantalizing historical document in our literature."[33] There is, however, one detail that has made it a lightning rod for controversy since its publication. It was issued anonymously, and the *Review*'s editor, Allen Rice, took the secret of its author to the grave in 1889.

This lack of attribution means that historians have spent 140 years trying to answer a series of thorny questions. Is *A Public Man* a genuine account of the secession crisis? And if it is only partly authentic, which parts can be trusted? If it is not what it claims to be, then is it a joke, a hoax, or something else? Who wrote it? And why was it published anonymously?

A Public Man appeared in four parts between August and November 1879 and runs to nearly 25,000 words—the equivalent of about 100 double-spaced typewritten pages. A few details about the author can be gleaned by simply skimming the text. Most of its 21 entries bear a date, and some also indicate a place, which is always Washington or New York. The names of many individuals have been replaced with dashes. The casual use of French and the placement of diereses over the vowels of English words (e.g., "reëstablishment") suggest an author who has more than a passing familiarity with that language. Perhaps most significantly, the anonymous observer is also a skillful writer, with a keen eye for detail and a remarkable ear for dialogue. The diary entries weave an account of those desperate days that is lucid, compelling, and suspenseful.

But who could have written it? There were undoubtedly scores of plugged-in politicians, journalists, business owners, and government functionaries who frequented both the nation's capital and New York and who had a knowledge of French. And Lincoln probably spoke with many, many people in the days leading up to his inauguration. This is not a promising start for compiling a short list of possible authors.

When the diary was published, the newspapers of the day were quick to propose a variety of suspects. Perhaps *A Public Man* was excerpted from the diary of Horatio King, the postmaster general in the Buchanan administration. Or maybe it was the work of Charles E. Stewart, a senator from Michigan. Or perhaps it had been penned by Thurlow Weed, the publisher of the Albany *Evening Journal*. Or how about Amos Kendall, the business agent of Samuel Morse? These and many other individuals were proposed and hotly debated.[34]

In the first few decades after its publication, many historians considered *A Public Man* to be a genuine contemporaneous account and made use of it in their own work. Some of its details were corroborated by later research, adding to its aura of authenticity. However, there was not much progress in determining the author's identity.[35]

In 1896, Edward L. Pierce weighed in with the opinion that the diary was largely spurious. *A Public Man* contains an account of a meeting between its author and Massachusetts senator Charles Sumner, the unbending abolitionist who had been physically attacked on the floor of the Senate. Pierce was the biographer of Sumner, and he cast doubt on the diarist's contention that Sumner was actively involved in the creation of Lincoln's cabinet. And if that detail wasn't correct, then why should the rest of *A Public Man* be trusted?[36]

Historian Frank Maloy Anderson, after years of painstaking research, brought renewed attention to the mystery. In 1949, he published a book in which he concluded that *A Public Man* was only partly genuine. He was able to rule out some suspects as authors because they were in the wrong place at key dates in the diary's account. Anderson's candidate for authorship was Washington insider and lobbyist Samuel Ward, popularly known as "the King of the Lobby." Ward lived next door to William H. Seward, who became Lincoln's secretary of state, and this would have given him access to some of the principals in *A Public Man*. Anderson concluded that notes taken by Ward during the secession crisis had been embellished with recollection and, in some places, "pure invention" at a later date.[37]

Writing for *The New England Quarterly* in 1949, Evelyn Page rejected *A Public Man* as an authentic diary because it falls too neatly into four acts, corresponding to the four installments in the *North American Review*. Page concluded that the author must have been a writer from New England and put forward the name of Henry Adams, son of Massachusetts congressional representative Charles Adams. The younger Adams served as his father's private secretary in Washington during the secession crisis. Not only was he in the right place at the right time, but *A Public Man* bears stylistic similarity to his other work. Page admitted, however, that the evidence was circumstantial.[38] Nonetheless, others found it compelling: in 1951, the lawyer Benjamin Price also cast his vote for Henry Adams.[39]

Debate continued for decades, with new suspects joining the lineup. In 1976, John M. Taylor proposed that the author was John Forney, a Pennsylvania journalist and politician.[40] Once again, however, this was based on circumstantial evidence—compelling but far from ironclad.

In 2010, the historian Daniel Crofts wrote the definitive book about the mystery. His careful analysis found little stylistic correspondence between the writing of Anderson's suspect, Samuel Ward, and the text of *A Public Man*. Instead, he attributed the diary to the journalist William Henry Hurlbert, best known as the editor of the *New York World*.

Crofts found that Hurlbert's writing possessed many of the characteristics found in the diary. For example, both display a fondness for extreme adjectives, such as "absurd" or "wretched," as well as those ending in "-ly" ("certainly," "perfectly"). Hurlbert's oeuvre and *A Public Man* are also studded with alliterative phrases ("deeply disturbed," "virtual vindication"). This seems promising, but could Hurlbert's authorship be proven?

In order to settle the matter definitively, Crofts teamed with statistician David Holmes, who conducted a stylometric analysis of the diary and the leading suspects. Specifically, he compared the diary with texts written by Hurlbert, Samuel Ward, Henry Adams, and James E. Harvey (the latter individual was a respected journalist before the war). For control texts, Crofts chose the writings of Salmon Chase, who served in Lincoln's cabinet, as well as George Templeton Strong and Gideon Welles (Lincoln's secretary of the navy). Both men had kept diaries during the war.

Holmes selected three to five 3,000-word samples from *A Public Man* as well as the four suspected and three control authors. He then determined the 50 most common function words that appear in the texts. In this case, the top five are "the," "of," "and," "to," and "a." Next, he made use of the stylometric technique developed by John Burrows described in chapter 2. This method, called Delta, compares function words to their occurrence in each text sample. This creates a multidimensional array for each text that is then reduced, via principal component analysis or cluster analysis, to a smaller number of dimensions—usually only two.

We can think of each text sample as a point on a two-dimensional map. As with a map of some part of the world, in which the physical distance between two cities represents how far apart they are, we can visualize the results of the multivariate analyses by seeing whether texts from the candidate authors cluster with *A Public Man* or end up somewhere else on the map.

To check the validity of this methodology, Holmes first compared the texts from each of the three control authors: Chase, Strong, and Welles. A given author should look more like themselves than anyone else, so a two-dimensional map of the multivariate results should group each author's texts together. And this is what he observed.

Next, Holmes performed the same analysis with three of the candidate authors: Adams, Harvey, and Ward. Once again, the points clustered into three distinct groups, demonstrating that these authors also have distinctive linguistic fingerprints. He then added a fourth group of texts: those taken from *A Public Man*. The texts from the diaries, however, formed a distinct group that was removed from the other three.

Finally, Holmes compared Ward, Hurlbert, and *A Public Man*, making use of another multivariate technique called discriminant analysis. And the results of this test were conclusive: the diary was clearly a better match with the writing of William Hurlbert than with Samuel Ward.[41]

If correct, this means that *A Public Man* can't be a diary. Hurlbert was living and working in New York during the winter of the secession crisis. Crofts suspects that he may have received some of his inside information from Samuel Barlow, a New York attorney. The most likely source, however, was a close friend who turns out to be Samuel Ward. Crofts concluded that *A Public Man* was probably composed, with Ward's active assistance, shortly before its publication in 1879. There had been no conversations with Lincoln: neither man had ever even met the president. But between the two of them, they were able to create exchanges that seemed authentic.

Hurlbert's motivations for writing *A Public Man* remain obscure. He doesn't seem to have been motivated by money: he earned a comfortable living as a writer and editor. Crofts suggested that he may have been engaging in some historical revisionism. He also points out that Hurlbert was a risk taker by nature. The newspaper editor may simply have enjoyed the challenge and the prospect of fooling those credulous enough to accept the diary as a genuine account of the crisis.[42]

Today, Hurlbert's most visible legacy is Cleopatra's Needle, the ancient Egyptian obelisk that he arranged to have erected in Central Park in 1880. His other claim to fame would remain hidden from view until it was unearthed and proven in the twenty-first century.

THOMAS PYNCHON, TECHNICAL WRITER

Several well-known American authors have become famous for their work as well as for being reclusive. Emily Dickinson would fit in both categories, as would J. D. Salinger. If living a cloistered life were a competition, however, then the celebrated novelist Thomas Pynchon would, without a doubt, be a contender for a top prize. Since the 1960s, he has assiduously avoided contact with the media and the general public. Sightings of him are as rare as those of Sasquatch or the Yeti. He is best known for his lengthy, densely plotted, and critically acclaimed novels, such as *Gravity's Rainbow* (1973) and *Mason & Dixon* (1997). His more recent work, such as *Against the Day*, *Inherent Vice*, and *Bleeding Edge*, has received more variable levels of praise.

Pynchon's life prior to his withdrawal from society is reasonably well documented. Born in 1937, he grew up on Long Island and enrolled at Cornell before dropping out. He served in the navy for two years and was stationed at Norfolk, Virginia.[43] Returning to Cornell, he completed a degree in English in 1958. Pynchon then moved to New York City[44] and began writing *V.*, his first novel, which was published in April 1963.[45] This picaresque and often abstruse work received the William Faulkner Foundation Award for best debut novel the following year and launched Pynchon's career.[46]

There is, however, an interesting footnote to this chronology. Between February 1960 and September 1962, while laboring over *V.*, Pynchon held down a day job as a technical writer. The would-be novelist was employed by Boeing in Seattle and contributed articles to the company's various newsletters. He is thought to have primarily written for one titled *Bomarc Service News*.[47]

Bomarc was a supersonic surface-to-air missile program developed to protect American cities and industrial sites from Soviet bombers. By the time it was finally deployed, however, the strategic threat had shifted from crewed planes to intercontinental ballistic missiles, essentially rendering the program obsolete. The deployed elements of the weapon system would be decommissioned in the early 1970s. In 1959, however, Boeing had received a $300 million contract for Bomarc from the Air Force, which would be the equivalent of $2.7 billon today.[48] Flush with cash, Boeing hired a small army to work on the program. This workforce included scientists, engineers, various subcontractors—and technical writers.

Echoes of Pynchon's stint at Boeing can be found in his early novels. Critics have speculated that the fictional defense contractor Yoyodyne, mentioned in both *V.* and *The Crying of Lot 49*, is a stand-in for the aerospace giant. Given that Pynchon was on Boeing's payroll for 31 months, it is likely that he contributed a number of articles to its publications. Identifying this early work by Pynchon would be a worthwhile undertaking because there is so little of it. A collection of five early short stories was published in 1984, and all but one of them were composed while he was in college. Otherwise, there is little else from that period of his life.[49] The articles that he wrote at Boeing would provide Pynchon scholars with an additional source of ore to mine. But there was a problem: the articles in the Bomarc newsletter were published without bylines.

Bomarc Service News was established in 1959 and was appearing once a month by the time Pynchon joined Boeing. Thirty-two issues, comprising more than 500 pages, were published during his tenure with the company. A given issue typically included four or five longer articles and two or three shorter ones. The newsletter's staff was small; there were only about five or six contributors. Would it be possible to identify Pynchon's anonymous contributions on stylistic or other grounds?

The necessary heavy lifting was performed by Adrian Wisnicki while he was a doctoral student at the City University of New York Graduate Center. He was able to obtain copies of the Bomarc newsletters and also to communicate with its retired editor, a man named Hixson. Hixson confirmed that Pynchon had been a staff writer and provided details about the newsletter's workflow.

Wisnicki pored over the approximately 200 articles published during Pynchon's tenure with Boeing and tried to identify those that had linguistic or stylistic similarities to the writer's early stories and novels. Rising above a background thrum of dry and often tedious prose, Wisnicki began to discern a voice that was recognizable as Pynchon's. The voice lacked a single defining characteristic but was signaled by a number of quirky elements that seemed out of place in a technical newsletter.

As it happened, Wisnicki also had a Rosetta stone of sorts. Pynchon *had* been credited with a byline for a piece titled *Togetherness*, which appeared in another Boeing publication, *Aerospace Safety*, in December 1960.[50] This 2,400-word article provided Wisnicki with a baseline for the style that Pynchon employed when writing about technical issues for Boeing. It crawled with clues that he could exploit in making attributions about the anonymous pieces in the Bomarc newsletter.

Throughout his career as a novelist, Pynchon would liberally punctuate his writing with em dashes (—) as well as with ellipses (. . .). These marks were undoubtedly employed by others on the Bomarc newsletter staff, but articles in which they appeared in profusion were worthy of a second look. Wisnicki also found that his quarry was fond of "scare quotes" and bullet point arrows, which echoed the dingbat characters that appear in the epilogue of *V.*—the book he was completing during his employment with Boeing.

In terms of style, Wisnicki found several articles that made liberal use of the second person in a didactic way, such as "We want you to be 100% perfect," which appeared in a piece on reliability. In some cases, these admonitions were accompanied by patronizing sarcasm, such as "Don't stick your head inside a gas tank so you can inhale its delightful aroma." Warnings such as these also seemed to be the spoor of his quarry. In addition, this writer would sometimes shift, in a jarring way, from the technical and the arcane to the conversational ("Now don't everybody yell at once").

With regard to content, Wisnicki found articles that made reference to fairly esoteric topics like Teflon or V-2 rockets. The German weapons system would become a central character in *Gravity's Rainbow* a decade later. Finally, the voice that Wisnicki was hearing displayed a predilection for authoring articles about safety, reliability, and maintainability.

None of these stylistic or content markers, however, were definitive proof of Pynchon's authorship on their own. But when two or more of them appeared in the same text, Wisnicki felt fairly confident that he knew who had written it. In the end, he was reasonably certain that 24 of the articles in his collection had been authored by Pynchon. Another 10, he thought, had possibly been written by him. If his attributions were correct, then Pynchon typically wrote one or two articles for each issue of the Bomarc newsletter during the time he was employed by Boeing.[51]

Katie Muth revisited the newsletter authorship issue in 2019 and applied a computational analysis to the attribution problem. She employed a machine learning technique called supervised learning, in which a computer program attempts to ferret out the elements that identify a set of texts as having been written by a particular author. The learning is referred to as "supervised" because the program receives feedback during a training phase about whether its guesses were correct or not. In this way, the software learns from its mistakes and improves its accuracy.

It should be noted that Muth's computational technique was diametrically opposed to the approach that Wisnicki had taken 18 years earlier. While he had attached great importance to typographical features like em dashes, quotation marks, and bullet points, all of this was stripped out of the supervised learning study, which analyzed only the words in the articles. This meant that any higher-level features, like figurative language, literary allusions, or even the theme of an essay, were dispensed with as well.

Muth trained her system on six pieces published in *Bomarc Service News* during 1959, which was before Pynchon joined Boeing. She also provided it with five essays that are known to have been written by Pynchon. (Three of these had been published in the 1960s, and two more appeared in the 1980s.) This allowed the program to construct stylistic profiles for both non-Pynchon and Pynchonesque prose. She then tested the system with 12 of the newsletter pieces that Wisnicki had attributed to Pynchon.

And the result? She found that eight of the 12 articles in the test set were highly correlated with the known Pynchon essays. However, two of the articles that Wisnicki was confident had been written by Pynchon—mostly because of their themes—didn't match the known Pynchon essays. Two other essays that Wisnicki had tagged as possibly written by Pynchon also failed to match Pynchon's known prose. In other words, Muth's analysis matched with Wisnicki's 80 percent of the time for the essays Wisnicki had been the most confident about. Given how different the two approaches are, this result is impressively high. However, there was no agreement for the two cases tested in which Wisnicki had only suspected Pynchon's authorship.

So what *did* Muth's program learn about the differences between the Pynchon and non-Pynchon texts? One intriguing finding is that Pynchon's average word length, at 4.6 characters, is significantly shorter than that of the staff writers of *Bomarc Service News*, who averaged 5.4. This is of interest because word length is a proxy for word frequency: common words are typically short, whereas uncommon or technical terms are longer.

In addition, the Boeing staff writers used past participles about a third of the time in their verb constructions. These are compound verbs with an "-ed" suffix, like "have talked" or "has lived." Pynchon, however, employed them less than 20 percent of the time. Instead, he made use of the simple past tense ("talked," "lived"), doing so more than three times as often as the newsletter staff. In addition, he employed personal pronouns ("I," "you," "she") nearly five times more often.[52]

To summarize these findings, Pynchon's nonfiction prose shows a predilection for simple terms deployed in direct and active constructions, whereas the staff writers were more likely to employ technical language with more complex verbs in passive constructions. Perhaps not surprisingly, therefore, Pynchon's Boeing coworkers remembered his writing as being concise and clear. As Muth herself observes, Pynchon's articles, in terms of their narrative structure and conversational style, read more like fiction than technical writing.[53]

It is worth noting that the contrasting approaches taken by Wisnicki and Muth largely converged on the same set of essays as having been written by Pynchon. Although their methods are polar opposites philosophically, they are also complementary in many respects. Wisnicki's approach included top-down elements, such as a consideration of an essay's theme, whereas Muth's bottom-up textual analysis reveals subtle differences in word frequency and verb choice that might elude even a close reading of a text or are simply too difficult to keep track of.

With regard to the discrepancies between Wisnicki's and Muth's attributions for four of the newsletter texts, a different sort of analysis may one day clarify whether Pynchon or someone else at Boeing wrote them. There is one way in which the authorship debate could be settled definitively, but that would require asking the author himself. And it would appear that he's not talking to anyone about anything.

THE TRUTH ABOUT *DOUBLE FALSEHOOD*

During the winter of 1727, the playwright Lewis Theobald caused a stir in London when he announced a new production for the Drury Lane Theatre. The reason for the commotion was the play's unusual provenance because the work wasn't technically "new." It was, Theobald asserted, based on a lost play by William Shakespeare. He claimed to have acquired three manuscript copies of the unnamed play, which he then "revised and adapted" for his production.[54]

Double Falsehood, the title that Theobald chose for the work, is based on the Cardenio episode from the first part of *Don Quixote*, in which the Man of la Mancha and Sancho Panza encounter a madman living in the Sierra Morena mountains. Part 1 of Cervantes' novel is known to have been published in an English translation in 1612 by Thomas Shelton.[55]

It is also known that a play titled *Cardenno* or *Cardenna* was performed at the court of James I in 1612 and 1613 by the King's Men.[56] This was the theater company that Shakespeare had been a member of. Although he may have retired to Stratford by this time, two other late works—*Henry VIII* and *Two*

Noble Kinsmen—are believed to have been written by him in collaboration with playwright John Fletcher, his successor with the King's Men.

Forty years after these performances, a play titled *The History of Cardenio* was entered into the London Stationer's Register and listed as having been written by Fletcher and Shakespeare. The registration, which was required before a work could be issued, was made by publisher Humphrey Moseley. Moseley's involvement in this story is problematic because he would later register three spurious works as having been written by Shakespeare. At any rate, he never seems to have gotten around to publishing his *Cardenio*, a fate that also befell several other plays he registered.

Theobald's claim that he had discovered an unpublished manuscript by Shakespeare was met with a certain degree of skepticism, in part because he had been credibly accused of plagiarism a decade earlier.[57] During the previous year, he had had a public spat with Alexander Pope about errors in an edition of the Bard's plays that Pope had published.[58] Furthermore, Theobald never showed anyone else the three original manuscripts that he claimed to possess. He was, however, a collector of old promptbooks, so it is possible that he could have stumbled across an unknown play or two.

In the decades following Shakespeare's death, publishers were not above trumpeting the discovery of previously lost works to increase sales. The Third Folio of 1664, for example, contains seven such "discovered" plays, although only one of these, *Pericles*, is thought to have any connection to the Bard. All of this means that a cloud of uncertainty hangs over *Double Falsehood* and *The History of Cardenio*. For nearly three centuries, there has been much debate over whether Theobald's account or Moseley's registration can be trusted.

Double Falsehood is a curious work in several respects. It is shorter than all of Shakespeare's other plays, comprising 1,771 lines, whereas the average for his oeuvre is about 2,900. It is also unique in that it lacks a subplot—an element that he often employed to comment on the main plot.[59]

Even if we accept Theobald's account at face value, it is unknown how much "improving" he performed on the text: this could have run the gamut from light editing to a wholesale reworking for a Georgian-era audience. He may, for example, have chosen to edit out a subplot, which would account for its brevity as well as the curious fact that Don Quixote and Sancho Panza, Cervantes' main characters, are nowhere to be found. Finally, in the eyes of many, the writing simply isn't up to Shakespeare's standards. But whether this is the result of Theobald's surgery or evidence that he manufactured the play out of whole cloth is unclear.

In recent years, the scholarly consensus has shifted in favor of accepting *Double Falsehood* as a genuine (or at least partly genuine) work of the Bard. In 2010, the play was published as part of the respected Arden Shakespeare series. The volume's editor, Brean Hammond, evaluated the evidence in a massive introduction and concluded that Theobald's story was likely more true than false.[60] Other prominent Shakespearians, such as Gary Taylor[61] and John Nance,[62] have also accepted *Double Falsehood* as a play at least partially written by Shakespeare.

Despite such endorsements, there are holdouts. These include the Shakespeare scholar Tiffany Stern and the critic Harold Bloom, who decried the play as a "palpable forgery" that Shakespeare had nothing to do with.[63] And Rod Rosenbaum, the self-styled "Shakespeare cop," agrees. Reacting to its appearance in the Arden Shakespeare series, he described *Double Falsehood* as a "profoundly worthless, virtually incoherent play" in a takedown that he published in *Slate*.[64]

At this remove, there may simply be no way to move forward regarding the external evidence: one either accepts the veracity of some long-dead and occasionally unscrupulous individuals or does not. However, additional internal evidence can be generated by analyzing the language of the play. And the list of potential suspects is short. Everyone seems to agree that *Double Falsehood* was written by either Shakespeare, Fletcher, Shakespeare with an assist by Fletcher, or Theobald. Furthermore, the play in question can be compared to the substantial body of dramatic work written by each of the three men.

In 2015, the authorship question was taken up by Ryan Boyd and James Pennebaker. The work of Pennebaker, his students, and collaborators represents a third approach to the study of language and identity. Unlike forensic linguists who seek to identify suspects or literary scholars who focus on stylistics, Pennebaker's approach is rooted in experimental psychology. For many years, he has studied how language use reflects people's personality traits, their relationship roles, and even their psychological and physical health.[65]

For their analysis of *Double Falsehood*, Boyd and Pennebaker chose to examine only plays that are believed to have been solo efforts. These included 33 works by Shakespeare, nine by Fletcher, and 12 by Theobald.

One of the tools that Pennebaker has created is a computer program called Linguistic Inquiry and Word Count (LIWC). At its core, LIWC is a simple counting program: it tallies the number of times that the words in a text fall into a predefined set of categories, such as the various parts of speech (e.g., pronouns or adjectives), words related to positive emotions ("love," "nice") or negative emotions ("hurt," "ugly"), or words related to the family ("daughter," "husband") or to insight ("think," "know"). Altogether, LIWC keeps track of the occurrence of words in 80 different categories.[66] All of the plays in the study were analyzed with LIWC to create unique content category signatures.

Another set of analyses involved counting eight types of function words in the plays. These include pronouns, articles, auxiliary verbs, and conjunctions. Previous research suggested that people who often use words from these categories are socially focused and dynamic thinkers; they enjoy telling stories. On the other hand, individuals who employ plenty of nouns, prepositions, and articles in their writing are classifiers; their thought processes are formal and analytic.

Inspired by Foster's work in unmasking the author of *Primary Colors*, the researchers also considered what they called low-base-rate tells. These are words that aren't used frequently by most people but appear on a regular basis throughout a given writer's body of work. They can be thought of as an author's "pet words": terms they like because of how they sound or what they mean. Such frequently deployed words provide a clear glimpse into the author's idiolect. Shakespeare, for example, used the word "sweet" hundreds of times in his works, while Joseph Conrad was enamored with "impenetrable."[67] Boyd and Pennebaker also employed more traditional stylometric tools, such as the average sentence length and the use of long words (i.e., more than six letters) in each text.

As in Katie Muth's analysis of Pynchon's writing in the previous section, Boyd and Pennebaker made use of supervised machine learning to classify the texts as the work of Shakespeare, Fletcher, or Theobald. There are many ways that this can be done, and the authors chose three complementary methods that are often used in author identification. In this case, the details don't really matter because all three models yielded virtually identical results: *Double Falsehood* most closely matched the plays of Shakespeare on 14 of the 15 tests that they performed. Theobald was the highest match on only one test involving LIWC content categories.

As a follow-up, Boyd and Pennebaker divided *Double Falsehood* into its five separate acts and compared them to equal-sized segments from the 54 plays by Shakespeare, Fletcher, and Theobald. With regard to *Double Falsehood*'s first act, 15 out of 15 comparisons suggest that Shakespeare was the best match. For Act II, the score was 12 for Shakespeare, two for Fletcher, and one for Theobald. Act III matched most closely with Shakespeare 12 times, with Theobald twice, and with Fletcher only once.

This pattern begins to change, however, with Act IV. Shakespeare was the highest match with *Double Falsehood* only five times and with Theobald only once. Fletcher carried the day with nine of the highest matches. And this pattern repeats in Act V, with a score of six for Shakespeare and nine for Fletcher. Boyd and Pennebaker concluded that Shakespeare may have been the principal composer of the beginning of the play and that Fletcher had primary responsibility for the later acts.[68] This finding is in line with earlier conclusions from several Shakespeare scholars.[69]

Does this mean that supporters of a Shakespeare/Fletcher authorship for *Double Falsehood* have carried the day? It is unclear how many doubters were swayed by Boyd and Pennebaker's analysis, although advocates for Shakespearian authorship were happy to cite it as evidence for their position. For them, attention shifted to creating a credible version of the work for the stage, which involves scraping the encrusted barnacles of Theobald from the hull of Shakespeare and Fletcher's drama.[70] *Double Falsehood* may not be a *King Lear* or even a *Timon of Athens*, but it does appear to belong on the same shelf as those works.

CHAPTER FOUR

WHICH?

Tales of Disputed Authorship

A DISPUTE IN OZ

Almost everyone has seen the film *The Wizard of Oz*, and many know that it is based on a book by Lyman Frank Baum. What is less well known is that it was the first of no fewer than 35 books written about that magical land. Baum himself wrote 12 Oz books that were published between 1900 and 1918, and two more that he finished before his death were released posthumously.

Before his success as the chronicler of Oz, Baum had been an actor, store owner, newspaper editor and reporter, and traveling salesman. In 1897, a book of Mother Goose rhymes had enjoyed some success, and he wrote a sequel to that book before striking gold with *The Wonderful Wizard of Oz* in 1900.[1] For the next two decades, Baum would be a prolific author. In addition to the Oz series, he wrote dozens of other books, primarily for children, and published under a variety of pen names. He also turned out short stories, poems, and movie scripts.[2]

Even before Judy Garland's star turn as Dorothy Gale, the world of Oz had expanded beyond the printed word. Baum and his illustrator, W. W. Denslow, helped to bring the first Oz book to the stage as a musical, and it enjoyed a successful run on Broadway in 1903. An adaptation of the second novel in the series, however, was a flop. A film of the seventh book, *The Patchwork Girl of Oz*, was released as a silent movie in 1914, but it too was a commercial failure.[3]

It was the massive success of the 1939 MGM movie that made Oz the cultural touchstone it has become, and it would be reimagined again and again. In 1974, it was reworked as a soul musical, *The Wiz*, and a film version

63

followed in 1978. The Wicked Witch of the West would receive a backstory in a 1995 novel by Gregory Maguire[4] and would become the basis for the musical *Wicked*, which premiered in 2003. It is now the second-highest-grossing Broadway show of all time, surpassed only by *The Lion King*.[5]

After Baum's death in 1919, his Chicago publisher approached children's author Ruth Plumly Thompson to see if she would continue the book series. She agreed to write new adventures in Oz and received the approval of Baum's widow, Maud.[6] Thompson would publish 19 sequels, at the rate of one a year, between 1921 and 1939. She returned to writing about Oz during the 1970s and penned two final books. The last of these was published in 1976, the year of her death.

Thompson's first book and the fifteenth in the series was *The Royal Book of Oz*. Appearing in 1921, it provides a backstory of sorts for the Scarecrow and a new adventure for Dorothy and her friends. In a short preface to the book, Maud Baum explained to the readers that Thompson had made a new Oz story based on "some unfinished notes" left by her husband "about Princess Ozma and Dorothy and the jolly people of the Wonderful Land of Oz." These notes, she explained, had been pulled together to create the new book. The title page indicated that it had been written by Baum and "enlarged and edited" by Thompson.[7]

The two chroniclers of Oz approached their storytelling somewhat differently. In general, Thompson's books are marked by a lightheartedness as well as a quicker pace. They are also more humorous and less complex than those in Baum's original series.[8] In these and other ways, *The Royal Book* is more similar to Thompson's later books than to Baum's earlier ones. This led some scholars of Oz to question whether Thompson's role had been to simply "enlarge and edit" what Baum had already written. It seemed more likely that she had written the entire book.[9] But if that supposition were true, how could it be proven?

Statisticians José Binongo and D'Arcy Mays attempted to settle *The Royal Book* authorship question by conducting a stylometric analysis. The case lends itself well to such an approach: there are only two potential candidates for authorship, and both produced a large amount of writing during their careers.[10]

The researchers were able to easily obtain machine-readable texts of Baum's original 14 books because they are now in the public domain and freely available online. At the time their study was conducted, however, this was true for only seven of Thompson's books about Oz, and print versions had to be obtained, scanned, and then proofread to fix errors introduced by the character recognition software. Many of Thompson's books in the series are now out of print, and the authors had no luck tracking down several of them.

As a next step, all the texts needed to be "cleaned." Baum, in particular, changed the spelling of some words to approximate different accents, and these creative misspellings were corrected. In addition, contractions were expanded: a word like "twasn't" was replaced by "it was not." At the end of this process, the researchers had created a corpus of more than 1.2 million words, consisting of Baum's 14 Oz books, another 14 written by Thompson, and *The Royal Book*. From this corpus, the researchers identified the 50 most common function words by counting the prepositions, conjunctions, determiners, and degree adjectives in the texts. Just five of these function words—"the," "and," "to," "a/an," and "of"—constitute one-sixth of the entire corpus.

The researchers then divided the texts into blocks of 5,000 words. Each of these 223 blocks was mapped to a position in a 50-dimensional space, corresponding to the degree to which they contained the 50 function words. This multidimensional space was reduced to two dimensions by a principal component analysis so that it could be visualized. The analysis accomplishes this by identifying the two dimensions that provide the best fit for the underlying data.[11]

And the result? A two-dimensional plot perfectly discriminated the two authors. Without exception, all of Baum's text blocks fell to one side of the resulting plot, and all of Thompson's fell on the other. Thus, the writing styles of the two historians of Oz can be discriminated by their use of function words alone.

In what ways do the two authors differ? Thompson shows a greater predilection for using positional words in her writing—terms such as "up," "down," "over," and "on"—than does Baum. Baum, on the other hand, was more likely to employ negative words, such as "but," "not," and "no," as well as the pronouns "that" and "which." It would be difficult to construct a meaningful theory for why this might be so, but that wasn't the point of the analysis: the goal of the researchers was discrimination, not explanation.

Next, Binongo and Mays created text blocks from five of Baum's non-Oz books. The blocks were drawn from his other novels, fairy tales, and short stories. When all the texts were analyzed, the same pattern emerged: all of Thompson's text blocks could be found on one side of a two-dimensional solution, and all of Baum's writing—both Oz and non-Oz—ended up on the other.

Finally, the researchers were ready to answer their primary question: would an analysis of text blocks from *The Royal Book* wind up plotted on the Thompson side of a two-dimensional solution or on the Baum side? The results were unequivocal: the work that had been published as an Oz book by L. Frank Baum appears to have been written entirely by Ruth Plumly Thompson.

There is an interesting coda to Binongo and Mays's study. Even though the results clearly point to Thompson as the author of *The Royal Book*, it is still possible that some other person could have written it since only her work and that of Baum were analyzed. Could a clever forger, perhaps someone extremely familiar with the series, have created a fraudulent new adventure in Oz? And if they did, would Binongo and Mays's approach be sensitive enough to catch them?

As it happens, Martin Gardner tried his hand at writing an Oz book. The well-known science popularizer was a lifelong fan of Baum's books, and in 1998, he published an homage titled *Visitors from Oz*. In its introduction, he wrote, "I have done my best to come close to Baum's simple style, and to be faithful to the whimsical land and characters he created."[12]

Following the same procedure as before, Binongo and Mays created 5,000-word text blocks from "Visitors" and ran them through an analysis with the texts of Baum and Thompson. Once again, two distinct groups of data points appeared in a two-dimensional solution. And again, one cluster represented the texts written by Baum, while the other belonged to Thompson—and to Gardner. When the researchers repeated the analysis with 10,000-word text blocks instead of 5,000, in order to extract more information from each text, the data points separated into three separate clusters, with one for each author. And Gardner's cluster was still closer to Thompson than to Baum.[13]

It is worth noting that Martin Gardner helped establish the International Wizard of Oz Club. He was a talented author in his own right and had written books in a variety of fictional genres. In his autobiography, he asserted that "I learned to read by looking over my mother's shoulder while she read aloud *The Wizard of Oz*. I simply followed the words as she spoke."[14] But when Gardner wrote his tribute to Baum, he wasn't able to do any better than Thompson—at least with regard to mimicking Baum's use of function words.

All of this leaves one question unanswered. If Thompson was the author of *The Royal Book*, then why wasn't she given credit for it? It seems likely that the motivation was financial. Baum had been heralded as "The Royal Historian of

Oz" and had created a valuable franchise. His publisher, Reilly and Lee, may have been worried that his readers would not accept a new chronicler. So as not to kill the golden goose, Reilly and Lee chose to put Baum's name on the title page of Thompson's book as well as his widow's approval in its preface.[15] Once they were assured that Thompson was up to the task of carrying on the series, the publisher released the later Oz books under her name. Despite Binongo and Mays's convincing detective work, however, some publishers continue to list Baum as an author on the cover of *The Royal Book*, whereas others list only Thompson.

POE-POURRI

Edgar Allan Poe stands as a commanding and controversial figure in nineteenth-century American literature. Although he is known primarily for his macabre stories and poems, public fascination has also attached itself to the unusual details of his biography, such as the marriage to his young cousin and the mysterious circumstances surrounding his death at age 40. Literary scholars credit Poe with having written the first detective story, *The Murders in the Rue Morgue*, as well as his contributions to the nascent genre of speculative fiction, which influenced writers such as Jules Verne and H. G. Wells.

During his short life, Poe was a prolific writer who churned out a large quantity of poems, short stories, and essays as well as one novel, *The Narrative of Arthur Gordon Pym*. His attempts to support himself solely through his writing, however, frequently left him in difficult financial straits. His first work, self-published in July 1827, was a 40-page collection of poems and credited only to "A Bostonian." The volume, titled *Tamerlane and Other Poems*, was virtually unknown during his lifetime and only rediscovered 10 years after his death. Other aspects of Poe's early career are similarly obscure.

In recent years, efforts have been made to identify Poe's early fiction. It has long been assumed that his first short story was *Metzengerstein: A Tale in Imitation of the German*, which appeared in Philadelphia's *Saturday Courier* magazine in January 1832. Like *Tamerlane*, it was published anonymously, although it would be republished under Poe's name during his lifetime. But was this his very first short story?

Paul Collins, an author and professor of English at Portland State University, has suggested that some of Poe's earliest fiction can be found in a volume devoted to Poe's older brother. This would be William Henry Leonard Poe, who had been born two years before Edgar. Henry, as he was called, was a sailor and later a poet who struggled with alcoholism and died from tuberculosis at age 24. The brothers were close and lived together for a time in Baltimore.

A collection of Henry Poe's work was published in 1926. It contains his poetry as well as two of his brother Edgar's poems that had appeared in *Tamerlane*.[16] The *Tamerlane* poems had also appeared in Baltimore's *North American*, where their author was listed as "W.H.P." It appears that Edgar—perhaps in an attempt to keep his creditors from tracking him down—published some of his early work using his brother's initials.

The *North American*, however, also published three short works of fiction by "W.H.P.," and these were also included in the Henry Poe volume. Stylistically, the pieces are similar: they are punctuated with a surfeit of exclamation points and em dashes. In terms of content, they exude the same sort of overwrought excitement that animates stories like *The Pit and the Pendulum* and *The Tell-Tale Heart*. Could they have been written by Edgar instead of his brother?

Collins attempted to answer this question by making use of the JGAAP program, which Patrick Juola had employed to unmask J. K. Rowling as the author of *Cuckoo's Calling* (described in chapter 3). His analyses included the three pieces from Henry's book that he suspected had been written by Edgar. These were *A Fragment*, *The Pirate*, and *Recollections*, which together make up about 4,000 words. For comparison authors, Collins chose works by six writers who were active in Poe's day: James Fenimore Cooper, Nathaniel Hawthorne, Washington Irving, George Lippard, John Neal, and William Gilmore Simms. To represent Poe, he chose *Tales of the Grotesque and Arabesque*, an 1840 collection of two dozen short stories. From each of these texts, he selected the first 10,000 words.

And the results? On 15 different measures, the texts by "W.H.P." were rated as most closely matching the writings of Edgar: he was ranked first on every test. To see how Poe the Younger would fare against his older brother, Collins replaced James Fenimore Cooper's *Twice-Told Tales* with Henry Poe's *Monte Video*. This is not an ideal comparison, as the latter text is only about 1,200 words long, but it seems to be the only work of prose that can be unambiguously attributed to Henry. Edgar was still ranked first, while his brother finished as high as second on some tests and as low as sixth on others. His average rank was 3.9 out of the seven authors—about what one might expect by chance.

Importantly, the outcome didn't change when Collins threw in works by other early nineteenth-century authors: Lydia Maria Child, Charles Fenno Hoffman, John Pendleton Kennedy, Augustus Longstreet, Catharine Maria Sedgwick, Robert Montgomery Bird, and N. P. Willis. In a 15-way slugfest, the younger Poe remained on top. The results changed a bit when Collins chose the *second* 10,000-word sample from Poe's short-story collection. In this case, Edgar's match with the pieces in the Henry Poe collection declined a bit, but the younger Poe was still judged the most likely candidate on some of the comparisons.[17]

It is possible to carp about Collins's analyses; he didn't, for example, establish formal criteria for accepting or rejecting the hypothesis that Edgar authored the works in question. Nonetheless, the results are lopsided enough that his conclusions are probably valid.[18] But if Edgar was the author of the three pieces, why didn't he include them in his *Tales of the Grotesque and Arabesque?* Collins speculates that Poe may not have been able to put his hands on them. He wasn't fastidious about retaining copies of his manuscripts, and the original publisher had suspended publication after half a year. It's also possible that he didn't consider these early efforts to be in the same league as his later work.

Another controversy about Poe's writing is more consequential. In 1835, he joined the *Southern Literary Messenger* as a staff writer and became its editor a few months later. The periodical had been established in Richmond, Virginia, during the previous year, and it published a potpourri of fiction, nonfiction, poetry, and reviews. Although his time with the *Messenger* was short, he contributed about three dozen reviews of books and periodicals to the publication as well as several short stories and portions of his novel.

In its April 1836 issue, during his tenure as editor, the *Messenger* ran what has become known as the "Paulding-Drayton Review." Ostensibly, it was an appraisal of two recently published books on slavery. For the unsigned reviewer, however, it served as a platform for a full-throated defense of the institution. This review was included in a 1902 edition of the complete works of Poe by James Harrison, which served as the standard edition of Poe's oeuvre for many years.[19]

Poe's attitudes about slavery and race are of more than passing interest to those who study the man and his work. On the one hand, Poe has traditionally been viewed as relatively nonpartisan and nonideological. In his precarious financial state, he could ill afford to alienate employers or readers by promulgating controversial points of view. In short, his perspective probably reflected the "average racism" of his time and place.[20]

On the other hand, Poe lived in Richmond for several years during his childhood[21] and was undoubtedly influenced by the ethos of the city that would become the capital of the Confederacy. And it is also worth noting that Poe dedicated his *Tales of the Grotesque and Arabesque* to the pro-slavery William Drayton, the author of one of the books in the "Paulding-Drayton Review."[22]

All of this has made the proslavery polemic a matter of debate among Poe scholars. An understanding of Poe's beliefs would inform the interpretation of several works that include characters of color. Toni Morrison, for example, has argued that Poe used the symbolism of blackness to represent the "Other" in his novel *The Narrative of Arthur Gordon Pym*.[23]

For many, external evidence seems to have settled the question. In 1941, William Doyle Hull made the case that the review had been written by Nathaniel Beverly Tucker, a law professor at the College of William & Mary. Hull based this attribution on a letter that Poe had written to Tucker a month after the "Paulding-Drayton Review" was published. In it, Poe refers to "your article on slavery."[24] This exculpatory evidence, however, wasn't published until 1924,[25] and even then, its importance seems to have overlooked by many Poe scholars.

One complicating factor is that, in his letter to Tucker, Poe sought forgiveness for "making a few immaterial alterations . . . with a view of so condensing it as to get it in the space remaining at the end of the number."[26] It is possible that Poe's changes to the piece were extensive, which has allowed some scholars, such as Bernard Rosenthal, to continue to claim that the review reflects Poe's own beliefs.[27] Others, such as J. V. Ridgely, have pushed back strongly against such an interpretation.[28]

Stefan Schöberlein, a professor at the University of Iowa, performed a stylometric analysis to determine the likelihood that Poe was responsible for the review. He assembled a corpus of texts by 15 authors associated with the *Southern Literary Messenger*, including Poe and Tucker. He then made use of a variety of approaches to compare these authors' texts. These included various classification algorithms as well as Burrows's Delta. And the results were clear: Tucker had authored the "Paulding-Drayton Review."

But what of editor Poe's "immaterial alterations" to Tucker's text? Schöberlein cut the review into 1,000-character chunks and compared them to Poe's and Tucker's corpora. The results suggest that, for the first half of the review, "Poe went beyond the usual tasks of an editor and apparently reworked Tucker's words into a final product that partially 'sounds' like Poe while still retaining Tucker's reasoning."[29]

It appears that Schöberlein's conclusions have provided partisans on both sides of this authorship debate with fresh ammunition. The "Paulding-Drayton Review" was probably penned by Tucker, but its first section appears to have been extensively altered by Poe. Would he have lavished such attention on a piece that he disagreed with? And since Tucker's original presumably no longer exists, it is impossible to know whether the review's defense of slavery was toned down by Poe or even amplified. Since the *Messenger* was ostensibly politically neutral,[30] the strident tone of the review seems out of place. Although stylometric analysis has shed some light on this mystery, it has not resolved it.

A LEGACY FROM LEWIS?

In 1977, a story by C. S. Lewis was published by Walter Hooper, a literary executor for the Lewis estate. Titled *The Dark Tower*, it is an unfinished work of science fiction. Whether it was truly written by Lewis, however, has been a matter of some debate since it first appeared in print.

Clive Staples Lewis, who died in 1963, was a scholar of English literature at Oxford and Cambridge as well as a prolific writer. He may be best known for his *Chronicles of Narnia*, a seven-volume fantasy series published during the 1950s. But he contributed to several genres during his career and also produced a great deal of nonfiction. His books and essays about Christianity and his faith have been inspiring for many. Lewis made a foray into science fiction with his Space Trilogy: *Out of the Silent Planet* (1938), *Perelandra* (1943), and *That Hideous Strength* (1945). *The Dark Tower* seems to be a sequel of sorts to the first volume in that series since the two books have several characters in common.

This incomplete work also has an unusual provenance. In the preface to the volume that includes it, Walter Hooper claims he obtained the manuscript in early 1964, two months after Lewis's death. According to Hooper's account, he came upon Lewis's brother Warren and his gardener while they were burning a pile of the author's old papers. Hooper was able to save the novel as well as a number of other works from the flames.

It was Hooper who named the untitled story *The Dark Tower*. He described the manuscript as consisting of 64 consecutively numbered handwritten pages, although two are missing. Its seven chapters consist of 26,700 words. The story breaks off in mid-sentence. Both the unfinished novel and *The Man Born Blind*, a short story from a notebook given to him by Lewis's brother, appeared in a volume along with previously published stories.[31]

The Dark Tower has a number of unusual elements, such as a form of time travel and a mind–body switch of the *Freaky Friday* variety. The novel's characters mention the year 1938, and it may have been composed around that time. While interpretations vary, the work could be read as a satire attacking bureaucracy and scientism.[32] The fact that Lewis did not publish it during his lifetime suggests that it was either abandoned or forgotten about.

The year after its publication, a devotee of Lewis's work named Kathryn Lindskoog called attention to what she claimed were issues in Hooper's biography and his relationship with Lewis. She also cast doubt on Hooper's account of the fire that nearly consumed the unpublished manuscript.[33]

In 1988, Lindskoog published a book that took her doubts about *The Dark Tower* to a whole new level. She claimed that the unfinished novel was a contemporary forgery that Hooper then passed off as a work by Lewis. She proposed that either Hooper or his close friend Tony Marchington had written it. The title of her book—*The C. S. Lewis Hoax*—was deliberately provocative.[34]

Among other claims, Lindskoog argued that the novel in question simply isn't up to Lewis's standards and that it doesn't match, in style or in content, the books in his Space Trilogy. She also called attention to similarities between *The Dark Tower* and Madeleine L'Engle's *A Wrinkle in Time*, even though that work wasn't published until 1962. Lindskoog repeated her accusations in revised and augmented editions that were published in 1994[35] and 2001.[36]

The allegations of fraud and forgery have been divisive for the community of Lewis scholars and devotees. Hooper, for his part, refused to engage with Lindskoog or to rebut her assertions.[37] In a review of Lindskoog's first book, the historian Nicolas Barker noted that the original manuscript for *The Dark Tower* is now at the Bodleian Library and that the handwriting is entirely consistent with Lewis's other originals. Lindskoog, however, claimed that this was not conclusive evidence because Hooper developed the ability to imitate Lewis's distinctive script—a point that Hooper himself has acknowledged. Notwithstanding that objection, Barker concluded that Lindskoog had written "a poisoned book."[38]

External evidence supports the claim that *The Dark Tower* was written by Lewis. Hooper reported that he showed the manuscript to Gervase Matthew, a lecturer in Byzantine studies at Oxford and a friend of Lewis's. Matthew said that he recognized the story and recollected having heard Lewis read excerpts of it aloud at a meeting of the Inklings—a literary discussion group that included J. R. R. Tolkien—in 1939 or 1940.[39] Lewis was also the doctoral adviser of Alastair Fowler, who became a professor at the University of Edinburgh. In a 2003 essay, he recalled Lewis having shown him *The Dark Tower*, along with other "unfinished or abandoned pieces," while he was his student in the 1950s.[40] However, both men provided their accounts long after these events occurred. It is possible, therefore, that they misremembered or confused the unfinished novel with other works by the prolific Lewis.

The controversy over *The Dark Tower* seems tailor-made for resolution via stylometry. And over the years, the text has been subjected to no fewer than four such analyses. These examinations, performed in four different decades, illustrate how stylometric techniques have grown in sophistication.

The first of these was conducted by Carla Faust Jones in 1989. She made use of a program called the Literary Detective, developed by Jim Tankard at the University of Texas, Austin.[41] It had fared reasonably well in earlier tests, such as by assigning the majority of the disputed *Federalist* essays to James Madison, as described in chapter 2. For any two texts, the program compares the frequency of individual letters, technically referred to as 1-grams, as well as letter pairs, or 2-grams. For example, the word "family" would be counted as having the five 2-grams: FA, MA, MI, IL, and LY.

Jones selected strings of between 16,000 and 20,000 characters—about seven to nine pages worth—from the first chapters of *The Dark Tower* and from the three books of the Space Trilogy: *Out of the Silent Planet, Perelandra*, and *That Hideous Strength*. She found that *The Dark Tower* was less like the other three books, particularly with regard to 2-grams, than the Space Trilogy books when compared to one another.[42]

In 1994, Andrew Morton employed the cusum (cumulative sum) technique to address *The Dark Tower* authorship question. (This controversial technique will be examined in chapter 7.) Morton claimed that this approach can identify discontinuities in a text, such as those that might occur when two authors write different parts of the same work. Morton compared the initial sentences of the first chapter of *The Dark Tower* with those of its fourth chapter as well as its seventh. He also analyzed sections from the first and third books in the Space Trilogy. He concluded that Lewis was not the author of the first and fourth chapters of *The Dark Tower* but that he did write the seventh.[43]

In 2009, statisticians Jeffrey Thompson and John Rasp explored *The Dark Tower* authorship question by performing analyses that compared the number of new words and rare words in the unfinished novel with the first two books of the Space Trilogy, which are thought to have been composed shortly before and after it. Their comparisons, particularly those involving new words, suggest that the word usage pattern in *The Dark Tower* is not consistent with either *Out of the Silent Planet* or *Perelandra*. However, they cautioned against drawing firm conclusions since *The Dark Tower* is thought to be the draft of an unfinished novel, whereas the other books are complete.[44]

The analyses described up to this point have only compared *The Dark Tower* with the most similar works in Lewis's oeuvre. But as we have seen, Lindskoog alleged that Walter Hooper or Tony Marchington was the true author. Would it be possible to compare the writing styles of the three men directly? The most recent stylometric analysis of *The Dark Tower* was undertaken to answer that question. It was performed by Michael Oakes, a computational linguist at the University of Wolverhampton, and published in 2017.

In his analyses, Oakes made use of a multitude of text samples. For Lewis, he selected stretches from *The Dark Tower*, the three volumes of the Space Trilogy, *The Chronicles of Narnia*, and the entirety of the short story *The Man Born Blind*. From Lewis's nonfiction work, he chose selections from *Mere Christianity* and *The Problem of Pain*. Oakes also chose stretches from Tolkien's *Lord of the Rings* and *The Hobbit* as well as L'Engle's *A Wrinkle in Time*. Samples from Hooper's writing were also analyzed: these were taken from *Through Joy and Beyond*, a biography of Lewis, and *Past Watchful Dragons*, a guide to the Narnia books. Finally, he threw in the only known text by Marchington: a 1,000-word hoax letter that had been published in *Christianity and Literature*.

In a series of preliminary analyses, making use of most frequent words and 4-grams (four-character sequences), Oakes was able to differentiate the works of the fiction writers—Lewis, Tolkien, and L'Engle—as points in distinct regions of a two-dimensional space via principal component analysis. This confirmed the soundness and sensitivity of his approach. Then he looked to see where samples from *The Dark Tower* and *A Man Born Blind* would cluster when compared to samples written by Lewis, Hooper, and Marchington.

A principal component analysis revealed that the first six chapters of *The Dark Tower*, as well as *The Man Born Blind*, clustered with Lewis's other writings. The last chapter of the unfinished novel, however, is more stylistically consistent with the samples from Hooper and Marchington. But this may be due to a shift from a narrative to an expository style in the work's final chapter as opposed to revealing the hand of a different author.[45] It is worth noting that Oakes's results are opposite the pattern that Morton obtained from his cusum analysis.

So did Lewis write *The Dark Tower*, or didn't he? It's a difficult question to answer definitively since the stylometric studies, using four different methodologies, arrive at somewhat different conclusions. However, it probably is an abandoned work written wholly or mostly by Lewis. The mixed stylometric results are unlikely to sway the Lewis skeptics or to provide much comfort to those who believe that Lewis wrote it. Kathryn Lindskoog died in 2003, and Tony Marchington passed away in 2011. Walter Hooper succumbed in 2020, a victim of the COVID-19 pandemic. As a result, the principal figures in this literary feud are no longer available to either attack or defend their positions.

A BRONTË IMBROGLIO

The novels *Jane Eyre* and *Wuthering Heights* are two of the tentpoles in the canon of British literature. Published within three months of one another in late 1847, they were penned by the sisters Charlotte and Emily Brontë. A third sister, Anne, also published a debut novel at the same time—the lesser-known but highly regarded *Agnes Grey*. The sisters were a literary dream team of sorts, but the dream didn't last long. Within a year and a half, Emily and Anne had died of tuberculosis. Charlotte would outlive her sisters by six years and succumb to complications from her first pregnancy. Neither Emily nor Anne lived past the age of 30, and Charlotte passed away before reaching 40.

The three sisters chose to publish their novels under male pseudonyms linked to the first letter of their given names. Charlotte was Currer Bell, Emily became Ellis Bell, and Anne took on the name Acton Bell. They passed themselves off as men because the subject matter of their works—which included lust, alcohol addiction, and brutality—was not considered appropriate for nineteenth-century women to be writing about.[46]

The second edition of *Wuthering Heights*, published in 1850 and following Emily's death, included a biographical note written by Charlotte. In it, she revealed that "Ellis Bell" was, in actuality, her sister Emily and provided a brief sketch of her life.[47] She also made some corrections to the text's punctuation and spelling and toned down the transcription of one character's strong Yorkshire dialect.[48]

Although not widely known today, there was a fourth Brontë sibling. Their brother, Patrick Branwell, worked as a tutor and portrait painter. He too, had a short life, dying at age 31 after struggling with addictions to opium and alcohol, three months before Emily's passing. He wrote a great deal of prose and poetry that went unpublished, although a few of his poems appeared in local newspapers under his pseudonym "Northangerland."[49]

Twenty years after *Wuthering Heights* appeared, the *Halifax Guardian* published a letter contributed by a William Oakendale. This was a pseudonym for William Dearden, who had been a friend of Branwell Brontë's. He claimed that Branwell had read to him the beginning of his own story that was much the same as Emily's novel. This reading is thought to have taken place in 1842, five years before *Wuthering Heights* was published. Dearden also claimed it was obvious that the book could "never have emanated from the pen of a young girl . . . it is beyond the imagination of an inexperienced girl to conceive."[50] The literary scholar Irene Cooper Willis would poke a number of holes in Dearden's story to such a degree that Branwell's authorship of *Wuthering Heights* is no longer taken seriously by most scholars.[51] This notion is, however, at the heart of a work of historical fiction by Chris Firth.[52]

And there have been other challenges to Emily Brontë's authorship as well. In 1911, John Malham-Dembleby alleged that Charlotte, not Emily, wrote *Wuthering Heights*. He asserted that the novel attributed to Emily has deep commonalities with Charlotte's *Jane Eyre*. He claimed, for example, that Heathcliffe and Rochester were "one and the same." He also proposed that a number of elements in *Wuthering Heights* were drawn from Charlotte's own life.[53] Most critics, however, have dismissed these claims out of hand.[54]

Two decades later, the British novelist and biographer Edward Frederic Benson published a chronicle of Charlotte Brontë's life. In it, he proposed that *Wuthering Heights* was a composite, written by Emily and Charlotte. This speculation was based on "differences not only in manner but also striking differences of phraseology," such as when the housekeeper Nelly Dean takes over the narration following the book's initial chapters.[55] "No single author," thundered Benson, "could have planned a book in so topsy-turvy a manner."[56]

A theory that Charlotte wrote *all* of the works attributed to the Brontë sisters was advanced in 2011 by Canadian author Michele Carter in a self-published work. Carter claimed that Charlotte had placed clues throughout the novels as proof of her authorship in the form of riddles, symbols, puns, and anagrams. Carter also proposed that Charlotte had "discovered a corrupt band of Freemasons in her village," which is certainly a novel thesis within the world of Brontë scholarship.[57] Carter also undertook a stylometric analysis of the Brontë sisters' work by employing Juola's JGAAP program. She reported her results in a blog posting in May 2017, which means that her methodology has not been peer reviewed.

Carter compared a 5,000-word sample from *Wuthering Heights*, published in 1847, against known writings by the three Brontë sisters. For Charlotte, she selected a 2,500-word sample from *The Professor* (1846). Comparisons for the other two sisters are problematic since Carter suspected that Anne's poems and two novels—*Agnes Grey* and *The Tenant of Wildfell Hall*—had been written by Charlotte as well. Besides her novel *Wuthering Heights*, Emily had published only a few poems. Therefore, Carter chose samples from the diaries of Emily (1,700 words) and Anne (1,100 words). For "detractors"—she meant distractors—Carter selected 5,000-word samples from Jane Austen's *Northanger Abbey* (1817), Elizabeth Gaskell's *Cranford* (1853), and Harriet Martineau's *Deerbrook* (1839).

The result of the first analysis was that Charlotte's *The Professor* was the top match with *Wuthering Heights* on 15 out of 15 comparisons. Martineau came in second eight times out of 15, while Emily was second four times. Austen placed second on three comparisons. When Carter repeated the analysis with *Agnes Grey* as the unknown document, the match with Charlotte was highest 14 times out of 15, with Austen taking the other first-place finish. Anne came in third place twice.

The final set of analyses, with *The Tenant of Wildfell Hall* as the unknown document, led to Austen finishing first 10 times, while Charlotte came in first five times and second 10 times. Anne was fifth six times and finished dead last, in sixth place, nine times.

As Carter pointed out, Austen died in 1817, and she couldn't be the author of any of the suspect Brontë novels. The relatively high match between *Wildfell Hall* and *Northanger Abbey* could mean that the author of *Wildfell Hall*—Anne or someone else—was influenced by or consciously made use of Austen's style.[58]

There is, however, a more fundamental problem with Carter's analysis that she doesn't acknowledge. By contrasting novels with diary entries, she might as well have been comparing apples to oranges. The two genres differ in a host of ways since diary entries typically don't contain dialogue and have relatively simple sentence structure. Whether Carter realized it or not, she stacked the deck against having either Anne or Emily Brontë recognized as the author of the three novels in question.

Fortunately, a peer-reviewed stylometric analysis of *Wuthering Heights* has been conducted. Rachel McCarthy and James O'Sullivan, researchers at University College Cork, faced the same limitations regarding the limited output from Emily, but they were able to assemble a writing sample of 1,200 words from her letters and diary entries. They also sought to address the claim that Branwell was the real author of *Wuthering Heights* by including in their study his unfinished novel *And the Weary Are at Rest*, which consists of 25,500 words. It is thought that Branwell drafted it around 1845, and the two parts of the autograph manuscript can be found today at the New York Public Library and the Princeton University Library. The work was privately printed in 1924.[59]

Both Branwell and Emily wrote many poems, but including them in an author identification study is problematic. McCarthy and O'Sullivan performed an analysis in which they included the siblings' poetry but found that the poems tended to cluster together regardless of who wrote them. They suspected that the linguistic fingerprints of the authors were being obscured by the effects of genre and tested their hypothesis with a separate analysis of other authors who wrote both fiction and poetry. After observing the same effect, they chose to include the Brontë family's novels but not their poems in their study.

Another issue in the analysis is the small number of words in Emily's sample. There has been a good deal of debate among stylometric researchers about how large a sample must be to provide accurate results. These estimates have ranged from 5,000 words down to 1,000: the size of Emily's sample in this study qualifies as acceptable (although just barely).

The researchers compared the 100 most frequent words in the original 1847 edition of *Wuthering Heights*, Branwell's novel, and Emily's letters and diary entries. They found that Emily's voice was the most prominent, although some sections of *Wuthering Heights* were a better match with Branwell.

McCarthy and O'Sullivan then compared *Wuthering Heights* with the three other Brontë siblings. Specifically, they added samples from Charlotte's four novels: *The Professor* (1857), *Jane Eyre* (1847), *Shirley* (1849), and *Villette* (1853). Anne was represented by *Agnes Grey* (1847) and *Tenant of Wildfell Hall* (1848), and Branwell once again by *And the Weary Are at Rest* (ca. 1845). A cluster analysis revealed that *Wuthering Heights* stands alone and is separate from the novels penned by Charlotte, Anne, and Branwell. The researchers conclude, by process of elimination, that *Wuthering Heights* was written by either Emily or someone else entirely. And the latter possibility seems highly unlikely.

The researchers also compared the four Brontës to eight other nineteenth-century British writers, such as Austen, Eliot, Dickens, and Thackery. Somewhat to their surprise, McCarthy and O'Sullivan found that the siblings clustered together, forming a distinct "Brontë group" that was separate from the other authors.[60]

The close connection between Anne, Branwell, Charlotte, and Emily Brontë makes stylometric distinctions particularly difficult. Attribution studies are not typically performed on authors who are related and who spent their childhoods writing about an invented world. The Brontë's juvenilia concerning the Kingdom of Angria and the Gondal saga was discovered by Charlotte's first biographer, Elizabeth Gaskell, although she gave them relatively short shrift.[61] It seems likely, however, that this fictional world building and collaboration affected their more mature writing. The linguistic fingerprints of the Brontë siblings may be intertwined to such a degree that traditional attributional methods may not be sensitive enough to differentiate them reliably.

IT'S STILL A MOCKINGBIRD

Which books should all students be exposed to? Novels by writers like Fitzgerald, Hemingway, or Steinbeck seem to rise and fall in popularity over time. Others are hardy perennials that appear on required reading lists year after year. One of the true stalwarts is Harper Lee's *To Kill a Mockingbird*, which has achieved a kind of literary immortality. It is a story told by a child in a disarmingly simple way, yet it grapples with the complex issues of racial prejudice, human dignity, and justice. It has always been critically acclaimed, and it has always been controversial. It was also the debut work of a college dropout and middle-aged dilettante who wouldn't publish another book until the end of her life, 55 years later. Like her novel, Lee's story is disarmingly complex.

The youngest of four children, Nelle Harper Lee was born in 1926 in Monroeville, Alabama, a small town of about 1,200. Her father was a lawyer and would later serve as the model for *Mockingbird*'s Atticus Finch. She was a tomboy and quite different from her childhood neighbor, a fastidious and bookish boy a year and a half older than she. Despite their differences, Harper

Lee and Truman Capote became close friends. They amused themselves by dictating stories to one another and pounding them out on a typewriter provided by Lee's father.[62]

Capote would move to New York City and enjoy considerable success as a writer. Lee would eventually relocate there as well. During the late 1950s, she wrote and then extensively rewrote the book that became *To Kill a Mockingbird*. In 1959, while awaiting its publication, she served as Capote's assistant in Kansas, helping him with research for his true crime novel *In Cold Blood*. Lee also edited the final draft of his book, which was published in 1966. She was hurt when Capote failed to acknowledge her contributions. Capote, for his part, was said to have been jealous of Lee's later success and disappointed that *In Cold Blood* wasn't considered worthy of a Pulitzer Prize, although it was nominated. He never published another book, although two of his unfinished novels would be released after his death.[63]

To Kill a Mockingbird, published in July 1960, was both a critical and a commercial triumph, selling two and a half million copies in its first year.[64] Lee was awarded the Pulitzer Prize for Fiction the following year, and a film version of the book was released at the end of 1962. Starring Gregory Peck, the movie was also critically acclaimed. It received eight Academy Award nominations and won three of them. Few writers have ever experienced such sudden success and acclaim.

At first, Lee seemed to enjoy the limelight: she served as a consultant for the movie, granted interviews, and visited schools. But by 1964, she had tired of the attention and withdrew almost completely from public life, retreating to Monroeville. There were high expectations for another book, but none appeared. During the early 1960s, she published a total of three magazine articles in *Vogue* and *McCall's*. And after that, there was nothing.

Then the whispering began. How was it that Lee had written such a powerful work despite never having published before? How much assistance had she received? Was it possible that someone else was the real author?

Rumors that Capote had penned *Mockingbird* began to circulate. Pearl Belle, a critic and editor, reported that Capote insinuated to her that he had written it. Capote's family went further. His father, Archulus Persons, claimed that Truman had written almost all of the story. In an interview with an Alabama newspaper, he claimed that Lee had contributed little more than an outline and that "it was his genius son that made the novel sing."[65] Lee never commented on such claims publicly, although her sister, Alice Finch Lee, spoke out angrily against them. In a 2002 interview, she referred to Capote's supposed authorship as "the biggest lie ever told."[66]

For many of Lee's detractors, these speculations were largely put to rest by some correspondence that surfaced in 2006. In July 1959, a year before *Mockingbird*'s publication, Capote wrote a letter to Mary Ida Carter, his aunt. Concerning Lee, he wrote, "I did not see Nelle last winter, but the previous year, she showed me as much of the book as she'd written, and I liked it very much. She has real talent."[67] He didn't say anything about having helped to write it. Given that Capote was not known for modesty, it seems unlikely that he would have failed to mention his involvement.

In 1978, Lee began to research a murder trial in Alexander City, Alabama, with an eye to writing an *In Cold Blood*–type nonfiction novel herself. Although she shared a few pages of her story, titled "The Reverend," with a lawyer involved in the case, nothing ever came of the project.[68] Thirty years later, Lee had a stroke that left her partly paralyzed. And in 2013, she filed suit against her literary agent over the copyright for *Mockingbird*.[69] The following year, she made news by disavowing an unauthorized biography that Marja Mills had written.[70] It seemed as if Lee were sinking into a morass of ill health and litigation.

It came as a shock, therefore, when HarperCollins announced that a new novel by Lee would be published in July 2015. Although sometimes described as a sequel, *Go Set a Watchman* is the first draft of *Mockingbird*, set 20 years later and told by Scout as an adult. Lee's editor at Lippincott, Tay Hohoff, had liked *Watchman*'s flashbacks to Scout's childhood and recommended that Lee retell her story from a child's perspective.[71] *Mockingbird* was the result of that revision. The original *Watchman* manuscript, long thought lost, was rediscovered by her lawyer Tonja Carter, although there are conflicting accounts about when and how it was found.[72]

What is clear, however, is that many readers were perplexed and disappointed by *Watchman*. In the jump from the 1930s to the 1950s, the saintly Atticus from *Mockingbird* is transformed into a white supremacist and a supporter of segregation.[73] There were also concerns that Lee had been coerced by others into agreeing to publish it, although an investigation found no support for this allegation.[74]

Although fans of *Mockingbird* may have been disheartened by the publication of the new work, it created a golden opportunity for stylometric aficionados. As soon as it was released, Polish researchers Maciej Eder and Jan Rybicki began to explore *Watchman*'s relationship to Lee's 1960 work as well as the writings of Capote and six other twentieth-century southern writers, including William Faulkner, Flannery O'Connor, William Styron, and Eudora Welty. They also compared it to *Cats and Other People*, the 1973 novel by Tay Hohoff, who had served as Lee's editor. As we have seen in other such analyses, the researchers computed the texts' most frequent words, excluding pronouns, and created a cluster analysis of the books written by the nine authors.

The researchers found that most of the novelists had unique voices: samples from five of Faulkner's books, for example, form a unique cluster, as do those from three of O'Connor's works. Also as expected, out of the 29 novels in the analysis, Lee's *Mockingbird* and *Watchman* are most like one another. And her closest neighbor? That turns out to be Eudora Welty. The resemblance isn't surprising: Lee greatly admired Welty and in her letters referred to her as "my goddess."[75] The samples from five novels by Capote also formed a distinct cluster, although Hohoff's *Cats* clusters with his works as well. Based on this analysis, it is clear that the whispers about Capote having written *Mockingbird* are false.

Eder and Rybicki also performed a network analysis that allowed them to assess more subtle affinities between the texts. And here they found a linkage between Lee's *Watchman* and Capote's *In Cold Blood*. A measure of similarity between *Blood* and *Mockingbird*, on the other hand, was much fainter. To examine such affinities more closely, they performed a separate analysis in which they sequentially compared the entire text from *Mockingbird* to *Watchman*, Capote's *Blood*, and Hohoff's *Cats*.

The sequential analysis revealed the strongest match between *Mockingbird* and *Watchman*: the authorial signal for the earlier book was strongest for the later one for a bit more than half of *Mockingbird*'s segments. In some sections, however, the strongest affinity to *Mockingbird* was to Hohoff's *Cats*. As we have already seen, Lee's editor encouraged her to recast *Watchman* into *Mockingbird*, and it is known that Hohoff worked extensively with Lee over an extended period of time. The strongest influence of Lee's editor can be seen in the climax of *Mockingbird*. This occurs in chapter 28, when Scout is attacked by Bob Ewell, who is then stabbed by "Boo" Radley. Lee seems to have received assistance from her editor in handling this crucial, violent scene.

But what about *Mockingbird*'s match with *In Cold Blood*? Since Lee helped Capote with both the research for and the editing of that book, we might expect to see some resemblance between the two works. In the sequential analysis, the signal from *Blood* is strongest—when compared to *Watchman* and *Cats*—only at the very beginning of *Mockingbird*. There may be, as the researchers put it, "a drop of Capote in Lee," but this influence appears to be quite limited.[76]

Even with the authorship question seemingly settled, *Mockingbird* continues to make news. It has become one of the most frequently challenged books in U.S. schools and libraries. Lee's inclusion of a particular racial slur (which appears about 50 times), other profanities, and the theme of sexual assault have made the novel a lightning rod for controversy. In 2017, *Mockingbird* was banned from an eighth-grade classroom in Biloxi, Mississippi, following similar removals from schools in Illinois, North Carolina, and Virginia.[77] In an interview, David Foster Wallace once declared that the job of good fiction is to "comfort the disturbed and disturb the comfortable." It appears that *Mockingbird* is still fulfilling that role.

PATTERSON'S PATTERNS

James Brendan Patterson is a force of nature in the literary world. As of this writing, he has published more than 400 novels, novellas, comic books, and short-story collections for adults and children. Although he isn't the world's wealthiest writer, he does fall somewhere between J. K. Rowling and Stephen King. He was also the best-selling author of the past decade: between 2010 and 2019, readers bought 84 million copies of his work in all formats.[78] During that period, he transformed the publishing process and even traditional models of authorship since the majority of his books—about 80 percent—are collaborations with others.

It is worth noting that Patterson wasn't an overnight success. He was born in 1947, the son of an insurance broker and a teacher. After earning a degree in English at Manhattan College, he dropped out of a doctoral program at Vanderbilt to become a junior copywriter at J. Walter Thompson, the New York advertising agency. Hoping to become a published author, he started writing every night after work and on weekends. His first effort, titled *The Thomas Berryman Number*, was rejected by 31 publishers before it sold to Little, Brown. This mystery thriller, released in 1976, was a modest success and won an Edgar Award. He published two more novels in the 1970s and then three during the 1980s. The public's reaction to his offerings was polite but indifferent.

Patterson didn't achieve commercial success until *Along Came a Spider*, his seventh book. It was the first to feature the Black forensic psychologist Alex Cross, who would become one of Patterson's best-known characters and appear in two dozen later works. *Spider* was published in 1993 when he was 46 years old. At that point, he began to write a book or more a year and soon retired from advertising to write full-time.

In the early 1990s, Patterson wrote a couple of nonfiction books with Peter Kim, and in 1996, he teamed up with Peter de Jonge to write *Miracle on the 17th Green*. Since then, he has collaborated with more than 90 authors. Although most of these associations have yielded only a book or two, he has released 40 titles with Maxine Paetro, 36 with Chris Grabenstein, and 21 with Michael Ledwidge. His coauthors are always acknowledged on the cover, although their names appear in smaller type than Patterson's own.

Until about 2004, Patterson was publishing three or four books a year and writing with a coauthor or two—an impressive number by any standard. But then, he greatly enlarged his stable of collaborators, and his production soared into the stratosphere. After releasing five books in 2005, he had almost tripled that figure by 2010. In 2015, he published 19 books, and of that number, 16 were written with coauthors. In 2017, Patterson's productivity reached its zenith: he released 65 books—more than one a week—with 55 collaborators. Now in his mid-seventies, Patterson has slowed down a bit: in 2021, he released "only" 16 books with 11 coauthors. Other writers savor each book deal, but Patterson has been known to sign off on 17 at once.[79]

Most of Patterson's collaborators have been relatively unknown authors, but he achieved a great deal of attention—and free publicity—by partnering with Bill Clinton to write *The President Is Missing*, published in 2018.[80] This was followed by another collaboration with the former president[81] as well as one with Dolly Parton in 2022.[82]

Far from resting on his laurels, the former adman is actively involved in all phases of his books' production, marketing, and branding. Patterson and his coauthors have even developed entire series aimed at specific segments of the book-buying public. His goal is to write something for everyone, from children to manga lovers to connoisseurs of mysteries.

His approach is data driven and pragmatic. When he discovered that John Grisham was outselling him on the West Coast, Patterson created a new series, the Women's Murder Club, and set it in San Francisco. When he found that his books weren't selling well in Nordic countries, he teamed with the well-known Swedish crime writer Liza Marklund to produce an international thriller.[83] This can be viewed as either shrewd marketing or the commodification of art—although Patterson has never claimed to be an artist.

One of his innovations has been to create BookShots—volumes of 25,000 to 35,000 words, or about 125 to 150 pages. Patterson believes that these shorter works, traditionally referred to as novellas, are a better fit with his readers' busy lives since they require less of a time commitment than longer works of fiction.[84] Such a book can be binge-read over a weekend, much like someone watching an entire season of a show on Netflix. Patterson believes that "taking the fat" out of commercial novels makes reading more palatable for a wider audience.[85]

Perhaps not surprisingly, many literary critics, as well as other writers, have failed to embrace his work. His emphasis on plot at the expense of characterization as well as his style—short sentences and short paragraphs—led Stephen King to describe him as "a terrible writer." When he encounters such reactions, Patterson will often say that "thousands of people hate my stuff, millions of people like it."[86]

How does Patterson's collaborative process work? In most cases, he produces an outline of a story for one of his coauthors. This is typically quite detailed and may run to 60 or 70 pages. His collaborators then draft and submit material to him about every two weeks, which he revises or reworks until he is satisfied.[87] Naturally, this raises the question of how much of the prose, in a book ostensibly coauthored by James Patterson, was truly written by the man who invariably receives the top billing on dust jackets.

Fortunately, this is a question that stylometric techniques can address. In 2017, Simon Fuller and James O'Sullivan published an analysis of Patterson's work and also tried to place it within the context of literary history. They pointed out that, even though Patterson's model of factory-level collaboration seems innovative, it dates back several hundred years. The Renaissance workshops that produced the likes of Michelangelo and da Vinci had a master and several apprentices: the newbies would perform the grunt work, while the old hands would oversee and execute the difficult parts of a painting or sculpture.

But perhaps the most relevant model of collaborative creation would be the output of Alexandre Dumas, the nineteenth-century French novelist and playwright, who employed many collaborators to keep up with the demand for his work. Much like Patterson, he wrote in a variety of genres and published a great amount of fiction, including 400 novels and 35 plays. Such an approach may not always produce great literary works, but Dumas's oeuvre does include enduring classics like *The Three Musketeers* and *The Count of Monte Cristo*.

Fuller and O'Sullivan chose to focus their attention on two of Patterson's collaborators. One of these is Peter de Jonge, a coauthor with Patterson on seven books published between 1996 and 2015. The other is Andrew Gross, who collaborated on six books that appeared between 2002 and 2006. Both men have also published novels for which they are the sole author.

For their analyses, the researchers selected two novels by Patterson and de Jonge and three by Patterson and Gross. They also included two books by de Jonge, five by Gross, and nine by Patterson as the sole author. To control for stylistic variation over time, Fuller and O'Sullivan avoided using any of Patterson's early works and opted instead for solo novels that appeared between 2001 and 2012—the same time span as his collaborations with the other two writers.

The researchers focused on the 100 to 1,000 most frequent words in the texts and then created a bootstrap consensus tree—a sort of similarity map—to see how the 21 books would cluster in terms of resemblance. If Patterson were the primary writer, then his linguistic fingerprints should overshadow the stylistic contributions of his collaborators. But if his coauthors were performing the lion's share of the labor, then we would expect to see both their solo efforts and their collaborations clustering together in the consensus tree.

For the most part, the results of the analyses support the idea that Patterson's coauthors are doing nearly all of the heavy lifting in their collaborations with him. Eight of the nine books written solely by Patterson form one branch of the consensus tree. A second branch consists of the works of Andrew Gross: his five solo works cluster together, and his three collaborations with Patterson form a secondary branch that is a bit closer to Patterson's sole-authored works than Gross's own books. A third branch is made up of the writing of de Jonge and includes his two solo efforts and the two books with Patterson.

The only real surprise is that one of Patterson's solo works, 2001's *First to Die*, is out of place in the consensus tree and grouped with the Gross–Patterson collaborations. *First to Die* was the first book in the Women's Murder Club series, with later installments coauthored by Andrew Gross and then Maxine Paetro. The analysis suggests that Gross played an unacknowledged role in the debut work of this series. But if that is the case, then why didn't Gross get credit as a coauthor? The researchers speculate that it may have been a simple issue of branding: publishing the first installment of a new series as written solely by Patterson might have been seen as increasing the prestige of the Women's Murder Club. Once it was established with a successful debut entry, coauthors could be added without adversely affecting its marque.[88]

There is reason to think that Patterson perceives his solo name as the "luxury" line in his many series. None of the 29 Alex Cross novels published to date have been collaborations, which suggests that Patterson fears adulterating his premier brand by writing them with collaborators.

O'Sullivan has taken pains to emphasize that the study was not designed to somehow expose Patterson as less than forthcoming about his role in these collaborations. On the contrary, Patterson has always made clear, when asked about his process, that his collaborators are doing most of the actual composition, albeit under his watchful eye.[89]

Patterson's collaborations with Bill Clinton provide an interesting test case for his branding. When one's coauthor is a well-known personality but not a fiction writer, does the seasoned author take the wheel, or does he allow his famous collaborator to write whatever he wants? An analysis by O'Sullivan of 2018's *The President Is Missing* clearly indicates that Patterson was the senior writing partner, with the notable exception of the finale, in which the linguistic signature shifts to that of the former president.[90] It is interesting to note that, unlike his other books, Patterson's and Clinton's names are the same size on the covers of their collaborative efforts.

CHAPTER FIVE

IT'S A CRIME!

A Forensic Linguistics Casebook

Now that we have seen examples of the methods developed by stylometrists for author attribution, let's turn our attention to those employed by forensic linguists. This chapter presents four well-known examples. They involve a suspect's confession, a terrorist's manifesto, a ransom note, and cell phone text messages. Each of these presents unique challenges for law enforcement and the legal system.

THE ORIGINATOR

On November 30, 1949, a Welsh laborer named Timothy John Evans walked into the police station in his hometown of Merthyr Tydfil to surrender to the authorities. He told the officers that he had "disposed" of his wife Beryl, whom he had married two years earlier. In his initial account, Evans, who lived with Beryl in the Notting Hill district of West London, stated that his wife had become pregnant. The family already had one young child and was struggling financially, and Beryl had decided to try to terminate her pregnancy. Evans claimed to have given Beryl something to drink that was supposed to induce an abortion, but the treatment had killed her.

Evans stated that he had hidden his wife's body in a sewer drain outside his residence. However, her corpse was not found when the drain was searched, and it took three men to remove the drain's heavy cover. A cursory inspection of his home found nothing remarkable. His family lived on the upper floor of a tenement at Ten Rillington Place—an address that would soon become infamous.

When informed that his wife's body could not be found, Evans changed his story. He now claimed that his downstairs neighbor, a postal clerk named John Christie, had offered to perform the abortion and that the desperate couple agreed to this plan. After Evans returned home from work on November 8, Christie told him that he had attempted the procedure but that something had gone wrong, and Beryl had died. Christie told Evans that he would dispose of her body and find someone to take care of the couple's young daughter, Geraldine. He advised Evans to leave town, and he departed for Wales to stay with relatives. He claimed that he hadn't mentioned Christie's role in the initial confession to protect him since abortions were illegal in the United Kingdom at that time.

The police returned to Evans's residence and, after a more thorough search of the premises, discovered the bodies of Beryl and 13-month-old Geraldine wrapped in a blanket and tablecloth. They were hidden in an outbuilding of the tenement's back garden. Evans's wife and daughter had been strangled. After hours of questioning, the distraught Evans confessed to killing his wife during an argument and strangling his daughter two days later.

Based on this confession, Evans was tried for murder. On the advice of counsel, he withdrew his final statement and claimed that Christie had been responsible, as he had alleged earlier. At Evans's three-day trial, John Christie and his wife Ethel served as star witnesses for the prosecution, reporting that Evans and his wife had often argued. Afterward, the jury deliberated for 40 minutes before finding Evans guilty. After an unsuccessful appeal, the 25-year-old Evans was hanged in HM Prison Pentonville in London on March 9, 1950.[1]

Three years later, after John Christie moved out of the downstairs apartment at Ten Rillington Place, a gruesome discovery was made. The remains of three women were found in a kitchen alcove that had been covered over with wallpaper. The skeletons of two more female victims were discovered in the garden, and the decomposing body of Ethel Christie was found hidden under the floorboards. When questioned, Christie confessed to having killed the women as well as Evans's wife. An insanity plea did not convince the jury at his trial, and Christie was hanged at Prison Pentonville for the murder of Ethel Christie on July 15, 1953.

Since there was now considerable doubt about Timothy Evans's guilt, two inquiries were conducted to reevaluate the evidence. The first review, conducted in just eight days during July 1953, concluded that Evans had murdered his wife and daughter. Public criticism of this verdict led to a second, more thorough investigation that occurred between November 1965 and January 1966. Significantly, the services of a Swedish linguist named Jan Svartvik were enlisted.

A lecturer at the University of Gothenburg, Svartvik had served as an assistant director of the Survey of English Usage at University College in London.[2] He would go on to become one of the world's foremost experts in corpus linguistics: the study of language as it is spoken and written as opposed to theoretical sentences far removed from real-world usage. Svartvik was asked to analyze the four statements Evans had made to the police: the first two that he had made at Merthyr Tydfil and two statements made days later at the Notting Hill police station.

In the second Notting Hill statement, Evans confessed to murdering his wife and child and described how he had disposed of their bodies. During his trial, however, Evans claimed that while three sections of his statement were genuine, two others, in which he confessed to the murders, had been coerced while he was highly emotional and afraid of physical violence from his interrogators. Was there any way to substantiate his claim based on the language the statements contained?

By closely comparing the Merthyr Tydfil and the Notting Hill statements, Svartvik found consistent differences in the language of the two transcripts. At the Merthyr Tydfil police station, for example, Evans was recorded making reference to time with phrases like "about half past six" or "about twenty to seven in the morning." In the Notting Hill statements, however, Evans employed phrases like "about 7.15 p.m." or "the 12.55 a.m. train." References to time made at Notting Hill almost invariably included an "a.m." or "p.m." descriptor, but Evans never did this in any of the two dozen temporal references recorded at Merthyr Tydfil.

It seems unlikely that Evans changed the way he typically referred to time between November 30, the date of the Merthyr Tydfil interrogations, and December 2, when he was questioned at Notting Hill. What did change were the detectives at the two locations where he made his statements. Svartvik's analysis of such differences suggests that the statements were not verbatim transcriptions of what Evans had said but rather higher-level interpretations of what the detectives thought he meant.

It is important to know, at this juncture, that Evans was functionally illiterate: beyond making out letters and numbers, he could not read or write. As a result, one might expect his spoken register to reflect this, and Svartvik found such evidence in Evans's statements. This included the use of double negatives ("She never said no more about it"), what Svartvik characterized as substandard verb forms ("I come back to the kitchen"), and substandard use of relative pronouns ("Different people from which I used to borrow").

At the same time, Svartvik documented other words and phrases that have a more literate, formal register, such as "incurring" (as in "incurring one debt after another"), "in a fit of temper," "in his presence," and "made my way." The unstated deduction is that those who recorded Evans's speech may have drawn on their own idiolect as they transcribed Evans's confessions.[3] And if the authorities manipulated Evans's words, might they have also changed his content? Given that Evans couldn't read, he couldn't verify his own statements but had to rely on the veracity of those who read them back to him.

A major issue in this and many other legal cases is that there isn't that much language to analyze. Evans's first statement to the Notting Hill police, for example, is only four sentences long, and his second, the longest of the four, consists of 109 sentences and 1,936 words. A close analysis of the words might suggest manipulation by the authorities but does not prove it. Could other units of analysis show systematic variation in a more rigorous and verifiable way?

Svartvik attempted to do this by comparing the purportedly "authentic" and "coerced" sections of Evans's second Notting Hill statement, which contains 298 clauses in total. He analyzed six different types of clauses and found large differences between the two sections. For example, 7 percent of the "authentic" sections contain the connective "then," whereas 30 percent of the "coerced" sections make use of this connective—a difference of more than four to one. And clauses linked by connectives, such as "so," "or," "but," and "and," occur 12 percent of the time in the "authentic" sections but make up only 2 percent of the clauses in the "coerced" sections—a difference of six to one. A statistical analysis across all the clause types suggests that such differences are unlikely to be due to chance.[4]

As a control, Svartvik also analyzed the clause types in the confession of John Christie. He divided Christie's statement of 139 clauses into three equal parts and compared the relative frequencies found in each. Unlike the language in the Evans statement, Christie's use of clausal types is much more consistent. For example, clauses linked by a connective occur at a rate of 9, 8, and 12 percent across the three sections. A statistical test suggests that such minor variation is likely the result of chance.[5]

Svartvik's analyses suggest that Evans's statements were not passively recorded by the officers who were interviewing him, as was required by English law at the time. According to the so-called Judges' Rules, suspects were supposed to dictate their statements to police officers, who were instructed not to interrupt or ask questions beyond simple requests for clarification. In practice, however, such rules were seldom followed. Suspects frequently described events out of order, repeated themselves, got sidetracked into minutiae, or left out key parts of the events they were narrating. To deal with such issues, the officers would interrupt the testimony to offer paraphrases and clarifications or to ask a whole series of their own questions.[6]

This is likely what happened to Evans, as his statements seem to be an admixture of his own words and a patois referred to as "police register." Research on this form of language has shown that its practitioners make liberal use of temporal adverbs, such as "subsequently" or "thereafter." Terms such as these, however, are deployed relatively rarely in everyday speech.[7]

The Evans case came to be widely seen as a miscarriage of justice, and the British Home Secretary proposed that Timothy Evans be granted a (posthumous) royal pardon in 1966. The case was also a contributing factor in the passage of the Murder (Abolition of Death Penalty) Act 1965. The act put an end to the death penalty for murder in Great Britain, with death sentences commuted to sentences of life imprisonment. Originally passed as a temporary measure, it was made permanent in 1969.[8]

Jan Svartvik's work on the Evans statements was a watershed event for the field that would come to be known as forensic linguistics. He even employed the phrase in the subtitle of his 1968 monograph on the case. His book introduced both the concept and the term to linguists and law enforcement officers, although the initial growth of this hybrid discipline was relatively slow.[9]

THE MAN IN THE WOODS

On April 3, 1996, three men walked up to a cabin in the woods near the village of Lincoln, Montana. Posing as surveyors, with maps in hand, they shouted a greeting. The door opened, and they could see that a bearded, unkempt man was the shack's sole occupant. He probably looked older than his 53 years. The trio asked for his help in determining the boundaries of the property. As he paused in the doorway, the other men grabbed and handcuffed him after a brief scuffle. The self-styled surveyors were, in reality, law enforcement officers from the U.S. Forest Service and the FBI.[10]

For the FBI, the arrest was the culmination of the most expensive—and longest—manhunt in American history. The man in the woods was responsible for crimes committed over a 17-year period. Bombs he had manufactured and then mailed or planted had killed three people. Nearly two dozen others had been injured. Those who lived had suffered serious burns or lost fingers, while others lost vision or hearing. The man in the woods had become a terrorist, although he had once been a mathematics prodigy and a university professor. His name was Theodore John Kaczynski, but he was far better known, both before and after his capture, as the Unabomber.

This moniker was the media's spin on the acronym UNABOM, the FBI's original case identifier. The amalgamation of letters referred to the organizations that the unknown bomber initially targeted: university employees and airlines. The attacks began in May 1978 and continued until April 1995. Law enforcement was convinced that the bombings were related because of similarities in the explosive devices themselves: they were carefully crafted and assembled from untraceable materials, such as batteries with their labels removed. The terrorist even manufactured his own glue from melted deer hooves.[11]

As the Unabomber perfected his technique, the devices became more sophisticated—and more lethal. The first 11 bombs he planted or sent through the mail resulted in cuts and burns. Some of these were serious, but there were no fatalities. The final six bombs, however, caused severe injuries and three deaths.

In 1987, investigators thought they finally had a break in the case. A witness came forward to say that she had seen the person who planted a bomb in the parking lot of a Salt Lake City computer store. Camouflaged to look like a piece of lumber, the device had detonated in the hand of the store's owner, riddling his body with shrapnel and causing severe nerve damage in one arm. The witness provided police with a description of a curly-haired man with a mustache, his face partially obscured by a pair of aviator sunglasses and a hood. A sketch of the bomber was widely circulated but did not lead to any further breakthroughs in the case.

By 1993, authorities were offering a million-dollar reward for information that would lead to the arrest of the Unabomber. This resulted in thousands of tips that had to be investigated. A trio of federal agencies was involved since the crimes stood at the intersection of three jurisdictions: the Bureau of Alcohol, Tobacco, and Firearms; the Postal Inspection Service; and the FBI.[12]

Perhaps not surprisingly, this massive dragnet scooped up a number of suspects who were completely innocent. William T. Vollmann, an author and National Book Award winner, was surprised to learn that he had been a suspect in the case, apparently because his publications included "anti-progress themes." He would come under suspicion again following the 2001 anthrax attacks—an episode described in chapter 7.[13]

In June 1995, the Unabomber sent the *New York Times* and the *Washington Post* a 35,000-word essay. Best described as a polemic, it railed against the evils created by modern technological society. Its author claimed that he would stop his attacks if his essay was published and warned that he would continue if it was not.[14] In hopes that he would keep his word—and because investigators were stumped—the two papers published excerpts on September 19. The *Post* ran the full text of the document, titled *Industrial Society and Its Future*, three days later.

Reactions to the decision to publish were mixed. Some critics argued that the newspapers had "abdicated journalistic responsibility by giving in to a terrorist."[15] And the Unabomber seemingly got what he wanted: the chance to broadcast his views on society's ills to the world. This lengthy screed, however, would also prove to be his undoing.

The essay was read in Schenectady, New York, by a college professor named Linda Patrik. It was she who first suspected that her reclusive brother-in-law might be the long-sought antitechnology terrorist. She encouraged her husband, a social worker named David Kaczynski, to take a look at it. He was initially skeptical, but when he read the Unabomber's essay, he detected similarities between his brother Ted's way of expressing himself and the terrorist's. For example, the essay includes the unusual phrase "cool-headed logician"—an epithet that he recalled his brother having employed.[16] Using an intermediary, the family contacted the FBI and turned over some of Ted's writing that had been found in the family home in Illinois. They also provided letters that Ted had written to his family.

Born in Chicago in 1942, Ted Kaczynski had grown up in a suburb of that city. He enrolled at Harvard when he was 16, then earned a doctorate in mathematics from the University of Michigan. He accepted a position at the University of California, Berkeley, and was the youngest mathematics professor in the school's history. He taught there for a couple of years but then resigned. He built a cabin in Montana with David and worked for him in Chicago for a time until David had to fire him for harassing a female coworker. However, the two stayed in touch until David's marriage to Linda—a match that Ted disapproved of.

Kaczynski returned to the cabin in Montana. It was more of a one-room shed that lacked electricity or running water. At the time of his arrest, he had been living alone in the woods, with periodic forays into a nearby town for supplies, for many years. It was there that his personality unraveled and where he built his deadly bombs and typed out *Industrial Society and Its Future*.

The manifesto—as it was dubbed by the media—is an odd disquisition. It runs to nearly 60 single-spaced pages and consists of 232 numbered paragraphs. These are followed by 36 footnotes. The document has a Flesch reading ease score of 41, which qualifies it as "fairly difficult."[17] It's not hard to imagine it springing from a well-educated, mathematically inclined mind. In terms of content, the first sentence provides a good summary of the hundreds that follow: "The Industrial Revolution and its consequences have been a disaster for the human race."[18]

The letters that Ted had written to his brother were analyzed by James Fitzgerald, a forensic linguist and criminal profiler employed by the FBI. Fitzgerald advocated for the publication of the essay by the newspapers in the hope that someone would recognize its author and come forward. And someone had.

Even without David's help, Fitzgerald had been able to make an educated guess about the Unabomber's age, based on his dated use of terms like "chick" for a woman and "negro" for an African American. The unknown author also used unusual terms, like "chimerical" and "anomic," which hinted at a high level of education.[19]

Other linguists, such as the Georgetown professor Roger Shuy, were also consulted on the Unabomber case. Shuy was given the manifesto as well as other known writings of the Unabomber since the terrorist had sometimes included short notes or letters with his bombs, and parts of some of these survived the blasts. In addition, the Unabomber had written letters to magazines and newspapers in an earlier attempt to find a publisher for his manifesto.

From this material, Shuy found additional clues about the Unabomber's background. He noticed that the bomber employed some unconventional spellings, like "clew" for "clue" and "wilfully" with only one "l" in the first pair. He recognized these neologisms as spelling reforms that had been promoted by the editor of the *Chicago Tribune* during the 1940s and 1950s. They had failed to catch on, but Shuy hypothesized that someone growing up in or near the Windy City during those decades might have been influenced by the *Tribune*'s style. Therefore, the odd spellings might hint at both the Unabomber's childhood home and his approximate age. Both of these suppositions turned out to be correct.

Shuy also noted that the Unabomber used the phrase "child-rearing" several times in his essay as opposed to "raising children." This is significant because the former phrase is characteristic of the Northern dialect of American English, whereas the latter phrase is more commonly employed by Midland speakers. And although the Northern dialect is spoken across a broad swath of the country from New England to the upper Midwest, it would be consistent with someone who had learned his mother tongue in Chicagoland.[20]

James Fitzgerald noticed something else in the manifesto that was intriguing. This was the odd phrase "You can't eat your cake and have it too."[21] Most people who use this expression would say, "You can't have your cake and eat it too." Strictly speaking, the more familiar version of this proverb doesn't make much sense. After all, how can you eat something that you don't have?[22] Fitzgerald would later learn that the altered form of this old chestnut had been employed by Ted and David's mother Wanda. It also appeared in a letter found in his mother's home.[23] Ultimately, Fitzgerald's superiors decided that there were sufficient grounds to issue a search warrant for Kaczynski's cabin.

The case against Kaczynski was airtight. In his cabin, authorities found plans and parts for making bombs as well as the original manifesto manuscript and, chillingly, two live bombs. One of these was identical to a device the Unabomber had employed previously.[24] Finally, a DNA match was found between saliva on a letter from the Unabomber and letters that Kaczynski had mailed to his family.[25]

In 1998, Kaczynski pleaded guilty to three counts of murder and a variety of other charges. Now in his early eighties, he is serving eight life sentences without the possibility of parole. The man who had lived in the woods is now incarcerated at a maximum-security prison in Florence, Colorado. It's ironic that someone who had been so careful to remove physical fingerprints from his deadly bombs had been unable to expunge the linguistic fingerprints from his magnum opus.

A (BEAUTY) QUEEN'S RANSOM

The 1996 homicide of six-year-old JonBenét Ramsey in her Boulder, Colorado, home has been a topic of popular fascination for more than 25 years. The death of the child beauty queen has been endlessly analyzed and debated in a stream of tabloid articles, tell-all books, and interviews. The murder has also been dissected by a legion of armchair detectives in online forums. With regard to suspects, two principal schools of thought have emerged: the child was killed either by a family member or by an intruder from outside the home.

Besides JonBenét, there were three other family members in the house on the night or morning that she died. These were her parents and her nine-year-old brother, Burke. Fifty-three-year-old John Ramsey was the well-to-do president and CEO of Access Graphics, a division of Lockheed-Martin that provided computer services. His second wife, Patsy, the daughter of a Union Carbide engineer, had turned 40 a few days after JonBenét's death. She had been crowned Miss West Virginia in 1977. Both were college graduates: John had earned an undergraduate degree in electrical engineering and a master's in business administration, and Patsy had majored in journalism with a minor in advertising. The family had lived in their 15-room house in Boulder for five years.

Just one aspect of this complex case is discussed here: the linguistic analysis of a ransom note ostensibly discovered by Patsy at the bottom of the house's circular stairwell early on the morning of December 26. After showing it to her husband, she made a 911 call and told the dispatcher that her daughter had been taken. Later that morning, however, JonBenét was found dead in the house's basement. She had been strangled, and her skull was fractured.

The ransom note was released by the Boulder County district attorney in September 1997. It appears below, with line numbers added for the identification of specific words and phrases. It was written with a Sharpie on pages torn from a notepad belonging to the Ramseys. Both the pen and the pad were later found in their home. Investigators also found a practice salutation on another page from the same pad.

Page 1

1   Mr. Ramsey,
2   Listen carefully! We are a
3   group of individuals that represent
4   a small foreign faction. We xx
5   respect your bussiness but not the
6   country that it serves. At this
7   time we have your daughter in our
8   posession. She is safe and unharmed

9   and if you want her to see 1997,
10 you must follow our instructions to
11 the letter.
12   You will withdraw $118,000.00
13 from your account. $100,000 will be
14 in $100 bills and the remaining
15 $18,000 in $20 bills. Make sure
16 that you bring an adequate size
17 attaché to the bank. When you
18 get home you will put the money
19 in a brown paper bag. I will
20 call you between 8 and 10 am
21 tomorrow to instruct you on delivery.
22 The delivery will be exhausting so
23 I advise you to be rested. If
24 we monitor you getting the money
25 early, we might call you early to
26 arrange an earlier delivery of the

Page 2

27 money and hence a earlier
28 ~~delivery~~ pick-up of your daughter.
29   Any deviation of my instructions
30 will result in the immediate
31 execution of your daughter. You
32 will also be denied her remains
33 for proper burial. The two
34 gentlemen watching over your daughter
        not
35 do v particularly like you so I
36 advise you not to provoke them.
37 Speaking to anyone about your
38 situation, such as Police, F.B.I., etc.,
39 will result in your daughter being
40 beheaded. If we catch you talking
41 to a stray dog, she dies. If you
42 alert bank authorities, she dies.
43 If the money is in any way
44 marked or tampered with, she

45 dies. You will be scanned for
46 electronic devices and if any are
47 found, she dies. You can try to
48 deceive us but be warned that
49 we are familiar with Law enforcement
50 countermeasures and tactics.
51 You stand a 99% chance of killing
52 your daughter if you try to out
53 smart us. Follow our instructions

Page 3

54 and you stand a 100% chance
55 of getting her back. You and
56 your family are under constant
57 scrutiny as well as the authorities.
58 Don't try to grow a brain
59 John. You are not the only
60 fat cat around so don't think that
61 killing will be difficult.
62 Don't underestimate us John.
63 Use that good southern common
64 sense of yours. It is up to
65 you now John!
66   Victory!
67   S.B.T.C.

The Ramsey ransom note is unusual in many respects. Most notable is its length: at 372 words, filling two and a half pages, it would have required about 29 minutes to write. Furthermore, it was not brought into the Ramsey home: it must have been written while its author was inside the house. In the years since JonBenét's murder, the language it contains has been subjected to numerous analyses. What follow are some of the major forensic conclusions, keyed to the relevant lines of the note.

Whereas most ransom notes provide only a terse set of directions, the Ramsey note has been described as "overly dramatic and much too wordy" and as containing "instructions that were laughable."[26] The note is also riddled with inconsistencies, such as a shift in tone from formal and polite at the beginning to informal and threatening by its end.

Judging from the relatively sophisticated vocabulary it contains, the note was penned by a well-educated person. This can be seen in the use of terms like "deviation," "scrutiny," and "countermeasures." Such language seemingly rules out JonBenét's nine-year-old brother as its author. Some analysts have called attention to the correct use of an accent mark over the e in "attaché" (line 17), but this may be the tail end of the y in "you" on the line above.

Forensic linguists have pointed to the note's mothering and admonishing language, as in "make sure that you bring" (lines 15 to 16) and "I advise you to be rested" (line 23). From these clues, it has been suggested that the author was probably female.

There are two misspellings: "bussiness" (line 5) and "posession" (line 8). Given that more esoteric terms are spelled correctly and that both misspellings occur in the first few lines, this suggests an attempt at deception. However, the author apparently forgot about committing more misspellings as the letter continued. There is also a shift in voice from the plural ("we," "our") to a mix of plural and singular ("I," "my") after line 18, suggesting that the author also periodically forgot about that detail as well.[27]

Also of interest is the use of a downward-pointing caret at line 35 to add the word "not" between "do" and "particularly." This proofreading mark for an insertion would certainly have been known by someone who majored in journalism, but its use is not, by itself, dispositive.

More telling, perhaps, are the references to people. The note is addressed to "Mr. Ramsey," although JonBenét's father is referred to by his first name later in the message. And shouldn't the letter have been addressed to both of the child's parents? In addition, JonBenét herself is never mentioned by name; instead, the phrase "your daughter" appears six times. It seems as if the author is trying to maintain a psychological distance from their subject.

The $118,000 requested as the ransom payment (line 12) seems modest given the family's wealth but also oddly specific. Investigators learned that John's deferred compensation from Access Graphics for 1995 had been $118,117.50. He received this amount in January 1996, and it was printed on every pay stub issued to him during that year.[28] This suggests that the note's author could have been a company employee with access to such information. More likely, however, is that the number is a red herring, designed to implicate one or more of John's coworkers as the "abductors." Other misleading clues include the writer's claim that they represent "a small foreign faction." It is difficult to imagine anyone describing themselves in that way.

As we saw in chapter 1, certain expressions are regional and can betray the geographic origins of those who employ them. Some analysts have suggested that the use of "bring" (line 16) instead of "take" is more common in the South than in other parts of the United States and that the use of "gentlemen" (line 34) to describe the individuals watching over JonBenét is also more common in southern states than elsewhere. Patsy grew up in West Virginia, whereas John was born in Nebraska and raised in Michigan. However, he and Patsy lived in Atlanta for several years, and the time spent in Georgia could have affected the dialect of either of them.

Some of the language in the note appears to have been lifted from movie dialogue. On the second page, for example, there are three instances of the construction "If [action], then she dies" (lines 42, 44, and 47). In the 1971 film *Dirty Harry*, there is a similar repetition: "If [action], the girl dies." That film also makes use of the admonition "Listen . . . carefully"—the first words of the ransom note. Even the odd insult (line 58) seems to have come from Hollywood: in 1994's *Speed*, the villain, played by Dennis Hopper, says "Do *not* attempt to grow a brain!"

And what to make of the initials S.B.T.C. (line 67)? Investigators noted that Patsy once signed her name as P.P.R.B.S.J. on a Christmas card to a friend—short for "Patsy Pugh Ramsey, Bachelor of Science in Journalism."[29] The initials on the note could stand for Subic Bay Training Center, a military base in the Philippines where John Ramsey had been stationed during his stint in the navy. Or perhaps it is short for "saved by the cross," an expression that would have been consistent with Patsy's deep religious faith.[30]

In February 1997, four forensic document examiners compared the handwritten printing of the ransom note with examples that John and Patsy Ramsey were asked to write as well as "course-of-business" exemplars in letters and lists written before their daughter's murder.

An analysis of the slant of the letters in the note is consistent with Patsy's writing but not with John's. John used an uppercase N at the beginning, middle, and ends of words, whereas neither Patsy nor the author of the ransom note did. The person who wrote the note also used rounded "o"s, as did Patsy but not John.

Patsy was an enthusiastic user of exclamation points, written at some distance from the preceding word. The same pattern can be seen in the ransom note. Her writing has similar indentation and spacing of words as in the note as well as an unusual, tailless "u" and a flourish on the lowercase "y."[31]

The four examiners agreed that the note hadn't been written by John but couldn't agree with regard to ruling out Patsy Ramsey. Two document examiners hired by the Ramseys, however, concluded that Patsy was not the author.[32]

A year and a half after JonBenét's death, a grand jury was empaneled and spent 13 months evaluating evidence and hearing testimony. Fourteen years later, in 2013, a portion of the grand jury's indictment was finally released to the public. It charged John and Patsy Ramsey with two counts of child abuse resulting in the death of their daughter, but the Boulder County district attorney chose not to prosecute them at that time for reasons that remain controversial.[33]

Patsy Ramsey died of ovarian cancer in June 2006 at age 49. John Ramsey remarried five years after that, and the couple moved to Michigan. As of this writing, no one has ever been tried for the murder of JonBenét. As a result, it is impossible to say how the various experts' analyses of the ransom note's language and writing would have fared in open court.

TRUTH IN TEXTING

Earlier in this chapter, we saw how relatively short texts, such as police statements or ransom notes, can make it difficult to identify or to profile the author. And these problems are magnified when a message is even shorter. A text sent via a cell phone, for example, might consist of a dozen words or fewer. Do such brief missives provide forensic linguists with enough grist for their analytical mills?

Consider the case of Julie Turner, a 40-year-old woman from Yorkshire, England, who disappeared on June 7, 2005. Before leaving the house at around 6 p.m., she told her partner, Darren Akers, that she was going to do some shopping. She never returned.

Turner was the mother of two and had been having an affair with a well-to-do gas delivery businessman named Howard Simmerson. The 43-year-old Simmerson had lavished up to £200,000 on her during their four-year relationship.[34] His blue Mercedes was frequently seen in the neighborhood, and Turner's partner was aware that the two were seeing each other.

When Turner left the house that evening, Akers assumed that it was to be with her lover. But five hours later, when she hadn't returned, Akers became alarmed and drove the 20 miles to Simmerson's home. His Mercedes was parked outside, but the house appeared to be empty. Four hours later, in the middle of the night, Akers called the police to report her as a missing person. A check of the area's hospitals and calls to family members failed to locate her.

On the afternoon of June 9, two days after she vanished, Akers was surprised to receive a brief text message on his phone. The message read, "Stopping at jills, back later need to sort my head out." It had been sent from a number that Akers didn't recognize, and nothing about it made any sense. He didn't know anyone named Jill, and Turner wasn't in the habit of communicating with him via text. He grew even more concerned.

Following up on the only lead he had, Akers returned to Simmerson's home and had a brief, unsatisfying conversation with him. The next day, he received another cryptic text message: "Tell kids not to worry. sorting my life out. be in touch to get some things."

The following day, the police interviewed Simmerson and seized two cell phones they found in his possession. One of these was apparently used only for contacting Turner. It contained a text that Turner had apparently sent the day before: "Sucker. im stopping at my friends. guess who. why do you think i wanted to rush back. don't bother looking for me." The authorities also took possession of a five-page letter found in Simmerson's home. It was unaddressed but made reference to a gun he was seeking to purchase and a wish to kill both Turner and himself.[35]

The text messages, Simmerson's letter, and a tape recording of the interview with the police were turned over to John Olsson for analysis. Olsson was the director of the Forensic Linguistic Institute, a consulting firm that specialized in such cases.

He noticed that the text supposedly sent by Turner was unusual: its writer had made use of periods in place of commas. And the letter written by Simmerson contained instances of the same quirk of punctuation, as in "Oh god what a tangle. but she is not getting away with my life." This seemed odd and possibly significant, although it might be the case that many people compose their texts in this way.

Olsson spent hours listening to the recordings of the police interviews but found little that seemed helpful. As he prepared to abandon the effort, he heard the detectives ask Simmerson about why he and Turner weren't living together since it appeared that both of them wanted to. In reply, Simmerson said, "She was on heavy medication and she said when she'd got her *head sorted out* and *sorted out her life* then it would happen."

As Olsson later told a reporter for the *New York Times*, "I jumped out of my skin, because this was exactly the same phrasing as the mobile phone texts" that Turner's partner Akers had received: "need to sort my head out" and "sorting my life out."[36] To Olsson's practiced eye and ear, the phrases seemed unusual. But how could he quantify the likelihood that someone would express themselves with these particular words?

Over the past few decades, linguists have amassed large collections of English from published materials and the internet. Such collections, or corpora, can contain millions of words. Linguists find these corpora useful because they can be searched to get a sense of how often particular words or phrases occur and in what contexts. They provided Olsson with a way of quantifying his intuitions about the unusual expressions in the mystery texts and in Simmerson's letter.

Olsson searched a corpus of 100 million words of running text and found one instance of the phrase "sort my life out" and one occurrence of "sorted his life out." He also tried a number of other variations, such as "sorted *my* life out," but came away empty-handed. And the same was true for "sort my head out" and its variant forms—they couldn't be found.

A problem with such corpora is that they are only as representative of language use as the documents that make them up. A corpus consisting of the plays written by Shakespeare, for example, would not be representative of how people in the twenty-first century use English to write letters or send text messages. Olsson made use of the next best thing: the Google search engine.

Although Google is designed to be a comprehensive index of the World Wide Web, it can also serve as a proxy of sorts for frequency counts in a given language. For example, the word "cromulent" was coined in a 1996 episode of *The Simpsons* as a synonym for acceptable or adequate. As of this writing, it appears about 144,000 times in Google's search results. That may sound like a lot, but the word "cautious" occurs about 476 million times. In other words, as a ballpark estimate, we can say that the latter term is nearly 3,000 times more common than the former, made-up one.

When Olsson used Google to search for the phrase "sort my life out," he found 23,000 instances. "Sort my head out" turned up only 600 times, which would seemingly qualify as extremely rare. He also checked to see how often both phrases had occurred within the same document—as they had in Simmerson's interview with the police. Only 17 such instances could be found across the entire World Wide Web.

Finally, Olsson was struck by the fact that the two phrases—"sort my head out" and "sort my life out"—occurred in the same order in the two anonymous text messages and in Simmerson's interview. All of this seemed too much to be a coincidence. In his report to the authorities, Olsson concluded that it was highly likely that Simmerson had sent the two anonymous text messages to Darren Akers. And when the authorities confronted him with this evidence, Simmerson confessed to having sent them.

The police involved in the case made an intensive search to locate Julie Turner—or her remains. Besides searching the countryside, a team of officers reviewed many hours of closed-circuit television recordings made by local businesses in the days after she disappeared. They noticed that a distinctive vehicle appeared frequently in these videos: a silver Ford Ranger with an oil drum in its truck bed. And one of Simmerson's clients reported that Simmerson had asked him if he could bury an oil drum on his property. Simmerson claimed that he needed to do this because he was trying to dispose of some weapons to keep the police from finding them. Simmerson's client, no doubt taken aback by the request, had turned him down.

Six weeks after Julie Turner disappeared, the oil drum seen in the videos was found at a junkyard in Derbyshire.[37] Inside it, they found her body. She had died from a gunshot wound to the head. After this discovery, Simmerson claimed that Turner had found his gun in the glove compartment of his vehicle and that she had accidentally shot herself while he was trying to take it away from her.

Howard Simmerson was tried for the murder of Julie Turner in late 2005. On the day she died, the man the British tabloids dubbed the "oil drum killer" had taken Turner to Leeds, where she spent nearly £3,000 on three handbags.[38] The prosecution contended that Turner had been killed by Simmerson after returning from this shopping spree. They presented evidence that traces of Turner's blood had been found in Simmerson's Mercedes and on the floor of his garage. This and the other evidence in the trial, which included Olsson's analysis of Simmerson's letter and text messages, convinced the jury that her death had not been accidental. He was found guilty of murder and sentenced to life in prison, with the recommendation that he serve at least 25 years.

John Olsson would go on to be involved in other high-profile forensic cases. He testified in a 2006 trial that Dan Brown had plagiarized portions of his thriller *The Da Vinci Code* from three earlier books written by Lewis Perdue.[39] Although Olsson's analysis found dozens of major similarities between Brown's and Perdue's books, a New York district court ruled against the plaintiff: the similarity was characterized as "generic and coincidental," and Perdue also lost on appeal.

Olsson also recognized the limitations of using existing English corpora for analyzing brief electronic communications like text messages. In 2009, he put out a call to have people send him their texts with the goal of collecting enough of them to establish baselines for this form of communication.[40]

He made good use of these data in 2013, when he provided evidence at the trial of David Ryan. Ryan stood accused of murdering his lover, Diana Lee. The prosecution claimed that Ryan sent texts from Lee's cell phone after he had killed her to make it seem that she was still alive. Ryan, however, had an unusual texting style: he would include two spaces after periods and question marks but no spaces after commas.[41]

By this time, Olsson had assembled a corpus of 5,000 text messages from 95 different contributors to his project and was able to testify that the use of no spaces after commas was rare—only about 4 percent of his texting contributors did so.[42] Olsson's analysis, combined with other forensic evidence, such as bloody footprints left at the scene of the crime, were enough to convince the jury. Lee was found guilty of murder and received a 34-year sentence.

Cases like these show that even a minuscule amount of text can, under the right circumstances, be as distinctive as a fingerprint. As in longer missives, people tend to express themselves in consistent ways, and their idiosyncratic use of punctuation can also be diagnostic. As we learn in Shakespeare's *Othello*, "Trifles light as air, are to the jealous confirmations strong, as proofs of holy writ."

CHAPTER SIX

FAKE!

Forgeries and Misattributions

THE COUNTERFEIT DECREE

What is the most consequential forgery in history? A strong contender for that title would be an Imperial Roman decree that gave away half of Europe to the pope. This bequest was supposedly made by Constantine the Great, the first Roman emperor to convert to Christianity. Referred to as the Donation of Constantine, it played a significant role in European history before being exposed as fraudulent. And the detective work that went into its unmasking represents one of the earliest examples of stylometric analysis.

Constantine ruled the Roman Empire for three decades at the beginning of the fourth century. Early in his reign, he fought against his brother-in-law Maxentius at the Milvian Bridge on the Tiber. Shortly before that battle, he had a vision. Accounts differ, but the most detailed version, recorded by the Greek historian Eusebius, relates that Constantine saw a cross of light above the midday sun. He also saw a phrase in Greek that translates as "by this conquer." The following night, he had a dream in which Christ told him to use this sign against his foes.[1] Constantine adopted the Chi-Rho monogram as his military standard, and his decisive victory over Maxentius gave him undisputed control of the Western Roman Empire. A few months later, Constantine issued the Edict of Milan, which officially recognized Christianity and ended the persecution of Christians.

Less than a year after the edict, Sylvester I became the bishop of Rome. Little is known about him, although several legends arose during the following centuries. These were propagated in works like *The Acts of Sylvester* and *The*

Golden Legend. In the latter, we learn that Constantine contracted leprosy and that pagan priests advised him that a cure could be obtained by bathing in the blood of 3,000 slain infants. However, the wails of the mothers about to lose their children caused him to reconsider. Instead, he appealed to Sylvester, who baptized him and miraculously cured his affliction.[2]

To show his gratitude, the emperor issued a decree in which he embraced Christianity and gave control of the Lateran Palace, Italy, and the western provinces of the Roman Empire to the Holy See for all time. This so-called Donation would play a prominent role in the investiture conflicts of the eleventh and twelfth centuries as religious and secular rulers sparred over the temporal power of the papacy. The Donation was also wielded in debates over the primacy of Rome or Constantinople in the pecking order of the Christian church. Altogether, the Donation was cited by at least 10 different popes as a trump card in these disputes.[3] There is even a dark, oblique reference to it in Dante's *Divine Comedy*.[4]

Given its importance, it is not surprising that the Donation's text came under scrutiny by those who suspected that it was a fabrication. And during the fifteenth century, scholars in three different countries claimed that the Donation was spurious. The first of these was Nicholas of Cusa, a German cardinal and philosopher. In 1433, he raised serious questions about the Donation because he could find no corroborating historical evidence.[5]

About a decade later, the authenticity of the Donation was called into question by Reginald Pecock, a Welsh bishop of Chichester. Approaching the problem of the decree from a different angle, he focused on Constantine's alleged baptism by Sylvester. In the Donation, Constantine states that he issued his decree four days after his baptism. The problem with this is that Eusebius, in his *Life of Constantine*, wrote that the emperor was baptized on his deathbed by a bishop in Nicomedia.[6] This would have been about 20 years after the date of the Donation's supposed proclamation.

Eusebius was a contemporary of Constantine's, and although the biography was written to flatter the emperor, many of its details were corroborated by others. Constantine's deathbed baptism by an Arian bishop is attested to by Saint Jerome and also by Saint Ambrose, who served as the archbishop of Milan and was born shortly after Constantine's death.

On the other hand, accounts of Constantine's baptism by Sylvester appear in the previously mentioned collections of stories about Sylvester. And these sources are problematic at best. In *The Golden Legend*, for example, we learn that Constantine also appealed to Sylvester to deliver Rome from a dragon that had taken up residence in the city. The beast's breath was said to be so foul that it was killing 300 people a day. Sylvester agreed to help and descended into the dragon's pit accompanied by two priests carrying lanterns. Following divine instruction, he bound up the dragon's mouth and thereby saved the city.[7] Perhaps not surprisingly, therefore, Pecock concluded that Eusebius was a more reliable source regarding the baptism of Constantine than the fanciful stories found in later hagiographies.

Pecock also called attention to the problematic dating of the Donation. The last line of the proclamation states that it was made during the fourth consulate of Constantine, which would have been 315 CE. But immediately after this, the text asserts that the grant was made during the consulate of Gallicanus, and this would have been 317. It seems like a strange error to go unnoticed in such an important imperial document. Pecock also asks why, if the popes held ultimate temporal power in the West, had it been necessary for their elections to be confirmed by the Holy Roman emperor?[8]

The definitive unmasking of the Donation, however, is attributed to Lorenzo Valla, an Italian priest and humanist. In 1440, he was serving in Naples as the secretary to King Alfonso V of Aragon. Over the strenuous objections of Pope Eugenius IV, the king had claimed control of the Kingdom of Sicily. And to block the pope from appealing to the Donation, he commissioned Valla to call its credibility into question. The work's title—*Oration on the Falsely-Believed and Forged Donation of Constantine*—leaves little doubt about his conclusions.[9]

Far from being a dry academic treatise, Valla's argument, as befits an oration, is full of passion. And his critique is as vicious as it is unsparing. At times, he enters into debate with the Donation's unknown forger and asks a series of sarcastic and rhetorical questions. He also doesn't hesitate to toss around epithets like "numskull" and "blockhead" while critiquing the forger's errors.

Valla offers a number of arguments against the Donation's legitimacy. Like Nicholas of Cusa, he points to the lack of historical evidence that would corroborate it. And what was known about Constantine's life contradicts the decree. For example, he cites historical claims that Constantine had been a Christian from boyhood.

Our focus, however, is on the two sections of the *Oration* that relate to errors of fact and terminology. There are several anachronisms in the text, but one that greatly vexes Valla is a reference to the four seats of the Church as being "Alexandria, Antioch, Jerusalem, and Constantinople." At the time the Donation was supposedly written, Constantinople was still Byzantium: it would not be renamed until 330. Valla sputters, "How in the world—this is much more absurd, and impossible in the nature of things—could one speak of Constantinople as one of the patriarchal sees, when it was not yet a patriarchate, nor a see, nor a Christian city, nor named Constantinople, nor founded, nor planned!"[10]

Another anachronism is a reference to "satraps" in the phrase "We—together with all our satraps and the whole Senate." This word is associated with Persian viceroys centuries after the fall of Rome.[11] Valla acidly comments, "Whoever heard of satraps being mentioned in the councils of the Romans? . . . But this fellow speaks of the Emperor's satraps and puts them in before the Senate."[12]

And as if all this wasn't enough, he writes scathingly about infelicities in the forger's language. Valla was well versed in classical Latin, which made it easy for him to spot issues in the Donation author's turns of phrase. For example, the decree contains the phrase "chief over the priests" when "chief *of* the priests" is clearly intended. In a similar vein, Valla calls attention to a sentence containing both "exiterit" and "existat," which is a confusion of meanings, moods, and tenses.[13] He concludes that the Donation is "comprised of contradictions, impossibilities, stupidities, barbarisms and absurdities."[14]

Surprisingly, perhaps, the Church's reaction to the *Oration* was fairly mild. In 1443, two cardinals encouraged Valla to make a retraction or to revise the work, but he refused. The following year, Valla was put on trial by the Inquisition, but this was for his other writings, in which he was critical of Aristotle and Saint Boethius. It took the intervention of the king of Naples to save him.[15] He then worked as an itinerant university lecturer before being called to Rome by Pope Nicholas V to teach rhetoric. He died in Rome in 1457.[16]

Valla's *Oration*, however, would take on a life of its own. It was finally published in 1517, and an English edition appeared in 1534. Three years later, Martin Luther translated it into German.[17] Since Valla's work could be read as a full-throated attack on the temporal power of the papacy, the *Oration* was championed by the leaders of the Protestant Reformation, and it was placed on the Vatican's List of Prohibited Books in 1559.[18] The Church continued to maintain the Donation was authentic for 30 more years until Cardinal Caesar Baronius, in his church history, admitted it was a forgery.[19]

So where did the Donation decree come from, and who wrote it? It may have been composed as early as 750, although the earliest surviving manuscript dates from the ninth century. Speculation about its author includes suggestions that they were Greek, Roman, or Frankish.[20] The Donation became included in a collection of documents called the False Decretals. Some of the records in this compilation were genuine, but many, like the Donation, were forgeries.[21]

Valla's careful study of the language making up the Donation of Constantine did not reveal its author, but that wasn't his intent. It was enough for his purposes to show that it could not have been a genuine imperial decree from the fourth century. And his exposure of the fraud, through the systematic identification of anachronisms, solecisms, and other errors, would not be out of place with the stylometric analyses of today.

CONSOLATION PRIZE

Although ancient Rome is often associated with military conquest, the arts and humanities also flourished during the republic and the empire. Historians such as Livy and Tacitus and poets such as Ovid and Virgil are well known and still read today. Perhaps the best known in modern times would be Marcus Tullius Cicero, widely regarded as one of the greatest orators of all time. Cicero's speeches and hundreds of his personal letters survived antiquity, and Petrarch's rediscovery of these letters in the fourteenth century helped to spark the Italian Renaissance. Other works of Cicero, including the majority of his philosophical treatises, have been lost.

In February of 45 BCE, Cicero's daughter Tullia died, a month after giving birth to her second son. Tullia had been her father's favorite, and he fell into deep depression over her death. Cicero stayed for a time with a friend, Titus Pomponius Atticus, and searched through his library for writings that would assuage his grief. Nothing that he found was helpful, and he withdrew to his villa to pen his own treatise on mourning and sorrow, which he titled *Consolatio* (Consolation).[22] Although he wrote it for himself, he came to believe that it could benefit others dealing with bereavement and the heartbreak of loss.

Cicero was inspired by the prior literature on consolation and mourning, including works such as *De Luctu* (On Grief). That treatise, popular in Roman times, was composed in the fourth century BCE by the Greek philosopher Crantor. The theme is similar, as Crantor was writing to console a friend on the death of his son. But in a letter to his friend Atticus, Cicero asserted that his own take on the subject was novel.[23] The *Consolatio* was influential, and several other Roman writers referred to it. Although fragments were preserved in Cicero's own *Tusculan Disputations*, as well as in the works of the early Christian writers Lactantius and Jerome, the complete work was thought to have been lost. There is a possibility that at least one copy survived into the Middle Ages: Ambrose Traversari mentions seeing the *Consolatio* during a visit to the monastery at Perugia in 1432.[24]

It was notable, therefore, when a manuscript of the long-lost work was published in Venice in early 1583. The Italian scholar and humanist Carlo Sigonio edited the manuscript for Francesco Vianello, who turned the manuscript over to the printer. Sigonio, a teacher at Bologna University, had previously published the known fragments of the *Consolatio*. However, he was not able to provide any details about the provenance of the manuscript. Its authenticity was challenged by a number of individuals, including Antonius Riccobonus, a professor at the University of Padua. He had been one of Sigonio's students and accused his former teacher of having written the work himself. The incident was an ugly one, fueled by a "prolonged exchange of controversial pamphlets"[25] in which Sigonio mounted a stout defense for the authenticity of the manuscript.

It soon emerged that Sigonio hadn't been the work's impartial editor: he was, in fact, the source of the manuscript that Vianello arranged to have published. For many who had been following the controversy, this development dealt a fatal blow to Sigonio's credibility. He would die the following year and was said to have confessed to the forgery on his deathbed, although this may have been little more than a rumor.[26]

Around 1785, the historian of Italian literature Girolamo Tiraboschi came across a letter by Sigonio from late 1582—before the publication of Cicero's work. Writing to a friend in Modena, he referred to the *Consolatio* as "a book of mine . . . which I wrote," and asked for the friend's opinion about it.[27] Although this might seem like damning evidence against Sigonio, not all scholars were willing to conclude that this was prima facie evidence of a forgery. He may have been referring to his extensive editing of Cicero's work.

In 1893, Robinson Ellis proposed that Sigonio had come across the same manuscript that Traversari had discovered at Perugia 150 years earlier and that it had somehow "found its way to Venice" in the intervening period.[28] Ellis also pointed out that the surviving fragments of the original *Consolatio*, recorded by Lactantius in the late third or early fourth century, matched the edition published by Sigonio. From these facts, Ellis theorized that Sigonio's manuscript was based on an ancient forgery, one that had been accepted uncritically by

Lactantius and by Jerome as Cicero's original work. This supposition was supported in an exhaustive study of the matter by Evan Sage in 1910.[29]

Ellis's theory of an ancient forgery solves a number of problems: it exonerates Sigonio, who had no history of duplicitous behavior, and also explains certain infelicities, such as the use of post-Ciceronian Latin, that are present in the manuscript that Sigonio discovered and published in 1583. And such forgeries are far from being a modern invention: the Roman world seems to have had its fair share of counterfeit and forged manuscripts. These are known to have included the works of Cicero.[30]

It is an open question, therefore, whether the *Consolatio* of 1583, forged then or at an earlier time, is a match with the writings of Cicero. A modern stylometric analysis could shed some light on the long-standing and complex questions surrounding the work's authenticity. It would also provide an opportunity to see whether methods that work well with modern English texts can be used when the author in question wrote in classical Latin. This challenge was taken up by Richard Forsyth, David Holmes, and Emily Tse, and they published the results of their analysis in 1999.

To create a corpus for their project, the researchers selected samples from the texts of Cicero and other classical writers, such as Caesar, Sallust, Seneca, and Tacitus. They also included samples of texts from Neo-Latin authors such as Sigonio (the primary suspect of the forgery), Muretus, Lauredanus, and Riccoboni. They were careful to remove the genuine fragments of Cicero from the 1583 *Consolatio*, but these amount to fewer than 400 words. The researchers ended up with 70 samples making up more than 300,000 words.

A subset of the texts, containing nearly 70,000 words, was analyzed to determine the most frequent function words, and the researchers decided to make use of the top 46 of these. These words constitute a full quarter of all words appearing in the subset and were employed in the subsequent analyses.

A preliminary study was conducted on the 25 samples from the speeches and other works of Cicero. A principal component analysis of the most frequent function words resulted in a two-dimensional plot that segregated Cicero's speeches largely to one side of the graph. His treatises and philosophical works mostly fell on the other side. This suggests that the analysis was sensitive enough to pick up on genre differences in classical Latin.

The researchers next turned their attention to two works that are believed to be spurious and falsely attributed to Cicero: *Epistula ad Octavianum*, which is known from a manuscript dating to the eleventh century,[31] and *Rhetorica ad Herennium II*, for which the oldest manuscript dates from the ninth century.[32] The researchers found that they were able to differentiate the genuine works by Cicero from the two doubtful texts by making use of three principal components.

How does Cicero compare to the other well-known Latin authors of antiquity? To answer this question, the researchers compared the sample texts of Cicero with samples from Caesar, Nepos, Sallust, Seneca, and Tacitus. With only one exception, a plot of the first two principal components separated Cicero's texts from the other authors and also separated most of the others from each other. The analysis also separated the military and biographical works from those that were philosophical in nature. On a second dimension, the spacing of the samples seems to reflect when the works were written: works composed during the republic (before 27 BCE) were segregated from those written during the empire.

Would this approach differentiate the Neo-Latin authors? The researchers also conducted an analysis that compared text samples from the five sixteenth-century writers in their corpus: Lauredanus, Muret, Riccoboni, Sigonio, and Vettori. The results in this case were strongly influenced by genre. A plot of the two principal components segregated Sigonio's histories from his orations; similarly, Muret's funeral and scholarly orations ended up in different clusters. The other three authors formed their own clusters on the resulting plot.

Finally, the researchers turned to their main research question: what would happen when the *Consolatio* of 1583 was compared to the writings of Cicero and Sigonio? The texts were subjected to a discriminant analysis, and it was found that the samples from Cicero and Sigonio could be classified into their correct groups 94 percent of the time. And when a discriminant function score was computed for the two samples drawn from the *Consolatio*, both were assigned to the group of Sigonio texts.

What does this result tell us? Simply put, the *Consolatio* of 1583 is far more likely to have been written by Sigonio—and falsely attributed to Cicero—than to have been written by Cicero himself. However, it doesn't rule out the possibility that someone else wrote the work either in antiquity or during the Renaissance.

To address a wider group of suspects, the researchers performed a discriminant analysis with all the classical Latin and Neo-Latin authors. Once again, this resulted in classification accuracy of 94 percent: three classical Latin samples were incorrectly assigned to the Neo-Latin group, and one Neo-Latin work was tagged as a classical Latin text. And the two *Consolatio* text samples? They clearly belong with the Neo-Latin works.

Having eliminated the classical authors as suspects, the researchers compared the *Consolatio* to four Renaissance authors. Once again, a discriminant analysis was employed, and the work in question matched most closely with Sigonio's writing when compared to text samples by Muretus, Riccoboni, or Vettori.[33]

Is it safe to conclude that Carlo Sigonio created a forgery of Cicero's *Consolatio* in the early 1580s? Although such a judgment seems warranted, it is important to keep in mind what author attribution studies can and cannot tell us. Sigonio is the likeliest suspect, but such analyses can't rule out the possibility that an unknown author—someone not included in the study described here—was channeling his inner Cicero. The creation of a credible forgery, however, would have required a deep knowledge of both classical Latin and Cicero's writing style, and this reduces the number of potential forgers considerably. In this case, the stylometric as well as the external evidence seem to point in the same direction.

SOLEMN MOCKERY

On April 2, 1796, theatergoers in London were treated to a spectacle that had not been seen in 180 years: the production of a new play by William Shakespeare. *Vortigern and Rowena* had been found—it was claimed—by a 19-year-old law clerk named William-Henry Ireland. He said he discovered the manuscript in a trunk filled with other old papers. These included letters to and from Shakespeare, a profession of his faith, a fragment of *Hamlet*, a complete version of *King Lear*, and even a lock of his hair enclosed in a love letter to his wife Anne Hathaway. The bounteous trunk containing these wonders was owned by a man known only as Mr. H, who insisted on remaining anonymous to protect his privacy.

All of this was a source of tremendous joy to William-Henry's father Samuel, a travel writer who also collected historical documents and relics. Along with many others in the late eighteenth century, he deified the works of Shakespeare as well as the man himself. Samuel had taken his son along on a pilgrimage to Stratford-upon-Avon when he credulously purchased a number of mementos that, he was assured, had a connection to Shakespeare or his family.

Drafts of the Bard's work in his own hand had never been discovered, and only four legal documents were known that contained his signature. Many believed—or at least hoped—that additional documents had survived and might be found in out-of-the-way places, such as in an archive or in someone's attic. How wonderful it was, then, when Ireland's son brought home a deed he had come across in Mr. H's trunk that bore Shakespeare's signature.

Naturally, William-Henry had made no such discoveries. Mr. H and his trunk of wonders did not exist. The young man was apprenticed to a conveyancer, or title lawyer, who provided little supervision, leaving him alone with his copying work. As a result, he had plenty of time on his hands as well as access to old legal documents. He amused himself by practicing his secretary hand—an old-fashioned script used in Shakespeare's day—and decided to try his hand at copying the Bard's signature. And once he had mastered that trick, why not create an entire document, such as a deed?

Old paper could be easily obtained from booksellers that he knew, and another acquaintance whipped up a supply of vintage ink. William-Henry found that holding his handiwork over a candle flame was sufficient to darken a document and make it appear far older than it was. The young man was motivated to seek his father's attention and approval, and this seemed like a good way of obtaining both. To put it simply, William-Henry had the means, the motive, and the opportunity for carrying out his deception.

Samuel Ireland received the signed deed rapturously, and his son told him that there was more where that came from. Over the next few months, he forged a series of documents, each more elaborate than the last, and then told his father that he had also discovered a complete and unperformed Shakespeare play in Mr. H's trunk of miracles. William-Henry delivered the play piecemeal, a few pages at a time, to his impatient father and a growing circle of true believers, which included luminaries like the biographer James Boswell and literary critic Joseph Warton.[34] In a frenzy of activity, William-Henry managed to finish writing the play in six weeks. Richard Sheridan, manager of the Drury Lane theater and an acquaintance of Samuel Ireland, agreed to stage a production of the play, titled *Vortigern and Rowena*, the following spring.

Why was Samuel Ireland willing to accept his son's stories about the seemingly bottomless trunk of Shakespeariana and the never-seen Mr. H? Why were his father's friends willing to accept as authentic an entire play that sprang from the mind of a young and callow law clerk? As with most confidence games, the answer is simple: the will to believe was strong. Shakespeare's original writings should exist, and this transmuted into a belief that they must exist and could be found.

Certainly, William-Henry did everything he could to maintain the charade. He "delivered" letters from his father to Mr. H and wrote replies, making sure to heap lavish praise on the son. As holes began to appear in the story, he would manufacture new documents to address them. And when ownership of the documents became an issue, he fabricated a new will for the Bard, in which he bequeathed his work to an Ireland ancestor who had once saved him from drowning. Caught up in a tangled web of lies and deceit, the skein of his deception became ever more difficult to maintain.

In the end, however, the desire to believe trumped everything else, including the Bard's somewhat unusual choice of subject matter for *Vortigern and Rowena*: a fifth-century warlord smitten by a Saxon leader's beautiful daughter. The work's unevenness, its inordinate length, and its seeming lack of polish were overlooked by those who wanted the play to be an authentic, lost work by the Sweet Swan of Avon.

Oddly enough, it was Shakespeare's hallowed stature that created difficulties for the doubters. If a consensus emerged that the other documents—and therefore *Vortigern* itself—were authentic, who would want to be seen as a vulgarian unable to recognize the Bard's genius? Perhaps *Vortigern* was Shakespearian juvenilia or an abandoned work, not in the same league as *Hamlet* or *Othello* perhaps but part of the Bard's canon nonetheless.

At the end of 1795, Samuel arranged to have published a lavish folio volume featuring engraved facsimiles of the Shakespeare documents.[35] This gave both supporters and doubters alike a chance to closely examine them since he had previously favored his supplicants with only brief glimpses of the papers. William-Henry had feared that careful scrutiny of his handiwork might reveal flaws, and he was right to be concerned about that possibility.

The doubters pounced quickly. The critic James Boaden noted that, in the *King Lear* manuscript, the French term "hélas" appeared instead of Shakespeare's "alas."[36] The Bard probably didn't know any foreign languages besides a bit of Latin and Greek, and it would have been odd for him to substitute the French exclamation for the English one. William-Henry, on the other hand, had studied for several years in Amiens and Eu and was fluent in French.[37] And there were other vocal doubters as well. Henry Bate Dudley, editor of *The Morning Herald*, published a number of satirical pieces about the Shakespeare documents and the overflowing cornucopia that was Mr. H's trunk.

The heaviest blows, however, fell two days before *Vortigern*'s premiere. The preeminent Shakespeare scholar Edmond Malone, who had long harbored doubts about the documents, chose that moment to publish a withering critique of young Ireland's discoveries. In a volume of more than 400 pages, he cataloged a multitude of sins, such as the bizarre spellings to be found in the documents. Although it is true that Elizabethan orthography was inconsistent at best, the documents in question had a surfeit of words with extraneous terminal "e"s and "y"s as well as too many doubled consonants. In addition, Malone pointed out odd phrases, historical inaccuracies, and issues with the handwriting.[38]

Those who believed that the Shakespeare documents were fakes, however, did not accuse William-Henry of being the forger. Many simply did not believe that the young man had the ability to produce such counterfeits, and the sheer quantity and diversity seemed to argue against a solitary fraudster. Some doubters suspected that the father had turned the family home into a foundry for producing Shakespearian knockoffs or that the shadowy Mr. H was perhaps the ringleader of a counterfeiting syndicate.

Forensic science as we know it today didn't exist in the 1790s, and Sherlock Holmes would not take his first bow until 90 years later. There was no way to analyze the ink and the paper of the documents, and scorch marks from William-Henry's clumsy attempts at aging them were interpreted as marks of authenticity. It was well known that other historic documents had ended up being consumed by flames. Providence, it would appear, had spared the work of the immortal Bard.

Given all the controversy, the atmosphere of *Vortigern*'s opening night at Drury Lane was electric. The enormous Theatre Royal was forced to turn away many would-be patrons, and those fortunate enough to secure seats included skeptics as well as champions. Both sides were vocal in their support or derision. Samuel even distributed a handbill that disputed Malone's critique to those in attendance. He and his family took prominent seats in the theater, while William-Henry, experiencing both elation and dread, haunted the stage's wings.

As it turned out, the greatest threat to *Vortigern*'s acceptance was not in the audience but on the stage. The actor in the play's titular role, John Philip Kemble, was firmly in the camp of the unbelievers. He had been performing Shakespeare for 20 years and had no difficulty discerning that *Vortigern* was not what it was claimed to be. He even proposed opening the play on April Fool's Day but was overruled. Its premiere—and, as it turned out, its sole performance—was scheduled for the following day.

Throughout the evening's entertainment, the unruly audience was loud and disorderly, although none of that was unusual for a Georgian-era theatrical piece. As the play lurched into its final act, Kemble made his feelings known. As King Vortigern, he began an extended soliloquy, addressing Death with lines that included the following:

And with rude laughter and fantastic tricks
Thou clapp'st thy rattling fingers to thy sides.
And when the solemn mockery is o'er,

Kemble intoned the last line in a ghoulish and drawn-out way, leaving no question about his opinion of the work.

According to William-Henry's own account of the proceedings, there was bedlam in the theater for 10 minutes following Kemble's derisive delivery of the line. And to make sure there was no doubt about his sentiments, once the play resumed, he repeated the line "with an even more solemn grimace than he had in the first instance displayed."[39] By the end of the performance, it was clear that the audience had rejected *Vortigern* as a genuine work by Shakespeare. The production closed that night, and the play would not be staged again until 2008. It was revived as a comedy, for one evening, by the Pembroke Players of Cambridge.[40]

After *Vortigern*'s disastrous premiere, William-Henry confessed to his two sisters, who in turn told their father. Samuel, however, refused to believe them. He simply could not accept that his son had the talent to fool him and his friends. Even after William-Henry publicly confessed, via a pamphlet,[41] his father would not accept the truth and even arranged to have *Vortigern* published shortly before his death in 1800.[42] William-Henry himself would publish two more self-serving confessions,[43] although he never apologized for his deception. Under a pseudonym, he would go on to pen a number of gothic novels and other works. His notoriety, however, would never again rise to the level it reached on the night that he channeled the ghost of Shakespeare.

CLEMENS BEFORE TWAIN

Samuel Clemens is universally known as the author of *The Adventures of Tom Sawyer*, published in 1876, and its sequel, *Adventures of Huckleberry Finn*, which appeared nine years later. Earlier in his writing career, Clemens published a number of short stories and travel books. These include *Roughing It*, which describes his adventures in the West during the 1860s. And before that, between 1858 and 1861, he was a freighter pilot on the Mississippi River.

But when did his writing career begin? Among the first pieces that he wrote for pay, Clemens scholars have identified three travel letters that appeared in the Keokuk (Iowa) *Saturday Post* and the *Keokuk Daily Post*. They were published in late 1856 and early 1857 under the pseudonym Thomas Jefferson Snodgrass. In them, the author provided humorous sketches of St. Louis, Chicago, and Cincinnati, told from the point of view of a "wide-eyed Keokuk bumpkin."[44] Although he later reported no memory of having written them, the son of the *Post*'s editor claimed that Clemens had been paid $5 for each of them.[45] They were rediscovered by reporter Charles Honce and published in 1928.[46] The letters have long been accepted as authentic and a part of Clemens's early literary canon.

In 1929, Clemens's biographer Minnie Brashear discovered four letters in the archives of the New Orleans *Daily Crescent* that were signed "Quintus Curtius Snodgrass."[47] Within a few years, six more letters would be found by Thomas Dabney and Ernest Leisy.[48] All 10 had been published in the *Crescent* between January 21 and March 30, 1861. This was a tumultuous time in Louisiana: the state seceded from the Union on January 26 and then officially joined the Confederacy two months later.

In the first of these letters, the editors describe Q. C. Snodgrass as "a prominent member of one of our newly organized military corps." Their correspondent reports on the holiday atmosphere surrounding the capture of the Federal garrison at Baton Rouge. A second installment chronicles a military ball. Most of the rest provide "hints to young campaigners," with Snodgrass signing himself as a "high old private of the Louisiana Guard." These letters can be characterized as gentle satires of the military and its training regimen. A letter dated March 7 is a fantasy: Snodgrass relates being a guest at the White House and having dinner with President Lincoln and his family. An excerpt from the ninth letter captures the overall tone of the series:

> In attacking a fortress it is well to hang back a little (you can be examining the lock of your musket or taking an imaginary stone out of your shoe) and let the eager ones get in first and draw the enemy's fire, after which you may enter with comparative impunity and take your full share of the glory.[49]

The humor is broad and a bit strained throughout; perhaps this is understandable given that Clemens would have been only 25 when they were written.

More interesting for Clemens scholars, however, is the light that the Q. C. Snodgrass letters might shed on the young man's allegiance as the nation was splitting apart. Twenty years after the Civil War ended, he would describe, in comedic terms, a two-week stint with the pro-Confederate Missouri State Guard during July 1861. He and some friends joined a unit called the Marion Rangers but saw no action. Clemens would publish a greatly embellished account of his service as an 8,000-word sketch in *Century* magazine titled "The Private History of a Campaign That Failed."[50]

If Clemens had been a member of the Louisiana Guard and participated in the seizure of the Federal garrison at Baton Rouge, this involvement could have damaged his later reputation. Although the commander surrendered the garrison and barracks without a fight, thousands of muskets and rifles, as well as a great deal of ammunition, fell into the hands of the separatists—arms that would soon be used against Union forces.[51] Clemens's breezy account of his brief involvement in the Missouri militia might have been designed to deflect criticism that he had not served in the war. And in an ironic twist of fate, Clemens would later play a role in the publication of Ulysses Grant's memoirs.

But did the Q. C. Snodgrass letters truly flow from Clemens's pen? In republishing the letters, the scholars hedged their bets. Brashear opined that "none of the *Crescent* letters suggest the later Mark Twain as satisfactorily as one wishes they did."[52] Leisy was also circumspect—although his doubts didn't stop him from emblazoning "Mark Twain" across the title page and on the spine of his volume. Reviewers of the published set of letters had no such qualms; one wrote that the letters were "beyond reasonable doubt the work of Twain,"[53] while another stated that "little doubt exists."[54]

In many ways, the letters seem consistent with Clemens's earlier series. Both sets of Snodgrass letters, for example, contain allusions to Shakespeare and to Thomas Paine. Stylistically, however, the Thomas Jefferson and the Quintus Curtius Snodgrass letters are markedly dissimilar. In keeping with his provincial persona, Clemens made extensive use of vernacular language—expressed through dialect and creative misspellings—in the earlier letters, as shown in the following excerpt:

It mought be that some people think your umble sarvent has "shuffled off this mortal quile" and bid an eternal adoo to this subloonary atmosphere—nary time. He ain't dead, but sleepeth. That expreshun are figurative, and go to signerfy that he's pooty much quit scribblin.[55]

Brashear argues that this change can be explained by Clemens becoming "convinced that the style of the earlier Snodgrass series was in poor taste, so he turned to what then seemed to him a more elegant style for satire."[56]

Was Clemens even in New Orleans during the first three months of 1861? It is known that he was there in late January or early February because on February 6, he sent a letter to his brother Orion in which he described visiting a fortune teller in the Crescent City.[57]

The Clemens authorship issue has been addressed via a stylometric analysis conducted by Claude Brinegar, a statistician and economist who would go on to serve Presidents Nixon and Ford as their secretary of transportation. His study was published in 1963—the same year that Mosteller and Wallace issued their analysis of the *Federalist* (chapter 2). As previously discussed, such studies were difficult to conduct in the early 1960s, and Brinegar chose to employ the relatively simple method pioneered by Mendenhall: the comparison of word-length frequencies described earlier.

First, Brinegar wanted to determine whether Clemens possessed Mendenhall's "characteristic curve of composition." He tallied the lengths of nearly 11,000 words in three sets of personal and public letters written by Clemens at about the same time the Q. C. Snodgrass letters were published. When he plotted the results, he found that the three word-length frequency curves matched almost precisely. He compared this result with two curves generated from samples from Clemens's later works—*Roughing It* and *Following the Equator*. Once again, he found that the curves matched almost perfectly: the author clearly had a "characteristic" curve of composition.

Next, Brinegar sought to determine whether the Q. C. Snodgrass letters themselves had a characteristic curve. He divided the set of letters, which contain about 13,000 words in total, into three equal-sized groups (letters 1 to 3, 4 to 6, and 7 to 10) and tallied their word lengths. When he compared the resulting word-length curves, their high degree of similarity strongly suggested that all 10 had been written by the same person.

The critical test, however, involved comparing Clemens's composition curve against one generated from the set of Q. C. Snodgrass letters. And here, things were a little off. The Snodgrass letters had more two-letter words than was typical for Clemens, and the number of three- and four-letter words was somewhat less. A series of goodness-of-fit tests confirmed that the differences were statistically significant. Brinegar's conclusion was unequivocal: Clemens was not the author of the Q. C. Snodgrass letters.[58]

One wishes that Brinegar had also created a composition curve for the T. J. Snodgrass letters and made the appropriate comparisons. However, he may have been discouraged by the complexities involved in how to count the idiosyncratic spellings that Clemens had employed.

While Brinegar was conducting his statistical analysis, Allan Bates, an enterprising doctoral student at the University of Chicago, was trying to answer the authorship question through different means. Through careful study of extant records, letters, and Clemens's own notebook, Bates was able to compile a chronology of his movements up and down the river during the period in question while Clemens was a pilot on the *Alonzo Child*.

In the first Q. C. Snodgrass letter, its author refers to a specific, verifiable incident: on January 10, he was aboard the *National*, steaming from New Orleans to Baton Rouge. At that time, however, Clemens was 1,200 miles upriver, approaching St. Louis on the *Alonzo Child*. And by correlating the publication dates for all 10 letters against Clemens's comings and goings, Bates found that the river pilot was in the right place on only two occasions. Like Brinegar, he confidently concluded that Clemens was not Quintus Curtius Snodgrass.[59] And although this opinion is not universally shared by contemporary Clemens scholars, most of them agree that the evidence is incontrovertible—much as they would like to have another early work by Clemens to dissect and study.

But then what are we to make of the remarkable fact that two different newspaper correspondents chose the name "Snodgrass" as their nom de plume? The odds of such a coincidence seem to strain credulity. However, the name Snodgrass was in the air at the time. Dickens's first novel, *The Pickwick Papers*, had been published when Clemens was a child and was popular in the American Midwest by mid-century.[60] Augustus Snodgrass, a self-styled poet, is a central figure in that book. The young Clemens probably chose his pen name as an homage to the British author, whose work he admired.[61] It's not impossible that someone else could have had a similar motivation.

Clemens left Missouri in mid-1861 to accompany his brother Orion to the Nevada Territory. Orion was a Republican and had been appointed secretary of the Nevada Territory by Lincoln. It was there and in California that Sam Clemens would assume a different moniker and begin writing short stories. His time on the Mississippi saw him take his first halting steps as a humorist, and he would mine and publish those experiences under a new pen name: Mark Twain.

PICKETT LINES

After the second day of the Battle of Gettysburg, Confederate commander Robert E. Lee made a fateful decision. He had come tantalizingly close to breaking the Union army by striking at its left and right flanks. Now, he decided, he could achieve victory by attacking the center of the Federal line. In ordering General James Longstreet to carry out this plan, Lee staked everything on a final frontal assault.

But the attack was a disaster. An artillery barrage against the Union position was largely ineffective, and Longstreet, who opposed Lee's plan, was dilatory in commencing it. When the assault finally began, some 12,500 infantrymen had to march across three-quarters of a mile of open ground to reach the Union army's position. The Confederate troops were exposed to withering fire from three sides, and yet some managed to reach the Federal line, where they were repulsed in bloody combat. The toll was horrific: more than 5,000 men were killed or wounded, and nearly 4,000 were captured. Lee's invasion of the North had failed, and a turning point in the war had been reached.

Through a quirk of fate, the failed assault would become known as Pickett's Charge. General George Pickett's forces were part of Longstreet's assault, but he was one of three divisional commanders involved in the attack. Pickett would continue to serve under Lee until the end of the war, although he suffered another major defeat when his division was mauled at the Battle of Five Forks. Lee was forced to abandon Richmond as a result and would surrender to Ulysses Grant at Appomattox eight days later.

George Edward Pickett was a colorful and controversial figure. He graduated last in his West Point class of 1846 but gained fame in the Mexican American War. His first wife died in childbirth in 1851 after less than a year of marriage. A second wife also died young. Two months after the Gettysburg campaign, the 38-year-old widower married the 20-year-old LaSalle "Sallie" Corbell, and they would have two children. The family fled to Canada after the war, fearing prosecution for Pickett's ordering the hanging of 22 soldiers as deserters during the war. After a year, they returned to Virginia, and Pickett found employment as a farmer and insurance salesman. He died of a liver abscess in 1875 at age 50.

Corbell Pickett would outlive her husband by some 55 years and supported herself and her surviving son by working as a government clerk in the Federal Pensions Office. She dedicated her life to a zealous campaign to repair and enhance her dead husband's reputation. Over time, she became a popular speaker and contributor to magazines. She also wrote several books about her husband and the war.[62]

In 1913, Corbell Pickett published *The Heart of a Soldier, as Revealed in the Intimate Letters of Gen'l George E. Pickett, C.S.A.* She claimed in the book's foreword that "for half a century these letters have lain locked away from the world, the lines fading upon yellowed pages, their every word enshrined in the heart of the noble woman to whom they were written."[63] The book consists of 44 letters that Pickett wrote to her during the conflict as well as a few written afterward. These missives, invariably signed "Your Soldier," include number XVIII, which was penned shortly before the charge at Gettysburg, which would be forever associated with him. Given the controversy surrounding the attack, such a first-person, real-time account has considerable historical value.

Several Civil War scholars, however, have expressed serious doubts about the letters' authenticity. Their tone throughout is fawning and mawkishly sentimental. Number XII, dated April 15, 1863, and headed "In Which He Urges His Betrothed to Marry Him at Once," contains the following lines:

> You know that I love you with a devotion that absorbs all else—a devotion so divine that when in dreams I see you it is as something too pure and sacred for mortal touch. And if you only knew the heavenly life which thrills me through when I make it real to myself that you love me, you would understand.[64]

It's not impossible that Pickett could have written this: he was a known romantic living in a romantic age and clearly besotted with his Sallie at the time. And many letters written during the war contain such cloying sentiments. But the phrasing inspires some doubt.

Of more concern is that the letters contain information that Pickett did not possess when they were ostensibly composed. The note written on the third day of the Battle of Gettysburg provides a good example of this: he refers to geographic features like Little Round Top and Culp's Hill, even though these names were not known to the Confederate commanders and do not appear in their after-action reports. In addition, the letter runs to six pages, which raises the question of how Pickett could possibly have found the time to compose it while preparing his troops for their assault on the Union line.[65]

Others have defended the letters as genuine. The Civil War historian Glenn Tucker addressed the issue in his 1968 book *Lee and Longstreet at Gettysburg*.

He concluded that Pickett's notes to his wife were mostly authentic. Tucker did allow that Corbell Pickett may have edited and altered them for purposes of clarity. Nonetheless, his judgment was that the words she published were those of her husband. Tucker also points out that in 1913, many of the men Pickett commanded would have still been alive and would have objected to an obvious forgery, but no one did.[66]

In a review of the controversy published in 1986, historian Gary Gallagher not only accused Corbell Pickett of having manufactured the letters but also claims to have identified the quarry that she mined for their content. Specifically, Gallagher points to remarkable similarities of thought between Pickett and his inspector general, Walter Harrison. Harrison published *Pickett's Men: A Fragment of War History* in 1870, and Gallagher identified "more than forty instances of nearly verbatim plagiarism ranging in length from one sentence to entire paragraphs, together with dozens of paraphrases."[67]

It didn't help LaSalle's case that she was known to play fast and loose with facts. For example, she claimed that she married George Pickett at age 15 instead of 20 and that she was therefore a child bride of the Confederacy.[68]

Despite such concerns, material from the letters appeared in Michael Shaara's "The Killer Angels," which won a Pulitzer Prize, and in Ken Burns's well-known PBS documentary about the Civil War.[69] It would be helpful, therefore, to determine whose linguistic fingerprints can be found on the letters: the general's or those of his devoted wife.

In 2001, David Holmes and his colleagues looked into the matter. (Other research by Holmes was mentioned earlier in this chapter and also in chapter 3.) As in other authorship attribution studies, what is needed are samples of text from the two Picketts in question—George and LaSalle—as well as control texts from the same period and genre. And in this case, everything needed is readily available.

Samples of texts written by George Pickett were drawn from his military reports during the war. The researchers chose three samples of about 2,000 words each. In addition, letters that Pickett wrote before and after the war to his family and friends were included. These were taken from 11 handwritten letters held by Brown University. The letters were divided into four samples of about 2,000 words each.

Corbell Pickett was a prolific author after her husband's death, and for her texts, Holmes's team chose samples from her autobiography *What Happened to Me* as well as her historical work *Pickett and His Men* and her novel *The Bugles of Gettysburg*. In addition, the researchers found letters that Corbell Pickett had written to her stepson and a close friend after the death of her husband, and these were added to her textual set. The researchers chose 17 samples of about 3,000 words each.

As mentioned earlier, Gallagher alleged that Corbell Pickett plagiarized from Walter Harrison's book to provide the material for the letters from her husband, and Holmes's team included three samples from *Pickett's Men*, ranging from 4,000 to 5,000 words each.

Finally, the researchers decided that the most appropriate control texts for comparison to *The Heart of a Soldier* would be letters written by other Confederate officers to their families. Accordingly, they selected letters written by Robert E. Lee, Dorsey Pender, and Richard Corbin. Holmes's team also included letters written by four Union army privates in the control sample. Three 3,000-word samples for each of the seven men constituted the control set.

As in similar studies, an initial set of analyses was conducted as a check on the validity of the stylometric approach for these texts. The researchers identified the 60 most frequently occurring words in the control sample of Confederate and Union letter writers. A principal component analysis yielded a two-dimensional solution in which the officers emerged on one side of the plot with the enlisted men arrayed on the other side. In addition, there were distinct clusters of samples for most of the seven correspondents. Corbin, Lee, and Pender were cleanly separated from one another, as were two of the four Union privates. For the other two enlisted men, there was some overlap.

A second analysis compared the 60 most frequently occurring function words in the samples from Pickett's military reports and correspondence with the samples from the Harrison book. A two-dimensional plot clearly separated Pickett's personal letters from Harrison's history, with Pickett's military writings falling between them. The technique was able to separate the military writings of the two men.

An analysis of Corbell Pickett's writing was able to segregate her letters from her autobiography, although there was substantial overlap between her historical work and novel, probably because there is great similarity in subject matter. And a comparison of the writings of the George and LaSalle texts, once again based on the 60 most frequently occurring function words, was able to differentiate the two Picketts and their various genres: military reporting and letters.

For the critical comparison—George Pickett versus LaSalle Corbell Pickett versus *Heart of a Soldier*—the researchers turned to another technique:

discriminant analysis. This provides a way of measuring the degree to which two or more groups can be segregated from one another. Using the 25 most frequently occurring function words in the corpus, the analysis was able to cleanly separate Corbell Pickett's published work from her letters and also from those of her husband. And when the researchers added in the samples from Pickett's handwritten letters, *Heart of a Soldier*, and the Harrison book, the results were clear. The samples from *Heart of a Soldier* didn't cluster with Pickett's known handwritten or other letters. Instead, the disputed letters clustered with Corbell Pickett's autobiography.[70]

In short, Holmes and his coauthors' findings provide empirical support for the suspicions of Gary Gallagher and others who have accused Corbell Pickett of inventing her husband's letters and then publishing them. It is unknown whether her motivation was financial—the book sold well—or simply another act in a decades-long attempt to burnish the reputation of Her Soldier.

CHAPTER SEVEN

OOPS!

Misses and False Positives

AN ELEGY FOR AN ELEGY

On a late afternoon in early 1984, a graduate student was scrolling through a reel of microfilm in one of the libraries at the University of California, Los Angeles. The student was someone we met in chapter 3 of this book: Don Foster, the Vassar professor who unmasked Joe Klein as the author of *Primary Colors*. Twelve years before that episode, he was a doctoral student of English literature at the University of California, Santa Barbara, researching early English book prefaces and dedications. As part of that project, he was working his way through a series titled *Early English Books, 1475–1640*. It comprised all of the surviving volumes, pamphlets, and broadsides from that era and had only recently been released as a research tool.

While hunting for dedications to examine, Foster came across a pamphlet, titled *A Funerall Elegye*, that had been published in 1612. As he scanned through its short salutation, he noticed that it was similar to William Shakespeare's dedications for *Venus and Adonis*, published in 1593, as well as *The Rape of Lucrece*, published in 1594. In its text, he thought he heard echoes of the Bard's plays, such as *Richard II*. The pamphlet had been printed by George Eld and Thomas Thorpe, who had published Shakespeare's sonnets three years earlier. The *Elegy* was unsigned, but the salutation bore the initials "W.S." Could it be that the *Elegy* was a lost work of William Shakespeare's?[1]

An extraordinary claim like this would require extraordinary evidence, and Foster dug in to see if he could find some. A bit of detective work revealed that the *Elegy* commemorated one William Peter of Devonshire, who had been murdered near Exeter on January 25, 1612. After a day of drinking, he had been stabbed in the back of the head and killed by a relative named Edward Drew. Only two copies of the *Elegy* had survived to the present day, and both were at Oxford. Foster obtained funding to travel to Oxford and examine the originals as well as to research the circumstances of Peter's murder. He found plenty of circumstantial evidence supporting his thesis but no smoking gun. He wrote about the discovery in his dissertation, which he defended in 1985, and in a book published four years later. In it, he was careful to lay out evidence both for and against an attribution to Shakespeare.[2]

It is unknown how much written material Shakespeare produced during his lifetime. Only about half of his plays were published before his death in 1616. The others appeared in the famous First Folio of 1623, a collection of 36 plays. Currently, three additional plays are thought to have at least partly been written by him, and two others are believed to have been lost. Other plays that had formerly been attributed to him did not gain wide acceptance. There exists more debate about a number of anonymous poems and other short works. Needless to say, scholars are loath to expand the Bard's oeuvre without substantial evidence, and a true consensus for a given claim can take decades to form.

As with many things related to Shakespeare, the dispute over Foster's *Elegy* is embedded in a larger debate concerning the authorship of the plays attributed to him. As mentioned in chapters 2 and 3, arguments about Shakespeare's identity have been raging for decades. This debate was the impetus for Thomas Mendenhall's pioneering work at a time when Francis Bacon was a prime suspect for having written the Bard's plays.

More recently, a favored candidate has been Edward de Vere, the 17th Earl of Oxford. De Vere, however, died in 1604. This is an inconvenient truth for his partisans because about a dozen of the plays seem to have been composed in the decade following the earl's demise. However, the exact dates of composition are unknown, and so there is some wiggle room in the chronology. The *Elegy*, however, has been dated precisely to February 1612. If it had been written by the same author as the plays, then the earl's supporters would be dealt a serious and possibly fatal blow.

In addition to circumstantial evidence, Foster based his attribution on the rare words that appear in the works of Shakespeare and other Elizabethan authors. (In this context, rare means uncommon in a given author's work as opposed to infrequent in general.) To assist him in identifying these terms, Foster created the Shaxicon: a computerized database that includes words appearing

12 times or fewer in the Bard's plays.[3] He also made use of a database of 80,000 lines from elegies published between 1612 and 1613.[4]

Foster's assumption was that Shakespeare's idiolect was being altered by what he was reading during the time he was composing his plays. The Shaxicon, for example, suggests that he was influenced by Ben Jonson's *Every Man in His Humour* (1598) because its rare words show up in works written by the Bard shortly thereafter, such as in *Henry IV, Part 2* (circa 1598) and *As You Like It* (circa 1599). Among the dramatic texts in his database, Foster found that *Henry VIII* (circa 1613) had the highest match to the *Elegy* in terms of rare words used. For nondramatic texts, the highest match was to Shakespeare's sonnets, which were published in 1609.[5]

Foster's claim and his methodology received decidedly mixed reviews. Some scholars were intrigued, while other reactions were scathing. The critic Stephen Wigler, writing for the *Baltimore Sun*, dismissed the Shakespeare attribution out of hand. His reasoning was based not on rare words or a close reading but on a holistic judgment: the *Elegy* simply isn't well written. Specifically, he described it as "incompetent, amateurish, and disorganized." He claimed that it could not have been written by the Bard for that reason alone.[6]

The *Elegy* is a strange document in several respects. Published as a 21-page pamphlet, it runs to nearly 600 lines and a little over 24,000 words. If it is a late work by Shakespeare, it clearly lacks the arresting metaphorical language that is the hallmark of his later plays. But given that the *Elegy* was listed in the Stationer's Register in London a mere 19 days after William Peter's death, perhaps its lack of substance and polish could be explained by the haste with which it was written. Besides, if Shakespeare didn't write it, then who did?

For a time, Foster's conjecture about the *Elegy's* authorship was ascendant, and it received considerable attention. Readers of the January 14, 1996, edition of the *New York Times* were greeted by a front-page story about Foster's claim. The article recapped the December meeting of the Modern Language Association in Washington, D.C. At that conference, a number of Shakespeare scholars had endorsed Foster's attribution. It appeared that a scholarly consensus was emerging.[7] The debate, however, also took on a decidedly nationalist cast, with Foster's supporters coming largely from the ranks of other American Shakespeare scholars, such as Richard Abrams, while the skeptics were British and French. In 1997, *A Funeral Elegy* was added to three of the complete editions of Shakespeare. All three of these editions were published in the United States.

By 2002, the tide began to turn in favor of the skeptics when Gilles Monsarrat weighed in on the debate. A professor at the University of Burgundy, Monsarrat was well known for his translations of Shakespeare into French. He also had a keen eye for the Bard's use of vocabulary. Monsarrat not only cast doubt on Foster's attribution but also named John Ford as the likeliest author of the *Elegy*. Ford had been born in Devon in 1586. He began to publish in 1606 and worked as a playwright after 1620. His best-known work is the incestuous drama *'Tis Pity She's a Whore*, which he penned in 1633. And the language Ford used in his poetic work bears a striking resemblance to that found in the *Elegy*.

To cite but one example, consider the simile "like a seeled dove." (This refers to the falconer's practice of sewing shut the eyelids of a bird to make it tame.) The phrase doesn't appear in Shakespeare but can be found in Ford's *The Broken Heart*, written in the 1620s. There are also clear parallels between the *Elegy* and Ford's religious poem *Christ's Bloody Sweat*, published in 1613. In total, Monsarrat points out 15 identical or nearly identical phrases that appear in both the *Elegy* and Ford's works. For his part, Don Foster had interpreted this as Ford borrowing from the *Elegy*, but an alternative explanation is that John Ford was the author of both. As Monsarrat bluntly put it, "Either Ford memorized much of the elegy, or he composed it himself."[8] Finally, circumstantial evidence supports this conjecture as well: Ford almost certainly knew William Peter, the murder victim and subject of the *Elegy*.

Ward Elliott and Robert Valenza weighed in on the debate by conducting a stylometric analysis. In a head-to-head comparison of Shakespeare and Ford, they examined the two writers' use of certain words, like "of," and phrases, like "such as," as well as their use of hendiadys (e.g., "cups and gold" instead of "golden cups"). They found that, in comparison to the *Elegy*, Shakespeare's language failed half of the tests they devised, whereas Ford failed only 3 percent.[9]

Foster himself found these critiques to be convincing. In June 2002, he publicly retracted his attribution about the *Elegy* in SHAKSPER, an online forum. (The *Times* reported this development as well, but unlike the initial claim in 1996, the main article was relegated to the Arts section on page 57.)[10] By that point, several other scholars had reached the same conclusion. Richard Kennedy had noted the similarity of the *Elegy* to Ford's writing, and Brian Vickers weighed in with a book-length analysis that supported Monsarrat's claims.[11]

But if Ford wrote the *Elegy*, then what are we to make of the initials "W. S." after the salutation? That remains a mystery.[12] Various theories have been offered, including even the notion that Ford ghostwrote the *Elegy* for Shakespeare.[13] At any rate, a scholarly consensus has now emerged, and American publishers have quietly excised the *Elegy* from their complete works of Shakespeare.

More important for our purposes, however, is why Foster and his data-driven methodology misattributed the authorship of the *Elegy* to Shakespeare. Perhaps the search for individual but diagnostic words is, in itself, problematic. But as we have seen, Foster would use this methodology with great success when he revealed Joe Klein as the author of *Primary Colors* in 1996. A granular, word-level approach has also succeeded with a number of forensic cases. Foster's procedure may have failed in this case because his body of comparison texts was simply too small. A corpus composed of thousands of lines may seem impressively large, but in this case, it proved insufficient to differentiate the voice of Shakespeare from one of his admirers.

THE RESISTER

On September 5, 2018, the *New York Times* published an op-ed under the headline "I Am Part of the Resistance inside the Trump Administration." The newspaper chose to shield the identity of the author, who was identified only as a "senior official in the Trump administration."[14] The reasons for this decision become clear within the first few sentences of the piece, which is a scathing critique of the forty-fifth president. The author describes Trump as amoral, impetuous, erratic, and antidemocratic—and those are only the epithets that begin with vowels. The unnamed official claimed to be part of a larger cabal of resisters who were actively working to thwart the president's more dangerous impulses. The editorial became a major news story and would go on to be the third-most-read article published by the *Times* during 2018.

At the White House, the piece set off a firestorm of controversy. The president referred to the editorial as "gutless," and the administration vowed to identify and punish the renegade in their midst for their apostasy.[15] Speculation about the author's identity was rampant. It was reminiscent of conjectures about the identity of Deep Throat, another government insider who had, 45 years earlier, helped to expose the crimes of the Nixon administration. That resister, Mark Felt, was able to keep his identity a secret for decades. Would this new whistleblower be as successful?

Those who wished to unmask the author—including both supporters and opponents of the president—didn't have a lot to work with. The editorial is only 958 words long. And as we have already seen, stylometrists typically need a few thousand words to work their attribution magic.

To complicate matters further, an individual identified only as a "senior official" could be one of dozens or even hundreds of people, depending on how liberally one chooses to bestow the term on the myriad functionaries that make up any presidential administration. In addition, the vast majority of such individuals are not published authors, so there is no public paper trail that would allow a comparison of their own writing with the language in the editorial.

As a result, the hunt for the Resister centered on the author's referents and potentially diagnostic textual clues. The op-ed ends with a paean to John McCain, which suggests that the author is a moderate Republican. It also describes McCain as a "lodestar," a figurative expression that refers to an inspiration or a guide. It is an unusual term and, as we have seen with other instances of *hapax legomena*, the sort of clue that might help reveal the author's identity.

Search engines like Google make it possible for almost anyone to play linguistic detective, and those seeking a link between the Arizona senator and lodestars turned up an intriguing connection. At McCain's memorial service at the National Cathedral, former secretary of state Henry Kissinger eulogized his friend by asserting that "honor was John's lodestar; it is an intangible quality." The memorial was held on September 1, and the Resister's editorial was published four days later. Had Anonymous been present at this service?

Although Trump himself chose not to attend the memorial, many of his advisers did. These included Chief of Staff John Kelly, lawyer Rudy Giuliani, National Security Adviser John Bolton, Director of National Intelligence Dan Coats, and ambassador to Russia Jon Huntsman. Trump's daughter Ivanka and son-in-law Jared Kushner were also noted to be in attendance.[16] But since videos of the service were soon available online, it would not have been necessary for the Resister to be physically present to hear Kissinger's remarks.

Online sleuths also discovered that Vice President Mike Pence had used the word "lodestar" in several of his speeches, whereas other suspects, such as Kelly or Secretary of Defense Jim Mattis, never seem to have done so in their public writing and speeches.[17] *Inside Edition* reported that Pence's Secret Service code name was "lodestar," which made an association with him seem even more likely, although the vice president's actual code name was "Hoosier."[18] Pence's office strongly denied that he was the author of the *Times* editorial. "The Vice President puts his name on his Op-Eds," tweeted Pence's chief of staff Jarrod Agen. "Our office is above such amateur acts."[19]

Omarosa Manigualt Newman, Trump's former adviser, took to Twitter naming four staffers she believed might be the Resister and asked people to vote for the likeliest suspect. She hinted that respondents should "choose the one who is looking to exit the White House soon." The four she listed were Andrew Bremberg, director of the Domestic Policy Council; Nick Ayers, Pence's chief of staff; Johnny DeStefano, counselor to the president; and Bill Stepien, White House director of political affairs. Ayers garnered the most votes, pulling in 37 percent, while DeStefano came in second, with 31 percent.[20]

In November 2019, 14 months after the op-ed appeared, the Resister published a book-length account of his concerns about Trump, giving it the ominous title *A Warning*.[21] The book's cover gave the author's name as Anonymous, followed by "A senior Trump administration official." It immediately shot to the top of the *Times* best-seller list. The 272-page tome was eagerly combed over by those seeking additional clues regarding the author's identity.

Reviewers Carlos Lozada and Jennifer Szalai zeroed in on the Resister's use of metaphor for evidence about their interests and background. They noted that the use of football and golfing imagery was suggestive of someone who was a sports fan. References to games like Twister and Battleship might mean that the author was a Gen Xer. And casual references to senior military officers Jim Mattis and National Security Adviser H. R. McMaster by their first names was indicative of someone who had not served in the military.[22] None of these speculations did much to narrow down the list of suspects, however.

David Kusnet, writing for *The New Republic*, suggested that the author could be former Pentagon aide Guy Snodgrass. He had been the chief speechwriter for Mattis and was known to be apolitical.[23]

During the same period, the White House was concluding its own investigation. In December 2019, Peter Navarro, the president's trade adviser, wrote a lengthy memo that was made public by *Politico* in March 2021.[24] In it, Navarro claimed that a forensic analysis of both the editorial and *A Warning* yielded a "likely profile" comprising 10 specific attributes, including that Anonymous was a woman with several children and a political appointee with expertise in national security, foreign policy, and the Middle East. An experienced writer, she worked in the White House National Security Council as a deputy or special assistant to the president and was not a senior administration official. She was pro-Israel, favored a hard line with Iran, and had ties to John Bolton. Navarro concluded that this profile pointed to at least one specific person of interest.[25]

Did Navarro have the necessary background to conduct such an analysis? He is a graduate of Tufts who served in the Peace Corps and later earned a master of public administration and a PhD in economics from Harvard. He taught for a number of years, principally at the University of California, Irvine, where he was a professor of economics and public policy. His areas of specialization are energy policy and U.S.–Asia relations. None of this suggests expertise or training in linguistics, author attribution, or forensic analysis.

It might be instructive to consider one of Navarro's claims: that Anonymous was a woman with several children. As evidence for this, he cites *A Warning*'s dedication ("to my children") and the author's criticism of the president's sexism and misogyny. He mentions a passage in which Anonymous is critical of the idea that Nikki Haley's appointment as UN ambassador would help Trump become more popular with women. Navarro concludes, "One presumes here that it takes a woman to know a woman."[26]

Politico's reporting concluded that Navarro concocted the memo to implicate a specific colleague: Deputy National Security Adviser Victoria Coates, with whom he had philosophical differences regarding trade. Although Coates isn't mentioned by name in his analysis, she is an almost exact match with Navarro's profile. One of *Politico*'s sources claimed that this memo made its way to Trump. What happened next is clear enough: Coates was transferred out of the White House and into a position at the Department of Energy. This occurred at the end of February 2020, a few weeks after Navarro had passed his memo around at the White House.[27]

In late October, six days before the 2020 election and with his permission, the *New York Times* revealed that Miles Taylor was the author of both the op-ed and *A Warning*. Taylor had worked for 16 months in the Trump administration at the Department of Homeland Security. During the final seven months of his tenure, he was chief of staff to the secretary of the department, serving under Kirstjen Nielsen and then Acting Secretary Kevin MacAleenan. In September 2019, Taylor had left the administration to work for Google as a government affairs and public policy manager. He took a leave from the company in August 2020 in order to campaign for Joe Biden.

In hindsight, Taylor's claim to have been a senior official in the Trump administration was a bit of an exaggeration. And he had been deliberately deceptive as well. Two months before coming clean, Anderson Cooper had asked him on his program if he was Anonymous. He had categorically denied it at that time, telling Cooper that "I wear a mask for two things: Halloweens and pandemics." In a statement he later posted to his website, he explained that he "wanted the attention to be on the arguments themselves" instead of on him.[28]

Janet Ainsworth and Patrick Juola have cited this episode as an object lesson of the potential dangers when nonprofessionals attempt to identify unknown authors.[29] Miles Taylor hadn't been on the radar of anyone in the Trump administration, and the journalists, pundits, and armchair linguists hadn't been able to identify him either. One could argue that no harm came from the deception and that anonymity was necessary for his warning to be heard. It is doubtful, however, that Victoria Coates feels that way. And there may have been others in the Trump administration whose careers were blunted by suspicions that they were Resisters. Taylor was successful at concealing his identity, but his anonymity was maintained primarily through his obscurity.

A NEAPOLITAN MYSTERY

Elena Ferrante has become one of Italy's most beloved novelists. Her first book, 1991's *L'amore molesto* (*Troubling Love*), has been followed by nearly a dozen others. Of these, she is best known for her Neapolitan Quartet, published between 2012 and 2015. The four books chronicle the lives of Elena Greco and Lila Cerullo, who grew up in difficult circumstances near postwar Naples. The critically acclaimed saga of friendship, motherhood, social class, and competition has been translated into 35 languages, and books in the series have sold more than 16 million copies worldwide.[30] It is an impressive track record for a novelist who doesn't exist. Elena Ferrante is a pseudonym, and the author's actual identity has been a closely guarded secret as well as the subject of intense speculation and debate.

Ferrante doesn't promote her novels: she has been quoted as saying that "books, once they are written, have no need of their authors."[31] She refuses to be interviewed but has, on occasion, provided written responses to questions from journalists. Some letters have been published, and certain elements of her novels are thought to be autobiographical. All of this has provided literary sleuths with tantalizing clues about her identity.

In January 2005, the journalist Luigi Galella proposed that Ferrante was a man: the Italian novelist Domenico Starnone. Galella based his thesis on a number of thematic and textual similarities between Ferrante's debut novel and Starnone's *Via gemito*, published in 2000. Starnone, for his part, issued an unequivocal denial. Undeterred, Galella teamed with physicists Vittorio Loreto and Andrea Baronchelli, who conducted a stylometric analysis of the works of Ferrante, Starnone, and four other authors who had been suggested, at one time or another, to be Ferrante. Their analysis found the highest match between the mystery author and Starnone.[32]

Over the next decade, numerous other candidates for Ferrante were proposed, with interest in her identity reaching a fever pitch in 2016. In March of that year, the scholar Marco Santagata proposed that Ferrante was Marcella Marmo, a history professor at a Neapolitan university. Marmo denied it, as did Ferrante's publisher.[33] Even Ferrante's English translator, Ann Goldstein, has been suspected of being the mystery author. Goldstein, an editor at *The New Yorker*, denied the attribution and asserted that even she didn't know Ferrante's true identity.[34]

In October 2016, the investigative reporter Claudio Gatti made news when he claimed to have solved the case. Unlike earlier attempts to unmask Ferrante, Gatti was guided by the advice of Deep Throat, the Watergate informant whose mantra was "follow the money." By tracing payments from Ferrante's publisher, which increased dramatically along with her readership, Gatti concluded that Ferrante was Anita Raja. Raja is a retired librarian and freelance translator who lives in Rome with her husband, who happens to be Domenico Starnone. Neither of Raja's professions is particularly remunerative, but she had somehow acquired the means to purchase valuable parcels of real estate.[35]

Case closed? Not necessarily. Ferrante claims that she grew up in Naples and that her mother was a seamstress. Raja's mother, on the other hand, was born into a Polish Jewish family who fled the Nazis in 1937. In Italy, she married a magistrate. The couple initially lived in Naples, and this is where their daughter Anita was born. Three years later, however, the family moved to Rome, where Anita grew up in a solidly middle-class home. Given the novels' vivid depiction of poverty and postwar Naples, could Ferrante really be Raja? Gatti went so far as to accuse Ferrante of lying about her parentage in her responses to the press.

In September 2017, a group of researchers met in Padua to see if they could converge on a definitive solution to the Ferrante mystery. To help them in their work, a team led by Arjuna Tuzzi and Michele Cortelazzo created a corpus of Italian novels for stylometric analysis; the corpus was dubbed the Padova Italian Corpus (PIC). It contains the novels of contemporary Italian authors who were critically acclaimed or commercially successful. The corpus includes Ferrante herself as well as all the authors who have been suspected of being her.

Altogether, the PIC contains 150 novels by 40 different writers. One-quarter of these authors hail from Naples or the Campania region. Two-thirds are men, and one-third are women. In total, the PIC includes nearly 10 million words of text.

This is an impressively large corpus, but as the researchers themselves acknowledged, having a vast body of text to analyze is no guarantee of success. If Ferrante is a collaboration of two or more authors, for example, this approach will not identify her. Similarly, if the mystery author never published anything besides the Ferrante novels, she would also be invisible to the analysis. The universe of talented Italian novelists is not infinite, but it is still large enough that there was no guarantee that Ferrante's other work—if it exists—was captured by this net.

The researchers pursued a multipronged strategy to identify Ferrante. One team applied an iterative procedure to calculate the similarity of text blocks drawn from the novels and then used hierarchical cluster analysis to identify novels that bunched with the Ferrante novels. They found there was a cluster that included all of the Ferrante books, and it also happened to include many of the novels of Domenico Starnone.[36]

Other researchers who took part in the conference, making use of a variety of techniques, converged on Starnone as well. Jacques Savoy, for example, employed a multivariate approach focusing on the most frequent words appearing in the PIC. Using a machine learning approach like the one employed in the Pynchon newsletter analysis of chapter 3, Savoy chose seven Ferrante novels as the test set while the rest of the corpus served as the training set. Savoy's results were conclusive: Starnone was the best match with Ferrante.[37]

Qualitative studies of Ferrante's work have reinforced the conclusions of the quantitative approaches. There are several instances of unusual or rare words popping up in the oeuvre of Ferrante's novels, and many of these are also seen in Starnone's work but not in the writing of other authors in the PIC. Out of the 9.8 million words in the corpus, the noun *risatella* ("little laugh") occurs 30 times. Twenty of these instances can be found in the novels of Ferrante, and the other 10 appear in the work of Starnone. The remaining 38 authors in the corpus never employ it. A similar pattern obtains for several other terms.[38]

So who is Domenico Starnone? He was born in 1943 to a seamstress in Saviano, 16 miles east of Naples. He has written for newspapers and the screen and has published a string of novels. He seems to fit the profile, but many Ferrante fans have pushed back strongly against this identification. The

Neapolitan Quartet is so perceptive about women, these admirers claim, that no man could have written it.[39] There are clear exceptions to this in the history of literature. Tolstoy's *Anna Karenina* and Flaubert's *Madame Bovary* are the obvious ones, but these may be the exceptions that prove the rule. It is certainly true that many men have written one-dimensional or unbelievable female characters.

But what of Anita Raja, the suspect identified by Gatti? She is not represented in the PIC because she isn't known to have published any novels. She has, however, been a prolific translator. Many of these translations were published by Edizioni E/O, which happens to be Ferrante's Italian publisher. Raja has translated 16 of Christa Wolf's novels from German into Italian, and for the 2017 conference, the scholar Jan Rybicki added these translated works into his own analyses of the PIC. Although he concluded, like the others, that Ferrante is most likely Starnone, Rybicki acknowledged the limitations of using this method to see if Raja is Ferrante. A translator's job is to transmute an author's words into another language while preserving the writer's unique voice and not to impose their own stylistic idiosyncrasies onto the text. Skilled translators can do this extremely well. But if Raja is both Ferrante and a faithful translator, then her own voice would be obscured by Wolf's: her own linguistic fingerprint would be smudged at best.[40]

The most interesting pushback against attempts to solve the Ferrante mystery have come from the novelist's most ardent fans. Many of them are comfortable with not knowing who Ferrante is, and they don't want to know.[41] Freed from having to consider the trappings of the creator's backstory, this agnosticism allows them to appreciate Ferrante's work on its own merits. And then there is the matter of prying into an anonymous author's life—a clear violation of their privacy. Many found it distasteful, for example, when Gatti used leaked documents and real estate records in an attempt to ferret out Ferrante's identity.[42]

But does a living author have the right to not be known? It's not a violation of Shakespeare's privacy to question whether he wrote a particular work; he's no longer able to have an opinion about the matter one way or another. Oddly, this doesn't seem to have been an issue in the unmasking of J. K. Rowling as the author of *A Cuckoo's Calling*, described in chapter 3. That is probably because, as one of the richest women in the world, Rowling is a celebrity in a way that Ferrante—whoever they are—is not. And celebrities have to contend with paparazzi whether they wield a camera or a computer. But does Ferrante qualify as a public figure? She clearly doesn't want to be one.

Some have also pushed back against the sexism implicit in equating Ferrante with Starnone: that if the Neapolitan novels are great works of literature, then they could have been written only by a man. Needless to say, this way of thinking conveniently ignores the outstanding work produced by female authors as well as the historical impediments to their ability to write and to publish.[43]

A final point to consider is that Ferrante's novels could be a collaborative effort by Raja and Starnone.[44] Rybicki acknowledges that if this is the case, then stylometric analyses may be unable to detect Raja's contribution to this collaboration.[45] If nothing else, the debate over Elena Ferrante has cast a harsh light on the methodological limitations of author identification as well as the questionable ethics of unmasking living writers who prefer to remain anonymous.

THE MAVERICK

The contributions of Andrew Q. Morton to stylometric analysis are deserving of special discussion because they illustrate both the promise and the peril of developing attribution techniques. Morton's work on the authorship of the Pauline epistles was described in chapter 2, and in the following years, he endeavored to extend his approach from ancient Greek texts to modern English ones. As someone working outside of the academic community—in his case as a minister for the Church of Scotland—he had the freedom to explore unconventional ideas. But he also had to deal with the skepticism of the academic community regarding his claims, evidence, and methodology.

In 1978, Morton published *Literary Detection*, a book describing several author attribution techniques he had developed.[46] A central idea animating Morton's work was his belief that everyone has unconscious habits of thought that are reflected in the words they choose when they write. Furthermore, he believed that such habits are fixed and unchanging, constituting a linguistic fingerprint that requires only the finding of a proper way to measure it. In his book, Morton declared that such telltale clues can be found in collocations and proportionate word pairs, which are words that occur together in a text. And in a study of 10 twentieth-century authors, he claimed to find evidence of such consistency, even for authors such as John Fowles, who claimed to write differently in a variety of different genres.

Close analysis of Morton's methods, however, has revealed serious flaws. Wilfred Smith of the University of Ulster, in a careful critique of this approach, objected to the "inadequacy of [Morton's] documentation, the haphazard methods for selecting data, and the limited number and incomplete nature of the tests for establishing the accuracy of the method."[47] But it was a claim about Shakespeare, by a different practitioner of Morton's methods, that brought such concerns to the fore.

In June 1980, the British weekly *The Observer* trumpeted news that a computer had "found" a new play by the Bard of Avon. Thomas Merriam, a lecturer in history at Basingstoke Technical College, had used Morton's methods to "prove" that the disputed play *The Book of Sir Thomas More*, thought by many scholars to be a joint work, had been written almost entirely by Shakespeare. Among other claims, Merriam asserted that patterns of common words in *Thomas More* were "statistically indistinguishable" from those found in the Bard's plays, including *Julius Caesar*, *Titus Andronicus*, and *Pericles*. Furthermore, the rare words appearing in the disputed play were highly similar to those in *Henry VI*. Merriam's conclusion was that *Thomas More* was, "give or take 10 percent . . . an early work of Shakespeare." This verdict would be endorsed by Morton based on an (unpublished) analysis of his own.[48]

Extraordinary claims like this one require extraordinary evidence as well as consensus within the scholarly community. And in the case of the disputed play, neither was forthcoming. For nearly a decade, Wilfred Smith would publish acerbic attacks on Merriam's work,[49] and Merriam would respond with increasingly bitter denunciations of Smith's broadsides.[50] It may have been an amusing spectacle for some, but as a dispute, it generated more heat than light. At the end of the day, the community of Shakespeare scholars found Merriam unconvincing. The majority opinion is that Shakespeare's contributions to *Thomas More* are relatively minor and constitute a revision to a collaborative effort involving five different playwrights. Furthermore, this attribution is based more on analyses of handwriting and ink than on stylometry.[51]

In the late 1980s, Morton teamed up with Sidney Michaelson, a professor of computer science at Edinburgh. And in 1990, their collaboration resulted in a new stylometric measure they called the cusum technique (mentioned in chapter 4). The fact that Morton and Michaelson described their technique in two university research reports means that the method was not subjected to the peer-review process that is the standard for academic publications.

Once again, the point of departure for this method is the belief that underlying and unchanging habits can be revealed through textual analysis. To analyze a particular passage, the researcher creates a plot that shows how much each sentence deviates from a text's average sentence length. For example, consider a case in which the author's average sentence is 10 words long and the text to be analyzed has five sentences that are four, 12, 10, 16, and eight words each. In this case, the plotted values would be negative six (four minus 10), two (12 minus 10), zero, six, and negative two. The number of sentences plotted would typically be more than this, but the calculation would be the same.

Once a sentence length plot has been created, measures of linguistic habits must be calculated. One commonly used measure is an author's use of short words. In cusum, short words are defined as those that are two or three letters in length. Words that begin with vowel sounds are also commonly measured. As with sentence length, the computations for these two measures involve finding the average for each and the deviations from this average for each sentence.

Morton never provided a clear theoretical rationale for why these two types of words should reveal a characteristic authorial fingerprint. In the case of two- or three-letter words, it is possible that they are functioning as a proxy for some other attribute, such as word frequency. Many two- and three-letter words are highly frequent in English. But there are also plenty of exceptions (such as "cam," cur," "lob," and "ox"). The use of words that start with vowels is even more of a puzzle. Many common words have this characteristic ("about," "into," and "other"), but so do plenty of rare or unusual terms ("apostasy," "idiopathic," and "obloquy"). A dragnet pulled through an author's sentences will haul in all such words without discrimination.

Finally, the short word deviations are typically combined with the initial vowel words to create a composite score. These deviations are plotted on a second graph. We now have two graphs: one of sentence length deviations and one showing the composite measure of the habit words. One graph can now be superimposed on the other. If the two plots lie atop each other, this means that the entire text was written by the same person. However, if there is significant separation between the two plotted lines, this suggests evidence of multiple authorship, such as the insertion of one writer's sentences into another's.

What counts as "significant separation"? Cusum is a visual representation of the author's habits, and it is up to the researcher to determine what constitutes a "blip"—a minor and temporary deviation in an author's habits—and what is a true deviation between the plotted lines. Anomalies can be caused by many factors, such as the beginning and ending of a text, and so it is suggested that such sections, as well as other sentences that appear problematic, be excluded from the cusum computations. Unusually long sentences can be broken into shorter clauses. And if two- and three-letter words don't produce a good result, well, how about using two, three, and four letters or three and four letters and so on?[52]

It should be clear by now that cusum analyses involve a great deal of subjectivity. Unlike Burrows's Delta, which will always generate the same numbers no matter who performs the computations, different cusum analysts may well produce different results. And it is this subjectivity and lack of replicability that is anathema to other stylometric researchers. However, it is possible to eliminate the step involving the visual comparison of graphs by using weighted cusum measures. This does make such analyses more objective and amenable to statistical analysis. However, when comparing texts of known authors, the weighted method generated incorrect results more than half the time.[53]

Several other studies from the early 1990s also failed to validate the technique. One study found that cusum identified three single-authored texts as having multiple authors, while it failed to identify 21 multiple-authored texts correctly as such.[54] Another showed that cusum analyses were unable to reliably detect the insertion of material into a given text.[55] In their 2007 review of forensic linguistics, Malcolm Coulthard and Alison Johnson characterized the weight of evidence against cusum as "devastating."[56]

Morton's cusum analysis of C. S. Lewis's *Dark Tower*, mentioned in chapter 4, was also never subjected to peer review: the results were simply included in Kathryn Lindskoog's book about Lewis, and she provided no details about which "linguistic habits" were examined.[57]

Even the foundation that cusum is built on—the purported existence of stable habits that writers make use of without conscious awareness—has been examined and found wanting. Research by psychologists has shown that linguistic variability within people is as great as variability between people.[58]

It would be a mistake, however, to dismiss the cusum controversy as an ivory tower debate with no real-world consequences. This is because during the early 1990s, the technique was accepted as expert evidence in British and Irish courts and in several high-profile cases.[59]

Consider the case of the Birmingham Six, who were sentenced to life imprisonment following their convictions for two terrorist bombings. The explosives had been placed in two Birmingham pubs and killed 21 people in November 1974. During an appeal of the case in 1991, Morton claimed that a cusum analysis of the statements made by the defendants had been altered at some later time by law enforcement. Morton's testimony helped to get the convictions quashed, and five surviving men were freed after serving 16 years of their sentences. One of the Six stated that Morton's testimony was "vital in overturning our convictions."[60]

For many years, the use of new scientific techniques in U.S. courtrooms was regulated by a 1923 decision called the Frye standard. It required that testimony put before a jury be based on "generally accepted" science. And due to the absence of peer-reviewed studies supporting cusum, Morton's technique would almost certainly fail to reach that standard. It should be noted, however, that the U.S. Supreme Court replaced Frye with the Daubert standard in 1993. Instead of requiring peer review, a decision about the admissibility of scientific evidence is now left up to individual judges in the United States.[61]

Andrew Morton died at age 99 in 2019. His obituaries highlighted successes like his legal victories.[62] The discredited cusum technique that he had pioneered and championed, however, stands as a cautionary tale of the dangers of going one's own way and blazing a trail that others refuse to follow.

ANTHRAX AND HUBRIS

During the fall of 2001, in the wake of the 9/11 terrorist attacks, many Americans braced for additional acts of extremism that might follow. Their worst fears seemed to be realized when letters containing deadly anthrax began to be sent through the mail. A first wave of five letters, dispatched in mid-September, targeted news and entertainment outlets. In early October, two additional letters were sent to U.S. Senators Tom Daschle and Pat Leahy. As a result of the mailings, 17 people were infected, and five of them died.

Anthrax infections are caused by bacteria found in the soil. Grazing animals are most likely to come into contact with these spores. Once ingested, they reproduce inside the host, and death usually follows in a matter of days or weeks. In humans, the spores can be consumed, inhaled, or absorbed through the skin. Airborne transmission via the lungs, when not treated promptly, is particularly lethal.

All the envelopes in the 2001 attacks bore a Trenton, New Jersey, postmark. Investigators checked hundreds of mailboxes in the area, but only one, in nearby Princeton, tested positive for anthrax. Besides the deadly spores themselves, the investigators didn't have much to go on. The letters sent to the senators bore the same return address, ostensibly a fourth-grade class at a fictitious school, and the addresses were printed in a way to make it appear that they had been written by schoolchildren.

In the envelopes, investigators found anthrax spores of the Ames strain—the type used in the American biodefense program. This material is carefully controlled, and only a few labs have access to it. Furthermore, the material was a highly refined dry powder. Only someone with a high degree of technical knowledge and access to specialized equipment could have produced it. In theory, this reduced the suspects to military and civilian biodefense workers, such as those at the U.S. Army's Medical Research Institute of Infectious Diseases (USAMRIID), located in Fort Detrick, Maryland. However, a total of more than 400 employees had access to the anthrax stocks.[63]

The contents of the four recovered letters gave investigators little to work with. Each bore the date "09-11-01" and was followed by only 15 to 24 words. The letters addressed to the *New York Post* and NBC newscaster Tom Brokaw were identical:

THIS IS NEXT
TAKE PENACILIN [*sic*] NOW
DEATH TO AMERICA
DEATH TO ISRAEL
ALLAH IS GREAT

Progress in the investigation was hampered by the pursuit of spurious leads, missed opportunities, and a number of copycats sending harmless powder through the mail. In its scope and duration, the investigation would come to resemble the hunt for the Unabomber. The investigation into the anthrax letters, however, would end differently.

Don Foster, the Vassar professor of English, would become involved in the investigation. This was after his successful unmasking of *Primary Colors* author Joe Klein in 1996, described in chapter 3. His attribution of the funeral elegy to Shakespeare had become front-page news in the same year. But his track record was decidedly mixed. And as we saw earlier in this chapter, he would retract his Shakespeare attribution in 2002.

Foster had also injected himself into the JonBenét Ramsey murder investigation and its curious ransom note, described in chapter 5. In June 1997, Foster took it on himself to write to Patsy Ramsey, the slain girl's mother, to tell her that he believed she was innocent. The following year, however, Foster changed his mind and argued for Patsy's guilt instead. He had been tapped by the Boulder, Colorado, district attorney's office to testify against JonBenét's mother, but when his earlier involvement came to light, he was dismissed from the case.[64]

Foster was brought onto the anthrax case by the FBI early on, in mid-October 2001. He was asked to analyze a letter that had been sent, in late September, to the Quantico, Virginia, police force. This was after the initial anthrax letters had been mailed but before they were reported on by the media. The letter's anonymous author expressed concerns about Ayaad Assaad, a researcher with USAMRIID. Foster concluded that it had been written by a female coworker of Assaad's at Fort Detrick. The FBI questioned Assaad early on but cleared him of any involvement.[65]

In October 2003, frustrated by a lack of progress in the anthrax case, Foster published a 9,500-word article in *Vanity Fair*. An abridged version would follow a few months later in *Reader's Digest*. In it, Foster opined that potential leads were not being investigated. And although his métier was stylometric analysis, he speculated about many other aspects of the case, the evidence, and possible suspects. Most significantly, Foster drew circumstantial connections between the anthrax attacks and Steven Hatfill, a hematologist and viral diseases researcher who had been identified as a person of interest in the ongoing investigation.[66]

What is lacking in Foster's piece, however, is any actual forensic linguistics. At one point, he links the expression "Get the hell out of Dodge," which appears in an unpublished novel by Hatfill, with a similar expression employed by Hatfill's associate, Bill Patrick ("Get out of Dodge City"). However, the expression is hardly unique. It is listed in the *Oxford English Dictionary* ("to leave quickly"), and the entry includes citations of the expression dating back to 1965. The Corpus of Historical American English shows that "Get out of Dodge" has appeared in print and on television dozens of times in recent decades. And even if the expression were a distinctive linguistic fingerprint, Foster links it to Patrick, a man who was never suspected of involvement in the anthrax letters, and not to Hatfill.

In August 2004, Hatfill filed suit against Foster, Vassar, Condé Nast (publisher of *Vanity Fair*), and *Reader's Digest*.[67] Claiming defamation of his character, his attorney sought $10 million for damage to his reputation. In the legal brief, the phrase "literary forensics" is repeatedly enclosed in scare quotes, creating the impression that it isn't a valid form of legal evidence. The result of *Hatfill v. Foster* was that Condé Nast settled out of court in February 2007, although the amount of the settlement is not known.[68] And in June 2008, a suit that Hatfill had brought against the U.S. government was settled for $4.6 million.[69]

Federal investigators were also pursuing other suspects. By 2006, the primary suspect had become biodefense researcher Bruce Ivins, who, like Hatfill, had worked at USAMRIID. He had even been enlisted to help with the initial investigation, testing mail sent by several copycats who were dispatching letters laced with harmless powder through the mail. However, he later became a person of interest and was surveilled by the FBI for several years. During this period, his phone was tapped, and he was fired from his consulting job. In November 2007, federal agents searched his residence. By the spring of 2008, Ivins began to exhibit mental instability and was committed to a psychiatric hospital for a time. In July of that year, as investigators prepared to file charges against him, he took his own life.[70]

After Ivins's suicide, many were critical of the government's investigation. Had a guilty man ended his life as his culpability became clear, or was an innocent and mentally fragile man hounded to his breaking point? The week after Ivins's death, the FBI laid out its case against him in a briefing and a release of records. A year and a half later, the Department of Justice (DOJ) released an investigative summary that ran to 200 pages. It contained a great deal of circumstantial evidence implicating Ivins. Most significantly, it was revealed that samples from Ivins's flask of Ames anthrax had a genetic signature, or morphs, that matched the powder used in the anthrax attacks.[71] In addition, the summary described purported similarities between the writings of Ivins and the language found in the anthrax letters.

In the report's section on linguistic affinities, the DOJ argued that the messages in the anthrax letters were similar to phrases used by Ivins in an email he sent to a colleague two weeks after 9/11: "I just heard tonight that the Bin Laden terrorists for sure have anthrax and sarin gas" and "Osama Bin Laden has just decreed death to all Jews and all Americans." And it is true that the letters sent to the *Post* and to Tom Brokaw mention anthrax, America, and Israel.

The DOJ also attached importance to the nine letters in the anthrax messages that had been bolded: in order, they are TTTAATTAT. This sequence, it was argued, spells out TTT AAT TAT, which is a shorthand for the amino acids phenylalanine, asparagine, and tyrosine. Their first letters spell out PAT, the nickname of one of Ivins's colleagues. Or if the single letter designators for the three amino acids are employed, the sequence becomes F, N, and Y. This could be shorthand for "F—— New York," a city that Ivins was said to dislike.

The existence of a hidden message in the letters was buttressed by the claim that Ivins had a fascination with codes and ciphers. Following the search of his home, Ivins threw out an issue of a 1992 journal that described genetic codes in DNA as well as a copy of *Gödel, Escher, Bach*, a 1979 book that, among many other things, deals with hidden messages in mathematics, art, and music. The investigative summary links these behaviors to Ivins's guilty conscience and a desire to dispose of incriminating evidence.[72]

Many who have examined the totality of the evidence against Ivins have concluded that he was the bioterrorist who sent the anthrax-laced letters out into the world. Pulitzer Prize–winning journalist David Willman, in his book on the anthrax attacks and Ivins, comes down on the side of the prosecutors.[73]

However, debate has continued about both the DOJ's investigation and its conclusions. Some reports have questioned the key contention that the strain of anthrax spores recovered from the letters could be definitively traced back to Ivins. A review of the case by the National Research Council in 2011 concluded that the analysis was suggestive but not ironclad.[74] And in 2014, the U.S. Government Accountability Office weighed in with similar concerns about the genetic tests that had been used.[75]

Throughout this book, we have seen many examples in which forensic linguistics and stylometry have helped to solve crimes, identify authors, and settle literary debates. The case of the anthrax letters, however, provides an example in which Don Foster, one of its foremost practitioners, ended up identifying the wrong suspect. As a result, he no longer consults for the FBI.[76] And the interpretation of the linguistic evidence in the DOJ's investigative summary is not a paragon of forensic science. The anthrax attacks, as well as the other cases described in this chapter, make clear some of the limitations of such work—as well as the potential for destroying the reputations of those falsely accused of serious crimes.

CHAPTER EIGHT

GHOST STORIES

A Voice of One's Own?

GIVING UP THE GHOST

Decades after his presidency, Ronald Reagan continues to cast a long shadow over American politics and public policy debates. His desire to limit the role of government in the lives of citizens was a guiding principle and one that animated the policies he put in place. The effects of some of these initiatives, like welfare reform, are still felt today. And many of his conservative notions have become mainstream governing principles within the modern Republican and Libertarian parties.

Reagan was born in Tampico, Illinois, a village with fewer than 1,000 inhabitants. His experiences growing up in small-town Middle America would prove formative. After graduating from college, he became a radio sports announcer in Iowa.[1] A screen test led to a contract with Warner Bros., and he would appear in more than 60 movies over a 20-year film career. He also moved into television roles and served as president of the Screen Actors Guild. The positive reception to a speech he gave in support of Barry Goldwater, the conservative Republican nominee for president in 1964, encouraged Reagan to try his hand at politics.

He was elected as the governor of California in 1966, unseating two-term incumbent Pat Brown. Reelection followed in 1970. When his second term ended in early 1975, he set his sights on the presidency. After being bested for the 1976 Republican nomination by the incumbent, Gerald Ford, he sought ways to remain in the public eye and to challenge Ford's victor, Jimmy Carter, in 1980. One of his strategies involved making use of an old technology as well as his first profession: he got back on the air and started making short radio broadcasts.

Reagan's training as an actor and his well-modulated voice were a natural fit with the medium. He was inspired by a previous president's fireside chats—30 radio addresses made by Franklin Roosevelt during the 12 years of his presidency. Roosevelt used these broadcasts to connect with the public during the dark days of the Great Depression and World War II.[2] As Reagan put it in his autobiography,

> Although the Democrats controlled the [California] legislature, it occurred to me that I had an opportunity to go over their heads. Franklin D. Roosevelt gave me the idea with his Fireside Chats, which made an indelible mark on me during the Depression.[3]

Reagan would deliver more than 1,000 radio commentaries during the late 1970s. These three-minute addresses were broadcast five days a week on about 300 radio stations with a combined audience of 20 to 30 million Americans.

Unlike town halls or press conferences, which require political figures to answer questions on the fly, the remarks in a radio address can be prepared beforehand by either the politician or a ghostwriter—someone they employ to give shape and eloquence to their thoughts. Given the large number of commentaries he recorded, it is reasonable to assume that Reagan had someone in his orbit who wrote them. It is known, for example, that his nationally syndicated newspaper columns, appearing twice a week during the same period, were drafted by others even though Reagan's name was on the byline.[4]

It came as something of a surprise, then, when Kiron Skinner, a political scientist at Carnegie Mellon University, stumbled across the drafts for many of these radio addresses in Reagan's private papers.[5] Altogether, Skinner unearthed drafts of 679 addresses, written in Reagan's distinctive script on pages torn from legal pads.

He would often draft these commentaries while traveling. They would be typed, edited, and then recorded by him in groups of 15—enough for three weeks' worth of weekday broadcasts. The recordings were then transferred to discs and sent out to radio stations. It is known that 1,032 commentaries were broadcast, which means that two-thirds of the radio addresses were unquestionably written by Reagan himself. The most common subjects of these addresses were foreign policy and national defense. He also often spoke about the

U.S. economy, energy, and the environment. And sometimes, he would simply tell an uplifting story.

More than 200 of these radio addresses were edited and published in a 2001 book[6] that became a *New York Times* bestseller. A second collection of more than 300 commentaries was released in 2004. But what about the hundreds of radio addresses for which no written draft existed? Had they also been penned by Reagan?

In 2003, Edoardo Airoldi was a graduate student in statistics at Carnegie Mellon. Kiron Skinner and her colleague Annelise Anderson told him about the Reagan radio addresses and gave him access to the texts. He set out to see if he could determine the author of the addresses for which no handwritten draft could be found in Reagan's papers.[7] It was possible, for example, that Reagan had written all of them but that the originals for this set had been lost. However, the fact that the drafts couldn't be found in his papers might imply that someone else in Reagan's circle had ghostwritten them.

Of the 353 radio addresses for which no draft exists, the researchers found archival evidence that 39 were written by members of Reagan's staff. John McClaughry, a policy adviser, was found to have authored 26 of them. Peter Hannaford, who served as Reagan's director of issues and research, contributed 12. And one was drafted by Martin Anderson, an economist and policy adviser. That leaves 314 commentaries unattributed. Could the authorship of the rest be determined?

The most obvious candidate for Reagan's ghosting was Peter Hannaford, the aide who wrote the first drafts of most of Reagan's newspaper columns.[8] In a 2003 interview for the Ronald Reagan Oral History Project, Hannaford was asked about his involvement with the radio broadcasts. Hannaford claimed to have drafted as many of the addresses as Reagan did early on. He also believed that a few had been written by Lynn Nofzinger, who served as Reagan's press secretary while he was governor. Hannaford also mentioned John McClaughry and Chuck Hobbes as contributors and said that there may have been a couple of others. He asserted that Reagan wrote almost all the later commentaries himself from the period after the August 1976 Republican National Convention until the end of the series in November 1979.[9] Given this evidence, it was decided to focus on attributing the anonymous broadcasts to either Reagan or Hannaford.

The researchers created a corpus consisting of the 679 commentaries known to have been written by Reagan, the 39 addresses drafted by his aides, and 30 newspaper columns written for Reagan by Hannaford. It was initially hoped that one man or the other had some distinctive linguistic tells, such as a predilection for certain abbreviations or idiosyncrasies in his spelling, such as writing "theatre" for "theater." An examination of Reagan's handwritten commentaries, however, revealed that the man was inconsistent in his spelling, shortenings, and punctuation. They also found that changes were made during the typing and editing processes. As a result, these sorts of shortcuts couldn't be used to determine who had written the unattributed commentaries.

At the word and phrase level, the researchers did find some differences between Reagan's characteristic way of expressing himself and the language used by his aides. In general, Reagan's style was more colloquial. Whereas his assistants might use words like "continuous," Reagan showed a preference for "over and over." And he rarely mentioned his opponent, Jimmy Carter, by name. Instead, he would make indirect reference to "the government" or to "Washington politicians."[10]

The researchers made use of a Bayesian model to address the authorship question. This was the method pioneered by Mosteller and Wallace in their landmark study of the *Federalist*, described in chapter 2. As in that earlier study, the researchers refined their probability estimates by examining the most frequently occurring function words in their corpus. Unlike the *Federalist* researchers, however, they were able to compare a much larger set of terms: 267 versus the 30 that Mosteller and Wallace had employed. They used these to compute the odds that Reagan or Hannaford had written each of the unsigned commentaries.

The researchers concluded that, in 1975, Reagan wrote 77 of the commentaries, while others drafted 71 of them. This matches Hannaford's recollection almost perfectly. For the period 1976–1979, they determined that Reagan drafted 90 of the addresses, while Hannaford was responsible for 74 of them— more than his aide remembered composing. In sum, the most probable author for more than half of the anonymous commentaries was Reagan himself.[11] This also means that Reagan was the author of more than 80 percent of the more than 1,000 addresses that he recorded during the late 1970s.

This finding is important because it helps deflate the stereotype of Reagan being incapable of writing his own prepared remarks. Reagan's opponents were fond of underestimating him. Clark Clifford, the Democratic political adviser, famously referred to him as an "amiable dunce,"[12] and many believed he was an empty suit, an actor reading the words put before him. Once he became president, he may have relied more on others to write his various speeches, but the radio addresses make clear that he could—and did—write most of his own material during his candidacy.

As president, Reagan again relied on radio broadcasts to get his message out: he made more than 300 weekly addresses while in office. These five-minute Saturday broadcasts effectively served as the social media of his day.[13] After a lapse under George H. W. Bush, Bill Clinton would follow in Reagan's footsteps and make more than 400 weekly addresses during his tenure in office.[14]

The practice has continued, although it has changed with the times. George W. Bush's administration began producing podcasts, and Barack Obama made video addresses. Donald Trump abandoned the practice after about a year and a half, but Joe Biden has revived it, holding "weekly conversations" during his presidency.[15] All of them, however, are following in the footsteps of the president known as the Great Communicator.

FRENCH TWIST

Thomas Paine is the paradoxical figure among the founders of the United States. He has become known as the father of the American Revolution for writing the new country's all-time bestseller to promote the cause of independence from Great Britain. And as a major supporter of the French Revolution, he wrote another wildly successful work to champion that cause. Despite these triumphs, he was almost executed in France, and his unpopular opinions caused him to be ostracized when he returned to America, where he would die virtually friendless.

Paine was born in England in 1737. A series of economic setbacks and personal misfortunes led to his emigration to Philadelphia in 1774.[16] In the following year, he became the editor of the *Pennsylvania Magazine*, the first successful publication of its kind in the colonies. And in January 1776, half a year before the Declaration of Independence, he published the pamphlet *Common Sense*, making a forceful case for throwing off the yoke of British colonial rule. Enormously successful, the 77-page tract sold half a million copies at a time when only 2 million people lived in the American colonies. *Common Sense* was often read aloud at public gatherings and served as a recruiting tool for the Continental Army. John Adams would write that "without the pen of the author of *Common Sense*, the sword of Washington would have been raised in vain."[17]

During the war, Paine wrote a series of 16 pamphlets titled *The American Crisis*. The first of these appeared in December 1776 at a time when the fledgling revolution was in serious danger of collapse. Its first line is renowned:

These are the times that try men's souls: The summer soldier and the sunshine patriot will, in this crisis, shrink from the service of his country; but he that stands by it NOW, deserves the love and thanks of man and woman.[18]

Following successful efforts to secure French funding during the Revolution, Paine left the United States for England in 1787. And when revolution broke out in France, he became its advocate. His contribution to the cause was *Rights of Man*, published in 1791. It was a refutation of Edmund Burke's *Reflections on the Revolution in France*, the conservative statesman's tract opposing anti-royalist developments on the continent.[19] No mere pamphlet, *Rights of Man* is a 90,000-word book that was highly successful in England, where it sold almost a million copies. A translation would become extremely popular in France, and Napoleon claimed to sleep with a copy under his pillow. A second part, in which Paine called for representative government and progressive taxation, was published the following year. The backlash from the British was so fierce that Paine was charged with seditious libel. As a result, he decamped for the continent in 1792.

In France, Paine ran afoul of the more radical factions of the Revolution, Robespierre in particular. He was arrested, thrown in prison, and scheduled to be executed. He avoided that fate through sheer luck. After nearly a year of imprisonment, Paine was released through the intercession of James Monroe. Alarmed by Napoleon's drift toward dictatorship, Paine returned to the United States in 1802. He published a letter in which he was highly critical of Washington, accusing him, among other things, of being a poor military commander. He ran afoul of religious leaders with his *Age of Reason*, a deist tract in which he railed against organized religion and the legitimacy of the Bible. Simply put, his stances were not popular. When Paine died in New York City in 1809, only six mourners attended his funeral.[20]

Scholars studying Paine's oeuvre have had to grapple with the fact that his tracts were often published anonymously. *Common Sense* was released without attribution, and its title became his pseudonym: the *American Crisis* pamphlets were signed "Common Sense." As a result, there may be anonymous pieces attributed to him in error as well as genuine works of his that have not yet been identified as such.[21]

The task of literary sleuths has been made easier by the distinctive way Paine expressed himself. When compared to other prerevolutionary pamphleteers, his approach has been characterized as "stylistically unique."[22] Specifically, unlike the other writers of his day, Paine employed short sentences and used few long words. In contrast with the turgid and ornate prose common in the eighteenth century, Paine's language was energetic, vigorous, and forceful.

In 2015, the British historian Jonathan Clark called into question the authorship of a 6,000-word passage in the middle of *Rights of Man*. The section concerns historical matters and differs in tone from the rest of the work. Instead of Paine's usual direct style, the narration largely shifts to the third person. Clark proposed that this part of the book had been written by Gilbert du Motier, better known as Marquis de Lafayette. He was the French aristocrat who famously served in the American Revolutionary War and who also happened to be a good friend of Paine's. Paine stayed with Lafayette after publishing the second part of *Rights* and also dedicated that work to him.

Clark believed that Lafayette was the real author because he is the clear hero of that section of *Rights*. Throughout it, Lafayette's role in events, both in America and in France, is consistently overstated. It may be that Lafayette took the opportunity Paine provided him to burnish his reputation. And there are additional clues as well; for example, in other parts of *Rights*, Paine explicitly acknowledges his friend's contributions. Finally, Clark points to a letter written to George Washington in 1790 in which Lafayette tells him that "you will See a part of My Adventures" in a book that Paine was writing.[23]

In a paper published in 2018, Richard Forsyth and David Holmes performed a stylometric analysis to see whether Clark's claim could be verified. They included in their study 29 texts of Thomas Paine, totaling more than 160,000 words. A second set consisted of letters and memoirs that Lafayette had written in English: these were 19 texts comprising 45,000 words. For control texts, the researchers chose selections from other founding fathers, including Ben Franklin, Alexander Hamilton, John Jay, Thomas Jefferson, and James Madison. These 45 texts amounted to nearly 130,000 words.

For their study, Forsyth and Holmes identified the 100 most frequent function words that appeared in a majority of the texts in their corpus. They also eliminated pronouns to reduce genre differences since letters and memoirs typically contain many first-person references.

Forsyth and Holmes's first goal was to see if they could differentiate between texts written by Hamilton, Jefferson, Madison, and Paine. A plot based on the first two principal components clearly showed differentiation among the four men. They found some overlap between Madison and Hamilton—a similarity that also bedeviled Mosteller and Wallace in their attribution study of the *Federalist*—but otherwise, there was a fairly high degree of separation between the four, with Paine showing a distinctive voice compared to the others.

A second analysis was performed using the texts written by Hamilton, Jefferson, Madison, and Lafayette. They found good separation between Lafayette and the others, but some of this may have been driven by genre since Lafayette's texts were autobiographical. Of some concern, however, was the fact that the three founding fathers were not well separated from one another.

The next step was to compare texts written by Lafayette and Paine as well as the undisputed and disputed sections of *Rights of Man*. Except for a letter that Paine wrote to Franklin, which drifts toward the Lafayette cluster, the two men were cleanly separated in a plot based on the first two principal components of their analysis. In addition, the undisputed section of *Rights* fell well within the cluster of texts by Paine. By contrast, the disputed section, which the researchers broke into two equal-sized texts, ended up plotted in a no-man's-land between the two men. A hierarchical cluster analysis assigned the undisputed section of *Rights* to Paine, whereas the two disputed texts behaved quite differently, clustering with texts written by both Lafayette and Paine. The researchers concluded that there is something peculiar going on in the middle section of *Rights* and that their data support Clark's contention that Lafayette was the author of the disputed section.

A follow-up study in which the researchers analyzed the text of *Rights* in overlapping 1,000-word segments once again found strong evidence for Lafayette's hand in the disputed 6,000-word passage. However, they also discovered two additional, shorter sections that are a better match with Lafayette's writing style than Paine's. The three passages share a particular characteristic: all describe important historical events. Given that Lafayette had firsthand knowledge of these episodes, it is easy to imagine Paine farming out the drafting of these portions to his friend. In the case of the two shorter passages, Paine seems to have used only parts of Lafayette's contributions or else to have heavily edited them. On the other hand, the longer section identified as suspicious by Clark seems to have been incorporated almost verbatim.[24]

Does it truly matter whether Lafayette wrote the historical sections of Paine's book? Given how widely *Rights* was read, both in English and in French, Clark suggests that Lafayette's exaggerations about his role in the American and French revolutions have been pernicious. His reputation, particularly in the United States, is about as high as that of any revolutionary figure with the exception of Washington himself. His sobriquet as "The Hero of Two Worlds" reflects this view.[25] Lafayette's contributions to both revolutions were significant—that is not in dispute—but Paine's book provided his friend with a forum to present himself in the best possible light. History may be written by the victors, but an even better trick may be to insert a flattering portrait of oneself into that history anonymously.

Other founding fathers have had their likenesses carved into stone on Mount Rushmore or printed on the nation's currency. Their homes have become major tourist attractions and their grave sites places of honor. Paine's fate has been different. Denied a burial in consecrated ground, he was interred at his farm in New Rochelle, New York.[26] His bones were dug up a decade after his death and then lost. His Greenwich Village home was demolished in 1930.[27] The remaining cottage in New Rochelle is visited primarily by local schoolchildren on field trips. A marble column was erected in Paine's honor, 30 years after his death, but it was repeatedly vandalized. The monument was eventually moved due to a street-widening project. The man whose voice animated both the American and the French revolutions would seem to deserve better.

TALL TALES FROM THE FRONTIER

With regard to certain historical figures, it is almost impossible to separate their actual lives from the legends that have grown up around their accomplishments. Such is the case with Davy Crockett, immortalized in film, television, and song as "King of the Wild Frontier." Almost every aspect of his life, from his childhood to his death at the Alamo, is encrusted in hyperbole and myth—a state of affairs that he actively promoted in his own biographical accounts.

Some details of his life are not in dispute. Although it is unlikely that he "killed him a b'ar when he was only three," as mentioned in the television theme song,[28] he was, for a fact, born in 1786 and grew up in rural eastern Tennessee, the sixth of nine children. From a young age, Crockett worked as a cattle driver, teamster, and farmer. He also apprenticed with a hatter for four years. He would try his hand at many ventures but was most successful as a bear hunter. Crockett would marry and have three children, although his wife died in her late twenties. He quickly remarried and fathered three more children. He served without distinction in the Creek War and the War of 1812.

After a stint as a justice of the peace, Crockett was elected to the Tennessee General Assembly, where he championed the cause of impoverished farmers. Elected to the U.S. House of Representatives, he broke with President Jackson over the latter's Indian Removal Act. After the failure of his reelection bid in 1834, he traveled to Texas and signed on as a volunteer in the revolt against Mexico. He famously helped to defend the Alamo Mission at San Antonio during its 13-day siege by Mexican troops. It is unclear whether he died fighting or surrendered and was executed: debate about his exact fate has continued for decades.[29] At the time of his death in March 1836, he was 49 years old and had been in Texas for two months.

The mythology surrounding Crockett began during his lifetime, with James Paulding's highly successful play *The Lion of the West*. First performed in 1831, its main character, Colonel Nimrod Wildfire, was thought by many to be a larger-than-life version of the frontiersman turned politician.[30] And a series of Crockett almanacs, published annually between 1835 and 1856, were full of stories about him. Some of these were true, some were embroidered, and others—such as superhuman feats of strength or skill—were manufactured out of whole cloth. These hyperbolic stories played an important role in turning Crockett into an American folk hero.[31]

Although Crockett benefited from his fame during the last five years of his life, he also found it to be a double-edged sword as others tried to profit from his popularity. In 1833, he was the subject of an unflattering—and unauthorized— biography,[32] and this motivated Crockett to set down an account of his own.[33] It was published the following year, his last in the House of Representatives. Although Crockett's extant letters suggest he was only marginally literate, the book's title page proclaimed that the story of his life was "written by himself."[34] Despite this assertion, the Crockett biographer James Shackford has discovered evidence that the work was ghosted by Kentucky congressman Thomas Chilton.[35]

Because of Crockett's opposition to Jackson, many Whigs began to view him as a potential presidential candidate for their party. To increase his appeal with northern industrialists, Crockett was invited to tour some of the textile factories of New England. This served as the raw material for a second book, in which he lauded the working conditions of the women who toiled in the mills.[36] It was cobbled together from newspaper articles, speeches, and notes by his friend William Clark, a congressman from Pennsylvania.[37]

A third book, ostensibly written by Crockett, was a satirical biography of one of his enemies, Martin Van Buren, and is widely believed to have been ghostwritten for him by Augustin Clayton, a congressman from Georgia.[38] This attribution is reinforced by the fact that it contains "a discussion of the finer points of Georgia politics."[39] It seems unlikely that Crockett would have been familiar with such details.

Finally, an account of Crockett's time in Texas, ostensibly taken from a journal recovered after his death, was enormously popular in both the United States and Great Britain.[40] The book describes the frontiersman's "many hairbreadth escapes" and played a major role in establishing the mythology of both Crockett and the Alamo. Nearly 50 years later, it was revealed to be a literary hoax, having been quickly produced by the playwright Richard Penn Smith to take advantage of the public's renewed interest in Crockett after his untimely demise.[41] Its first section, however, does contain some material written by Crockett, such as letters he wrote to his publisher.

In an attempt to resolve the claims about Crockett's authorship, David and Dena Salsburg performed the first stylometric analysis of his writings in 1999. They chose to examine the autobiography written with the help of Chilton (hereafter the *Narrative*), the account describing the New England factories ghosted by Clark (*Tour*), and the text purportedly taken from his final journal (*Texas*). Crockett had written little else during his lifetime, and the researchers decided that his extant letters were too few and too short to be of much help. *Texas* contains many pages written in dialect, and the researchers chose to exclude those. They also included the speeches that Crockett made while a member of Congress.

Following the example of Mosteller and Wallace's analysis of the *Federalist*, the Salsburgs searched for common function words that appeared in all three books and the set of speeches, and they identified nine of these. To equate the lengths of the texts, only the first few chapters of the *Narrative* were included. The speeches are problematic because they were recorded mostly in the third person. As a result, the researchers selected only the first-person sections. These passages total only about 2,000 words.

An analysis of the function words in the three books strongly suggests that they were not written by the same person. In addition, it was clear that the author of the *Narrative* was not the same person as the author of *Texas*. The speeches also differ significantly from *Texas*. The Salsburgs also compared *Texas* to two other contemporaneous authors, James Fenimore Cooper and Nathaniel Hawthorne, and found that they were poor matches. Their conclusion was that the same person probably wrote both the *Narrative* and the *Tour*, and that person was most likely Crockett.[42]

Twenty years later, a more comprehensive stylometric analysis was published by David Holmes and Ferris Samara. Their analysis included the four books attributed to Crockett as well as the unauthorized biography. The researchers also included works written by two of Crockett's suspected ghosts: Augustin Clayton (the Van Buren satire) and Richard Penn Smith (*Texas*). Apparently, the researchers were unable to identify anything else written by Thomas Chilton, the suspected ghost for Crockett's *Narrative*, or William Clark, who is thought to have written the *Tour*. They chose not to include Crockett's congressional speeches because they were recorded in paraphrase, which would have expunged the unique characteristics of Crockett's voice.

As controls, Holmes and Samara included works written by three of Crockett's contemporaries: James Fenimore Cooper (*Pioneers, Last of the Mohicans*, and *The Deerslayer*), Nathaniel Hawthorne (*Twice-Told Stories, The Scarlet Letter*, and *The House of Seven Gables*), and Herman Melville (*Moby Dick, The Piazza Tales*, and *Confidence-Man*). The researchers included 4,000-word sections from the beginning, middle, and end of each selected work. The 70 most frequently employed function words were identified and included in multivariate analyses to determine the overall similarity of the authors.

Holmes and Samara created a bootstrap consensus tree with the texts from each of the three control authors. As expected, they found that the works of Cooper, Hawthorne, and Melville separated cleanly into the three major branches of the tree. In addition, the sections from each author's individual books tended to cluster together. The two sections from Melville's *Confidence-Man*, for example, form a separate twig on Melville's tree, as do two of the three sections of *Moby Dick*. The analysis verified the sensitivity of this approach for sorting out Crockett and his ghostwriters.

A cluster analysis that included Crockett's disputed works confirmed the external evidence gathered by the historians: Augustin Clayton was identified as the likeliest author of the Van Buren satire, and Richard Penn Smith wrote the middle section of *Texas*. The first section of *Texas*, which contains letters written by Crockett, clustered with *Tour*.[43]

These findings suggest that Crockett played a greater role in the writing of *Tour* than historians had previously believed. Such a conclusion, however, must be treated with caution because *Tour* is a mélange of diverse material, including speeches that Crockett gave while on his circuit of factory visits. Crockett's ghost, William Clark, may have relied extensively on these addresses, as well as notes provided by Crockett. *Tour* is believed to have been composed in haste, as Crockett was in need of money, and Clark was ill at the time of its completion.[44] Given these circumstances, *Tour* may consist more of undigested source material from Crockett than of prose carefully shaped by his ghost.

Crockett-mania would return periodically during the twentieth century, fueled in part by the tall tales repeated during the nineteenth. Renewed interest was initially driven by the Disney television series of the mid-1950s that starred Fess Parker wearing a coonskin cap. His sartorial choice became a fashion craze: at its height, 5,000 coonskin caps were being bought by children every day.[45]

In 1960, John Wayne produced a film about the defense of the Alamo and assigned himself the starring role of Crockett. Influenced by the fictional account in *Texas*, the movie was panned by historians for its many inaccuracies, including Crockett's appearance and the way that he met his end: in the film version, he dies after causing a powder magazine to explode. Disney would release a more historically accurate version in 2004, with Billy Bob Thornton portraying Crockett, but it received mixed reviews and performed poorly at the box office. In the twenty-first century, the superhuman version of Crockett may be the only one that audiences find authentic.

GHOSTS IN THE MACHINE

Can writing a successful book help someone get elected as a U.S. president? It can—and it has. John F. Kennedy was many things: a handsome playboy, the scion of a wealthy family, a war hero, and ultimately the nation's chief executive. And while he was a senator, he published a best-selling, award-winning book that greatly elevated his standing within the Democratic Party. That work, titled *Profiles in Courage: Decisive Moments in the Lives of Celebrated Americans*, provided the charismatic young politician with the intellectual gravitas he craved.[46] It would also nearly derail his political career and ultimately complicate his legacy.

The project began in 1954 as an idea for a magazine article, but it would morph into a nearly 300-page book. It tells the stories of eight U.S. senators who defied their colleagues and constituents to take principled but unpopular stands. In some cases, these positions engendered intense criticism and blunted the politicians' political aspirations. Senator Robert Taft, for example, opposed the prosecution of Nazi war criminals at Nuremberg, characterizing the trials as victor's justice.[47] Taft's position was out of step with popular sentiment and probably cost him the 1948 Republican presidential nomination.

Profiles in Courage was not Kennedy's first book. He had published *Why England Slept* in 1940.[48] The title was an homage to Churchill's *While England Slept,* and its contents dealt with the British policy of appeasement in the years leading up to World War II. Written as his senior thesis at Harvard in 1938, it was redrafted by the Pulitzer Prize–winning journalist Arthur Krock at the behest of Kennedy's father. Another family friend, the magazine magnate Henry Luce, was pressed into service to write the book's foreword. Its release in August 1940, immediately after the fall of France to the Nazis, made it seem prescient and provided the young Kennedy with his first taste of notoriety and literary success. In 1953, he would tell the writer Margaret Coit that he "would rather win a Pulitzer Prize than be president of the United States."[49]

Soon after his election to the Senate in 1952, Kennedy hired Ted Sorensen, a lawyer from Nebraska, to help him draft legislation. Sorensen quickly became one of his chief assistants. Among other duties, Kennedy directed him to churn out a steady stream of articles, published under the senator's name, that appeared in the leading magazines of the day. The purpose of these pieces was to burnish the young senator's reputation and to raise his visibility. Although Sorensen, as the ghost in his boss's political machine, didn't get bylines, he had an arrangement with Kennedy to receive at least 50 percent of any royalties. He was excited by the *Profiles* project and dove headfirst into it.

How much of the actual writing did Kennedy contribute to the book? Only a little, it would seem. During the first half of 1955, when most of the drafting and editing was done, Kennedy wasn't even in Washington—he was in Palm Beach, Florida, flat on his back and recovering from surgery. After that, he was in Europe vacationing with Jackie. Sorensen, in contrast, was putting in 12-hour days as he labored over the manuscript and worked with the publisher.

The historian Jules Davids, a Georgetown professor of diplomatic history, also played an important role in the crafting of *Profiles.* He was one of Jackie Kennedy's teachers, and she told her husband about him.[50] Kennedy approached Davids to ask for his assistance, and he ended up contributing drafts for the chapters on Sam Houston, Lucius Lamar, and George Norris. Davids was paid $700 for his efforts—an amount that, given the success of the book, he later characterized as "pitifully small."[51]

Arthur Schlesinger, the well-known historian, provided extensive feedback, as did Arthur Holcomb and Walter Johnson. Evan Thomas, Kennedy's editor at Harper & Brothers, was responsible for the final title (at various times, it was called *These Great Men* and *Call the Roll*). It seemingly took a village to raise Kennedy's brainchild.

Kennedy lobbied his publisher to release the book before the end of 1955 to make it eligible for a Pulitzer Prize the following year but was unsuccessful. *Profiles* appeared during the first week of 1956 and received good reviews. And almost immediately, Kennedy's father began the campaign for the book to receive major recognition. Arthur Krock, who had reshaped Kennedy's college thesis, was enlisted to work behind the scenes to lobby the Pulitzer Committee. *Profiles* didn't even make it into the group of finalists, but some last-minute politicking led to it being selected as the winner of the Pulitzer Prize for Biography in May 1956. It appeared on the *New York Times* bestseller list for 95 weeks during 1956 and 1957.

Through intermediaries, Kennedy's father reached out to Sorensen in May 1957 and essentially offered to buy his silence about his role in writing *Profiles*. The elder Kennedy realized that the truth about the book would torpedo his son's political career, and he made the problem go away by offering Sorensen a structured settlement to be paid out over several years. The deal was thought to have been for at least $100,000 and would be worth 10 times that amount today.[52]

Despite the arrangement with Sorensen, there was speculation inside the Beltway that Kennedy had played only a minimal role in writing *Profiles*. These doubts were made public in December 1957, when the journalist Drew Pearson appeared on Mike Wallace's popular television interview program. When asked about *Profiles*, Pearson identified Sorensen as its author. Afterward, the Kennedy family threatened to sue ABC—Wallace's network—and the company issued a rare retraction and an apology.[53]

In December 1960, when President-elect Kennedy was assembling his cabinet, he met with Robert McNamara, who would become his secretary of defense. The first question that McNamara asked him was whether he had written *Profiles*. Kennedy assured him that he had—a response full of irony given that the subject of *Profiles* is doing the right thing, even though it might mean putting one's political future at risk.[54]

Curiosity about *Profiles* continued after the young president's death. During the 1970s, historian Herbert Parmet of the City University of New York conducted extensive research in the Kennedy archives and found evidence confirming that JFK's role in *Profiles* had been minimal.[55] For whatever reason, this conclusion did not receive much attention when it appeared in his 1980 book about Kennedy.

In 2001, Ted Sorensen suffered a stroke that made it difficult for him to read, but with assistance, he managed to compile his memoirs, and these were published in 2008.[56] Sorensen wrote that he drafted most of the chapters in *Profiles* and that he "helped choose the words in many of its sentences."[57] That statement may be as artful as any that he wrote for his employer. He passed away in 2010.

Between Parmet's research and Sorensen's mealymouthed confession, it appears that the case is closed. It would be interesting, however, to see what a stylometric analysis of writings by Kennedy, Sorensen, and Davids would reveal, particularly for the first and last chapters of *Profiles*, as Sorensen claimed that Kennedy had "worked long and hard" on these.[58]

It is instructive to contrast Kennedy's book with another tome that materially assisted a future president. In 1987, Random House released *Trump: The Art of the Deal*.[59] The book was entirely ghostwritten, but its real author, Tony Schwartz, did receive explicit acknowledgment: the author credit on the cover is "Donald J. Trump with Tony Schwartz." When it was published, Trump was a 41-year-old New York City real estate developer—a prominent man in his field but largely unknown outside of it. *Deal* became a runaway hit: it spent 48 weeks on the *New York Times* bestseller list and sold more than a million copies.[60] The book created an entire mythology for Trump as the savvy entrepreneur who takes big risks and reaps the rewards.[61]

As with *Profiles* and Kennedy, Schwartz's book wasn't solely responsible for Trump's ascent to the White House. But its success marked the beginning of his transformation. Trump would become a national figure through numerous venues. His involvement with professional wrestling, appearances on the *Howard Stern Show*, service as host of *The Apprentice*, and enthusiastic embrace of social media all played a part. But in hindsight, all of it seems to trace back to his ghostwritten book about deal making.

Deal was the brainchild of the media magnate Si Newhouse. When he observed that sales of *GQ* had been goosed by a cover story about Trump, Newhouse contacted the developer to see if he was interested in writing a book and offered him an advance of half a million dollars.

At the time, Schwartz was a journalist who had written an unflattering piece about Trump in 1985. Much to his surprise, Trump loved it because the article portrayed him as tough and uncompromising. When Schwartz approached him again, this time for a *Playboy* interview, Trump had recently signed the contract with Newhouse for a book. During their conversation, he suddenly asked Schwartz to write his autobiography. Schwartz countered with a suggestion that the book focus on his deal making instead, and Trump was agreeable. Schwartz was conflicted but signed on to the project when Trump offered him 50 percent of the royalties—the same deal that Kennedy had made with Sorensen. This included half of the advance, which suggests that Schwartz was a fair deal maker himself.

Schwartz came to regret agreeing to the project. Trump's short attention span and almost reflexive mendacity made interviewing his subject close to impossible. Instead, Schwartz spent a year and a half following Trump around, observing him and listening in on his phone calls. The final product was more fiction than fact.[62] After the success of *Deal*, Trump asked Schwartz if he wanted to write a sequel, but this time, he offered him only one-third of the royalties, and Schwartz declined.

On June 16, 2015, Trump announced his candidacy for president. He made a number of claims in his speech that day, but one of them caught Schwartz's attention:

> Now, our country needs—our country needs a truly great leader, and we need a truly great leader now. We need a leader that wrote *The Art of the Deal*.[63]

Hearing this, Schwartz tweeted thanks to Trump for suggesting that he throw his hat into the political ring. Trump, for his part, now claimed that he had authored the book himself.[64] And when Schwartz criticized Trump's candidacy, he was threatened with a lawsuit.[65]

Sorensen and Schwartz present an interesting contrast. One saw his contributions go unacknowledged, but he nevertheless remained loyal—and silent—until the end of his life. The other was acknowledged but became an outspoken critic. Together, they illustrate the dangers of serving as ghosts in the political machine.

Epilogue

As the cases described in this book make clear, the practitioners of stylometry have had many notable successes—as well as a few glaring failures—in identifying the authors of anonymous and disputed works, unmasking ghost writers, and identifying criminal suspects. And the field continues to evolve as more powerful computational techniques are developed and pressed into service. Even Burrows's Delta, described in chapter 2 as the gold standard for multivariate attribution studies, is giving way to more powerful methods based on machine learning. These artificial intelligence methods are already in wide use and were employed in several of the cases appearing in this book. These include the studies of Edgar Allan Poe, Thomas Pynchon, and *Double Falsehood* in chapter 3 as well as the identity of the pseudonymous Elena Ferrante in chapter 7.

At its heart, author attribution is a classification problem, and machine learning systems excel at this task since they can make use of thousands of features in their search for similarities and differences.[1] A major drawback of machine learning, at least for humans, is that it is a black-box technique. In other words, an artificial intelligence system may intuit that a particular author wrote a given text, but it can't explain how it arrived at this deduction. The information that such systems encode and then exploit can be found only in the connection weights assigned to the so-called hidden units of a neural network as opposed to explicit strategies that can be articulated and explained to the program's creators.

But the black-box problem isn't unique to stylometry: it is found in many other domains as well. Consider modern chess programs, which use machine learning to figure out their own strategies for playing the game. Instead of being taught how humans play chess, these neural networks learn on their own as they play millions of games against themselves, altering connection weights after losses and strengthening them when they win.[2] As is well known, these programs have learned to push wood better than even the strongest human players, but the strategies they have acquired can't be distilled into a form that people can understand.[3]

And there are new challenges for the practitioners of stylometry as well. Researchers are already at work identifying the authors of messages on social media and microblog sites.[4] Initially, Twitter restricted its users to tweets of 140 characters or fewer, which is about 20 to 40 words. Messages as short as these make author attribution extremely difficult. It is comparable to the challenges faced by law enforcement when trying to determine the authorship of text messages, as we saw in chapter 5. The researchers' task was made considerably easier in late 2017, when Twitter doubled the maximum length of messages, from 140 to 280 characters.

As we saw in chapter 8, politicians have long used ghost writers, and they often make use of them in their online communications as well. Before he lost his Twitter privileges, Donald Trump delighted in posting on the platform and became well known for his loose approach to capitalization, spelling, punctuation, and logic. It is believed that Trump's staff, when using his account to send out messages during his presidency, did their best to mimic this idiosyncratic style. However, the ghosted tweets can be identified by comparing them to those that he composed before he became a political candidate. This attribution process, however, became more difficult over time as Trump's underlings got better at mimicking their boss.[5]

Efforts are also under way to discover effective methods of author anonymization or obfuscation.[6] At a time when privacy has become a precious commodity, how can one craft a message that will successfully conceal its author? Although such technologies can be misused, dissidents in countries with repressive regimes would find them useful and even lifesaving. However, it is easy to imagine a stylometric arms race in which increasingly sophisticated efforts at obfuscation are matched by equally effective methods for detection.[7]

Clearly, stylometry raises serious privacy concerns, and we have seen these issues play out in several of the cases described in this book. Must an author who chooses to employ a pen name live in fear of being outed by nosy researchers using neural networks? As in many other fields, the methods employed have received more attention than the underlying ethics of using them. Perhaps somewhat belatedly, researchers are beginning to discuss these issues in a serious way.[8] At the end of the day, stylometry is simply a tool, and, as with any other tool, it can be used for good or ill. A certain degree of humility will be required to make wise decisions about wielding it.

Notes

PROLOGUE

1. David D. Kirkpatrick, "Who Is behind QAnon? Linguistic Detectives Find Fingerprints," *New York Times*, February 19, 2022.

2. Leah McGrath Goodman, "The Face behind Bitcoin," *Newsweek*, March 6, 2014.

3. Matthew Herper, "Linguistic Analysis Says Newsweek Named the Wrong Man as Bitcoin's Creator," *Forbes*, March 10, 2014.

4. Wincenty Lutosławski, *The Origin and Growth of Plato's Logic, With an Account of Plato's Style and of the Chronology of His Writings* (London: Longman, Green and Co., 1897).

5. Leonard Brandwood, *The Chronology of Plato's Dialogues* (Cambridge: Cambridge University Press, 1990).

CHAPTER ONE

1. Sargur N. Srihari, Harish Srinivasan, and Gang Fang, "Discriminability of Fingerprints of Twins," *Journal of Forensic Identification* 58, no. 1 (2008): 109–27.

2. John Olsson, *Forensic Linguistics: An Introduction to Language, Crime, and the Law* (London: Continuum, 2004).

3. John Olsson, *Wordcrime: Solving Crime through Forensic Linguistics* (London: Continuum, 2009).

4. Maria Konnikova, "When Authors Disown Their Work, Should Readers Care?," *The Atlantic*, August 28, 2012.

5. Malcom Coulthard, "Explorations in Applied Linguistics 3: Forensic Stylistics," in *Principle and Practice in Applied Linguistics: Studies in Honour of H. G. Widdowson*, ed. Guy Cook and Barbara Seidlhofer (Oxford: Oxford University Press, 1995), 229–43.

6. Matthew J. X. Malady, "Fingerprint Words: The Verbal Tics That Make Up Who We Are—and How They Spread to Others," *Slate*, September 11, 2014, https://slate.com/human-interest/2014/09/fingerprint-words-verbal-tics-that-define-us-and-how-they-spread-to-others.html.

7. Erik C. Cook, Jessica L. Schleider, and Leah H. Somerville, "A Linguistic Signature of Psychological Distancing in Emotion Regulation," *Journal of Experimental Psychology: General* 46, no. 3 (2017): 337–46.

8. Bernard Bloch, "A Set of Postulates for Phonemic Analysis," *Language* 24, no. 1 (1948): 7.

9. Malcom Coulthard, "Author Identification, Idiolect, and Linguistic Uniqueness," *Applied Linguistics* 25, no. 4 (2004): 431–47.

10. Eugene Kinkead and Russell Maloney, "Dr. Smith," *The New Yorker*, November 30, 1940, 12.

11. *Time*, "Radio: Where Are You From?," May 6, 1940.

12. George Bernard Shaw, *Pygmalion* (New York: Dover, 1994).

13. Charlotte A. Farley-Winer, "Henry Lee Smith Jr. (1913–1972): A *Nachruf* Twenty Years After." *Historiographia Linguistica* 19, no. 1 (1992): 187–98.

14. Josh Katz and Wilson Andrews, "How Y'all, Youse and You Guys Talk." *New York Times*, December 21, 2013.

15. Josh Katz, *Speaking American: How Y'all, Youse, and You Guys Talk: A Visual Guide* (New York: Houghton Mifflin Harcourt, 2016).

16. Ewa Jacewicz and Robert A. Fox, "Acoustics of Regionally Accented Speech," *Acoustics Today* 12, no. 2 (2016): 31–38.

17. Charles Harrington Elster, *The Big Book of Beastly Mispronunciations: The Complete Guide for the Careful Speaker* (Boston: Houghton Mifflin, 2005).

18. Bert Vaux and Scott Golder, "How Do You Pronounce Mary/Merry/Marry?," *The Harvard Dialect Survey* (Cambridge, MA: Harvard University Linguistics Department, 2003).

19. Oliver Gramling, *Free Men Are Fighting: The Story of World War II* (New York: Farrar and Rinehart, 1942), 315.

20. Hans Kurath, Bernard Bloch, Marcus Lee Hansen, and Julia Bloch, *Linguistic Atlas of New England: Handbook of the Linguistic Geography of New England* (Providence, RI: Brown University Press, 1939).

21. Caroline Floccia, Claire Delle Luche, Samantha Durrant, Joseph Butler, and Jeremy Goslin, "Parent or Community: Where Do 20-Month-Olds Exposed to Two Accents Acquire Their Representation of Words?," *Cognition* 124, no. 1 (2012): 95–100.

22. Angie Williams, Peter Garrett, and Nikolas Coupland, "Dialect Recognition," in *Handbook of Perceptual Dialectology*, vol. 1, ed. Dennis R. Preston (Amsterdam: John Benjamins, 1999), 345–58.

23. Shiri Lev-Ari and Boaz Keysar, "Why Don't We Believe Non-Native Speakers? The Influence of Accent on Credibility," *Journal of Experimental Social Psychology* 46, no. 6 (2010): 1093–96.

24. Andrew J. Pantos and Andrew W. Perkins, "Measuring Implicit and Explicit Attitudes toward Foreign Accented Speech," *Journal of Language and Social Psychology* 32, no. 1 (2013): 3–20.

25. Anthony DiLollo, Julie Scherz, and Robert A. Neimeyer, "Psychosocial Implications of Foreign Accent Syndrome: Two Case Examples," *Journal of Constructivist Psychology* 27, no. 1 (2014): 14–30.

26. Lara A. Frumkin and Anna Stone, "Not All Eyewitnesses Are Equal: Accent Status, Race and Age Interact to Influence Evaluations of Testimony," *Journal of Ethnicity in Criminal Justice* 18, no. 2 (2020): 123–45.

27. Katherine D. Kinzler, *How You Say It: Why We Judge Others by the Way They Talk—And the Costs of This Hidden Bias* (New York: Houghton Mifflin Harcourt, 2020).

28. Ben Crystal and David Crystal, *You Say Potato: A Book about Accents* (New York: Macmillan, 2015).

29. Walt Wolfram and Natale Schilling, *American English: Dialects and Variation*, 3rd ed. (New York: Wiley, 2016).

30. William Labov, Sharon Ash, and Charles Boberg, *The Atlas of North American English: Phonetics, Phonology and Sound Change* (Berlin: Mouton de Gruyter, 2006).

31. G. Oliveira, A. Davidson, R. Holcezer, S. Kaplan, and A. Paretzky, "A Comparison of the Use of Glottal Fry in the Spontaneous Speech of Young and Middle-Aged American Women," *Journal of Voice* 30, no. 6 (2016): 684–87.

32. R. C. Anderson, C. A. Klofstad, W. J. Mayew, and M. Venkatachalam, "Vocal Fry May Undermine the Success of Young Women in the Labor Market," *PLoS One* 9, no. 5 (2014): e97506.

33. James W. Pennebaker, *The Secret Life of Pronouns: What Our Words Say about Us* (New York: Bloomsbury Press, 2011).

34. Erik R. Thomas, "Phonological and Phonetic Characteristics of African American Vernacular English," *Language and Linguistics Compass* 1, no. 5 (2007): 450–75.

35. Jay G. Wilpon and Claus N. Jacobsen, "A Study of Speech Recognition for Children and the Elderly," in *1996 IEEE International Conference on Acoustics, Speech, and Signal Processing Conference Proceedings*, vol. 1 (New York: IEEE, 1996), 349–52.

36. John R. Rickford and Sharese King, "Language and Linguistics on Trial: Hearing Rachel Jeantel (and Other Vernacular Speakers) in the Courtroom and Beyond," *Language* 92, no. 4 (2016): 948–88.

37. James Taranto, "The Dialect Dialectic: Is It Racist to Translate a Black Speaker's Quote into Standard English—or Racist Not To?," *Wall Street Journal*, September 27, 2011.

38. Michiko Kakutani, "Light Out Huck, They Still Want to Sivilize You," *New York Times*, January 6, 2011.

39. Lawrence Howe, "Property and Dialect Narrative in 'Huckleberry Finn': The 'Jim Dilemma' Revisited," *The Mark Twain Annual* 7 (2009): 5–21.

40. Mark Twain, *The Adventures of Huckleberry Finn* (New York: Harper & Brothers, 1884).

41. William Labov, *A Study of Non-Standard English* (Washington, DC: Center for Applied Linguistics, 1969).

42. Aly Wiesman, "Samuel L. Jackson Slams Obama: 'Stop Trying to Relate and Be More Presidential,'" *Insider*, September 24, 2013.

43. Peggy Noonan, "Out of Many, Two?," *Wall Street Journal*, July 31, 2014.

44. Grace Wyler, "CREEPY: Mitt Romney Is Asking for Hugs from Southern Girls," *Insider*, March 13, 2012, https://www.businessinsider.com/mitt -romney-asks-for-hugs-from-southern-girls-2012-3.

45. Jennifer Zettle, "UW Linguists Analyze Palin's Accent," *The Badger Herald*, November 17, 2009.

46. Jason Georgy, "What Kind of Accent Is That, Anyway?," *Chicago Tribune*, September 18, 2008.

47. Geoff Nunberg, "For Candidates, an Accent on Authenticity," *Fresh Air*, WHYY-FM, Philadelphia, October 15, 2008.

48. Ralph W. Fasold, "The Relation between Black and White Speech in the South," *American Speech* 56, no. 3 (1981): 163–89.

49. Penelope Gardner-Chloros, *Code-Switching* (Cambridge: Cambridge University Press, 2009).

50. Monica Hesse, "Elizabeth Holmes's Weird Possibly Fake Baritone Is Actually Her Least Baffling Quality," *Washington Post*, March 21, 2019.

CHAPTER TWO

1. Donald Ostrowski, *Who Wrote That? Authorship Controversies from Moses to Sholokhov* (Ithaca, NY: Cornell University Press, 2020).

2. Sybil Drew, *Self Styled Genius: The Life of Thomas Corwin Mendenhall* (Jan & Brooklyn, 2016).

3. Drew, *Self Styled Genius*.

4. T. C. Mendenhall, "The Characteristic Curves of Composition," *Science* 9, no. 214 (March 11, 1887): 237–46.

5. R. D. Lord, "Studies in the History of Probability and Statistics. VIII: De Morgan and the Statistical Study of Literary Style," *Biometrika* 48 (1958): 282.

6. Mendenhall, "The Characteristic Curves of Composition," 239.

7. Mendenhall, "The Characteristic Curves of Composition," 245.

8. Joseph C. Hart, *The Romance of Yachting: Voyage the First* (New York: Harper and Brothers, 1848).

9. T. C. Mendenhall, "A Mechanical Solution of a Literary Problem," *The Popular Science Monthly* 60 (December 1901): 105.

10. Peter Farey, "Playing Dead: An Updated Review of the Case for Christopher Marlowe," *Journal of Marlovian Research* 3 (2011): 1–13.

11. C. B. Williams, "Studies in the History of Probability and Statistics: IV. A Note on an Early Statistical Study of Literary Style," *Biometrika* 43 (1956): 248–56.

12. Peter Grzybek, "History and Methodology of Word Length Studies: The State of the Art," in *Contributions to the Science of Language: Word Length Studies and Related Issues*, ed. Peter Grzybek (Dordrecht: Springer, 2007), 15–90.

13. C. B. Williams, "Mendenhall's Studies of Word-Length Distribution in the Works of Shakespeare and Bacon," *Biometrika* 62 (1975): 207–12.

14. William C. Creasy, *The Imitation of Christ: A New Reading of the 1441 Latin Autograph Manuscript* (Macon, GA: Mercer University Press, 2007).

15. Creasy, *The Imitation of Christ.*

16. Francis Richard Cruise, *Who Was the Author of "The Imitation of Christ?"* (London: Catholic Truth Society, 1898).

17. Cruise, *Who Was the Author of "The Imitation of Christ?"*

18. *New York Times*, "Denies A-Kempis Is Author," December 19, 1925, 3.

19. F. Yates. "George Udny Yule 1871–1951," *Obituary Notices of the Fellows of the Royal Society* 8, no. 21 (1952): 308–23.

20. Terence C. Mills, *A Statistical Biography of George Udny Yule: A Loafer of the World* (Cambridge: Cambridge Scholars Publishing, 2017).

21. M. G. Kendall, "George Udny Yule C.B.E, F.R.S.," *Journal of the Royal Statistical Society: Series A (General)* 115, no. 1 (1952): 156–61.

22. G. Udny Yule, "On Sentence-Length as a Statistical Characteristic of Style in Prose: With Application to Two Cases of Disputed Authorship," *Biometrika* 30, no. 3/4 (1939): 370.

23. Yule, "On Sentence-Length as a Statistical Characteristic of Style in Prose," 373–74.

24. G. Udny Yule, *The Statistical Study of Literary Vocabulary* (Cambridge: Cambridge University Press, 1944).

25. Yule, *The Statistical Study of Literary Vocabulary*, 21.

26. Kumiko Tanaka-Ishii and Shunsuke Aihara, "Computational Constancy Measures of Texts—Yule's K and Rényi's Entropy," *Computational Linguistics* 41, no. 3 (2015): 481–502.

27. E. Earle Ellis, "The Authorship of the Pastorals: A Résumé and Assessment of Current Trends," *Evangelical Quarterly* 32 (1960): 151–61.

28. Jermo Van Nes, "On the Origin of the Pastorals' Authenticity Criticism: A 'New' Perspective," *New Testament Studies* 62, no. 2 (2016): 315–20.

29. Heinrich J. Holtzmann, *Die Pastoralbriefe: Kritisch und Exgentisch Behandelt* (Leipzig: Wilhelm Engelmann, 1880).

30. Jacques Savoy, "Authorship of Pauline Epistles Revisited," *Journal of the Association for Information Science and Technology* 70, no. 10 (2019): 1089–97.

31. David Leon Higdon, "The Concordance: Mere Index or Needful Census?," *Text* 15 (2003): 51–68.

32. P. N. Harrison, *The Problem of the Pastoral Epistles* (Oxford: Oxford University Press, 1921).

33. W. P. Workman, "The Hapax Legomena of St. Paul," *The Expository Times* (1896): 418–19.

34. Jermo Van Nes, "Hapax Legomena in Disputed Pauline Letters: A Reassessment," *Zeitschrift für die Neutestamentliche Wissenschaft* 109, no. 1 (2018): 118–37.

35. Andrew Q. Morton, "The Authorship of Greek Prose," *Journal of the Royal Statistical Society Series A (General)* 128, no. 2 (1965): 169–233.

36. Sidney Michaelson and Andrew Q. Morton, "The New Stylometry: A One-Word Test of Authorship for Greek Writers," *The Classical Quarterly* 22, no. 1 (1972): 89–102.

37. Paul Foster, "Who Wrote 2 Thessalonians? A Fresh Look at an Old Problem," *Journal for the Study of the New Testament* 35, no. 2 (2012): 150–75.

38. Savoy, "Authorship of Pauline Epistles Revisited."

39. H. H. Greenwood, "St. Paul Revisited—A Computational Result," *Literary and Linguistic Computing* 7, no. 1 (1992): 43–47.

40. James A. Libby, "The Pauline Canon Sung in a Linguistic Key: Visualizing New Testament Text Proximity by Linguistic Structure, System, and Strata," *Biblical and Ancient Greek Linguistics* 5 (2016): 122–201.

41. Douglass Adair, "The Authorship of the Disputed Federalist Papers: Part II." *The William and Mary Quarterly* 1, no. 3 (July 1944): 235–64.

42. Stephen L. Schechter, ed., *The Reluctant Pillar: New York and the Adoption of the Federal Constitution* (New York: New York State Commission on the Bicentennial of the United States Constitution, 1985).

43. Pamela C. Corley, J. D. Robert, M. Howard, and David C. Nixon, "The Supreme Court and Opinion Content: The Use of the Federalist Papers," *Political Research Quarterly* 58, no. 2 (2005): 329–40.

44. Douglass Adair, "The Authorship of the Disputed Federalist Papers," *The William and Mary Quarterly* 1, no. 2 (April 1944): 97–122.

45. S. A. Bailey, "Notes on Authorship of Disputed Numbers of the Federalist," *Case and Content* 22, no. 8 (1916): 675.

NOTES

46. Stephen E. Fienberg, David C. Hoaglin, and Judith M. Tanur, eds., *The Pleasures of Statistics: An Autobiography of Frederick Mosteller* (New York: Springer, 2010).

47. Sharon Bertsch McGrayne, *The Theory That Would Not Die* (New Haven, CT: Yale University Press, 2011).

48. Frederick Mosteller and David L. Wallace, "Inference in an Authorship Problem," *Journal of the American Statistical Association* 58, no. 302 (1963): 275–309.

49. *Time*, "Education: Madison's Avenue," September 21, 1962.

50. Frederick Mosteller and David L. Wallace, *Inference and Disputed Authorship: The Federalist* (Reading, MA: Addison-Wesley, 1964), vii.

51. Stephen E. Fienberg, "Review of 'Inference and Disputed Authorship: The Federalist,'" *Journal of Interdisciplinary History* 1, no. 3 (1971): 557–60.

52. D. I. Holmes and R. S. Forsyth, "'The Federalist' Revisited: New Directions in Authorship Attribution," *Literary and Linguistic Computing* 10, no. 2 (2010): 111–27.

53. Julianne Nyhan and Andrew Flinn, *Computation and the Humanities: Towards an Oral History of Digital Humanities* (Cham: Springer, 2016).

54. John F. Burrows, *Computation into Criticism: A Study of Jane Austen's Novels and an Experiment in Method* (Oxford: Clarendon Press, 1987).

55. John Wiltshire, "Jane Austen: Computation or Criticism?," *The Cambridge Quarterly* 17, no. 4 (1988): 380.

56. John F. Burrows, "Not Unless You Ask Nicely: The Interpretative Nexus between Analysis and Information," *Literary and Linguistic Computing* 7, no. 2 (1992): 91.

57. John F. Burrows and Anthony J. Hassall, "'Anna Boleyn' and the Authenticity of Fielding's Feminine Narratives," *Eighteenth-Century Studies* 21, no. 4 (1988): 427–53.

58. Hugh Craig, "John Burrows, AM, FAHA," in *Australian Academy of the Humanities, Obituaries 2019–2020*, https://www.humanities.org.au/wp-content/uploads/2020/12/BURROWS-Final-2.pdf.

59. John F. Burrows, "Computers and the Study of Literature," in *Computers and Written Texts*, ed. Christopher S. Butler (Oxford: Blackwell, 1992), 167–204.

60. Roberto Busa, "The Annals of Computing: The Index Thomisticus," *Computers and the Humanities* 14, no. 2 (1980): 83–90.

61. John F. Burrows, "Questions of Authorship: Attribution and Beyond," *Computers and the Humanities* 37, no. 1 (2003): 5–32.

62. Stefan Evert, Thomas Proisl, Fotis Jannidis, Isabella Reger, Steffen Pielström, Christof Schöch, and Thorsten Vitt, "Understanding and Explaining Delta Measures for Authorship Attribution," *Digital Scholarship in the Humanities* 32, suppl. 2 (2017): ii4–16.

63. John F. Burrows, "'Delta': A Measure of Stylistic Difference and a Guide to Likely Authorship," *Literary and Linguistic Computing* 17, no. 3 (2002): 267–87.

64. John F. Burrows, "All the Way Through: Testing for Authorship in Different Frequency Strata," *Literary and Linguistic Computing* 22, no. 1 (2007): 27–47.

65. Jan Rybicki and Maciej Eder, "Deeper Delta across Genres and Languages: Do We Really Need the Most Frequent Words?," *Literary and Linguistic Computing* 26, no. 3 (2011): 315–21.

66. Nan Z. Da, "The Computational Case against Computational Literary Studies," *Critical Inquiry* 45 (Spring 2019): 601–39.

67. Joseph Rudman, "Cherry Picking in Nontraditional Authorship Attribution Studies," *Chance* 16, no. 2 (2003): 28.

68. Craig, "John Burrows, AM, FAHA."

69. David I. Holmes and Judit Kardos, "Who Was the Author? An Introduction to Stylometry," *Chance* 16, no. 2 (2003): 7.

CHAPTER THREE

1. Anonymous/Joe Klein, *Primary Colors: A Novel of Politics* (New York: Random House, 1996).

2. *Publishers Weekly*, "Review of *Primary Colors: A Novel of Politics*," January 1, 1996.

3. Mary B. W. Tabor, "'Anonymous' Gets $1 Million in a Film Deal," *New York Times*, February 9, 1996, A18.

4. *Washington Post*, "Wanted Anonymous: Sure, They Deny It. But if They Didn't Do It, Who Did?," February 2, 1996, B01.

5. Donald Foster, "Who Is Anonymous?," *New York Magazine*, February 26, 1996, 50–57.

6. David Kusnet, "'Primary Colors'—Outside the White House beyond the Beltway; Unmasking 'Anonymous': A Suspect Lays the Book at Joe Klein's Doorstep," *Baltimore Sun*, February 11, 1996.

7. Mary B. W. Tabor, "Politics: Campaign '92; Author, Subject of Article, Denies He Wrote 'Colors,'" *New York Times*, February 21, 1996, A14.

8. Joel Garreau and Linton Weeks, "'Anonymous' Sleuths Get a Byte Fishing by Computer: Is the Author About to Be Reeled In?," *Washington Post*, February 16, 1996.

9. Anonymous/Joe Klein, "No, Really, I Am Anonymous," *New York Times*, May 19, 1996, sec. 7, p. 43.

10. *Chicago Tribune*, "Handwriting Gives Clues to 'Primary' Author, Paper Says," July 17, 1996.

11. Warren St. John, "Serif Sleuth," *The New Yorker*, July 28, 1996.

12. *Washington Post*, "Wanted Anonymous."

13. David Streitfeld, "'Anonymous' Undone by His Own Hand?," *Washington Post*, July 17, 1996.

NOTES

14. Caryn James, "July 14–20; Anonymous Shows His Colors," *New York Times*, July 21, 1996, sec. 4, p. 2.

15. Lawrie Mifflin, "'Primary Colors' Author Resigns as Commentator at CBS News," *New York Times*, July 26, 1996, A17.

16. Maureen Corrigan, "The Only Surprise in Rowling's 'Cuckoo's Calling' Is the Author," National Public Radio, July 18, 2013.

17. Sarah Lyall, "The Detective Novel's Story Doesn't Add Up," *New York Times*, July 14, 2013.

18. Julie Bosman, "Rowling Leak Mystery: The Lawyer Did It," *New York Times*, July 18, 2013, C3.

19. Julie Bosman, "Rowling Book Skyrockets to Instant Hit," *New York Times*, July 16, 2013.

20. Lyall, "The Detective Novel's Story Doesn't Add Up."

21. Patrick Juola, John Noecker, Mike Ryan, and Mengjia Zhao, "JGAAP3.0—Authorship Attribution for the Rest of Us," in *Digital Humanities 2008* (Oulu: Association for Literary and Linguistic Computing, 2008), 250–51.

22. Virginia Hughes, "How Forensic Linguistics Outed J. K. Rowling (Not to Mention James Madison, Barack Obama, and the Rest of Us)," *National Geographic*, July 19, 2013.

23. Patrick Juola, "How a Computer Program Helped Show J. K. Rowling Write a Cuckoo's Calling," *Scientific American*, August 20, 2013.

24. Anya Sostke, "Duquesne Professor Helps ID Rowling as Author of 'The Cuckoo's Calling,'" *Pittsburgh Post-Gazette*, July 16, 2013.

25. Hughes, "How Forensic Linguistics Outed J. K. Rowling."

26. Richard Books and Cal Flyn, "JK Rowling, the Cuckoo in Crime Novel Nest," *The Sunday Times*, July 14, 2013.

27. Reuters, "Lawyer Fined for Revealing JK Rowling as Secret Author," *Irish Times*, January 2, 2014.

28. Jamaluddin, "The Cuckoo's Calling: Good under Robert Galbraith, Excellent under JK Rowling," *Express Tribune*, September 5, 2013.

29. Sarah Shaffi, "Rowling's Galbraith Sales Reach 1.5m," *The Bookseller*, October 12, 2015.

30. Maev Kennedy, "Lawyer Who Uncovered JK Rowling's Robert Galbraith Alter Ego Fined £1,000," *The Guardian*, December 10, 2013.

31. Lyall, "The Detective Novel's Story Doesn't Add Up,"

32. James B. Stewart, "Long Odds for Authors Newly Published," *New York Times*, August 30, 2013.

33. David C. Mearns, "'Diary of a Public Man'—Whodunit?," *New York Times*, January 16, 1949, 104.

34. Roy N. Lokken, "Has the Mystery of 'A Public Man' Been Solved?," *Mississippi Valley Historical Review* 40, no. 3 (1953): 419–40.

35. Daniel W. Crofts, *A Secession Crisis Enigma: William Henry Hurlbert and "The Diary of a Public Man"* (Baton Rouge: Louisiana State University Press, 2010).

36. Lokken, "Has the Mystery of 'A Public Man' Been Solved?"

37. Frank Maloy Anderson, *The Mystery of "A Public Man": A Historical Detective Story* (Minneapolis: University of Minnesota Press, 1948), 169.

38. Evelyn Page, "The Diary and the Public Man," *The New England Quarterly* 22, no. 2 (1949): 147–92.

39. Benjamin M. Price, "Who Wrote 'The Diary of a Public Man?' A Seventy-Two-Year-Old Mystery," *American Bar Association Journal* 37, no. 8 (1951): 579–81.

40. John M. Taylor, "The Diary of 'A Public Man,'" *North American Review* 261, no. 2 (1976): 78–80.

41. David I. Holmes and Daniel W. Crofts, "The Diary of a Public Man: A Case Study in Traditional and Non-Traditional Authorship Attribution," *Literary and Linguistic Computing* 25 (2010): 179–97.

42. Crofts, *A Secession Crisis Enigma*.

43. Paul Royster, *Thomas Pynchon: A Brief Chronology* (Lincoln: Faculty Publications, University of Nebraska-Lincoln Libraries, 2005), https://digitalcommons.unl.edu/libraryscience/2.

44. David Cowart, *Thomas Pynchon and the Dark Passages of History* (Athens: University of Georgia Press, 2011).

45. Thomas Pynchon, *V* (New York: J. B. Lippincott, 1963).

46. *New York Times*, "Faulkner Novel Award Given," February 3, 1964, 25.

47. Adrian Wisnicki, "A Trove of New Works by Thomas Pynchon? 'Bomarc Service News' Rediscovered," *Pynchon Notes* 46 (2001): 9–34.

48. *New York Times*, "New Bomarc Contract," March 22, 1959, 40.

49. Thomas Pynchon, *Slow Learner: Early Stories* (Boston: Little, Brown, 1984).

50. Thomas Pynchon, "Togetherness," *Aerospace Safety* 16, no. 12 (1960): 6–8.

51. Wisnicki, "A Trove of New Works by Thomas Pynchon?"

52. Katie Muth, "The Grammars of the System: Thomas Pynchon at Boeing," *Textual Practice* 33, no. 3 (2019): 473–93.

53. Muth, "The Grammars of the System."

54. Lewis Theobald, *Double Falsehood; or the Distrest Lovers* (London: J. Watts, 1728).

55. Harriet C. Frazier, "Theobald's 'The Double Falsehood': A Revision of Shakespeare's 'Cardenio'?," *Comparative Drama* 1, no. 3 (1967): 219–33.

56. John Freehafer, "'Cardenio,' by Shakespeare and Fletcher," *Publications of the Modern Language Association of America* 84, no. 3 (1969): 501–13.

57. Tiffany Stern, "'The Forgery of Some Modern Author'? Theobald's Shakespeare and Cadenio's 'Double Falsehood,'" *Shakespeare Quarterly* 62, no. 4 (2011): 555–93.

58. Carly Watson, "From Restorer to Editor: The Evolution of Lewis Theobald's Textual Critical Practice," *The Library* 20, no. 2 (2019): 147–71.

59. Peter Herman, "'Is This Winning?' Prince Henry's Death and the Problem of Chivalry in 'The Two Noble Kinsmen,'" *South Atlantic Review* 62, no. 1 (1997): 1–31.

60. Brean Hammond, ed., *Double Falsehood or The Distressed Lovers* (London: Methuen Drama, 2010).

61. David Carnegie and Gary Taylor, *The Quest for Cardenio: Shakespeare, Fletcher, Cervantes, and the Lost Play* (Oxford: Oxford University Press, 2012).

62. John V. Nance, "Shakespeare, Theobald, and the Prose Problem in 'Double Falsehood,'" in *The Creation and Re-Creation of Cardenio: Performing Shakespeare, Transforming Cervantes*, ed. Terri Bourus and Gary Talor (New York: Palgrave Macmillan, 2013), 109–23.

63. Alexis Soloski, "A Lost Shakespeare? It's a Mystery," *New York Times*, March 10, 2011, AR4.

64. Ron Rosenbaum, "The Double Falsehood of Double Falsehood," *Slate*, May 13, 2010, https://slate.com/human-interest/2010/05/the-terrible-decision-to-include -a-bogus-play-double-falsehood-in-the-arden-shakespeare.html.

65. James Pennebaker, *The Secret Life of Pronouns: What Our Words Say about Us* (New York: Bloomsbury Press, 2011).

66. Yla R. Tausczik and James W. Pennebaker, "The Psychological Meaning of Words: LIWC and Computerized Text Analysis Methods," *Journal of Language and Social Psychology* 29, no. 1 (2010): 24–54.

67. Brad Leithauser, "Pet Words," *The New Yorker*, September 11, 2013.

68. Ryan L. Boyd and James W. Pennebaker, "Did Shakespeare Write 'Double Falsehood'? Identifying Individuals by Creating Psychological Signatures with Text Analysis," *Psychological Science* 26, no. 5 (2015): 570–82.

69. Robert Folkenflik, "'Shakespearesque': The Arden 'Double Falsehood,'" *Huntington Library Quarterly* 75, no. 1 (2012): 131–43.

70. Gary Taylor, "Fake Shakespeare," *Journal of Early Modern Studies* 5 (2016): 353–79.

CHAPTER FOUR

1. David Dempsey, "The Wizard of Baum," *New York Times*, May 13, 1956, 255.

2. Rebecca Loncraine, *The Real Wizard of Oz: The Life and Times of L. Frank Baum* (New York: Gotham Books, 2009).

3. Mark E. Swartz, *Oz before the Rainbow: L. Frank Baum's The Wonderful Wizard of Oz on Stage and Screen to 1939* (Baltimore: Johns Hopkins University Press, 2000).

4. Gregory Maguire, *Wicked: The Life and Times of the Wicked Witch of the West* (New York: ReganBooks, 1995).

5. Laura Woods, "25 of the Highest-Grossing Broadway Shows Ever," April 1, 2021, https://www.yahoo.com/lifestyle/25-highest-grossing-broadway-shows-230020553.html.

6. Ruth Plumly Thompson, "How I Came to Write Nineteen of the Oz Books," *The Baum Bugle* 1, no. 2 (1957).

7. L. Frank Baum and Ruth Plumly Thompson, *The Royal Book of Oz* (Chicago: Reilly & Lee, 1921).

8. Russel B. Nye, "The Wizardess of Oz," *The Baum Bugle*, Autumn 1965, 119–22.

9. J. Snow, *Who's Who in Oz* (Chicago: Reilly & Lee, 1954).

10. José N. G. Binongo and D'arcy P. Mays III, "A Study of the Authorship of the Books of Oz Using Nested Linear Models," *Computations in Statistics—Simulation and Computation* 34 (2005): 293–308.

11. Erica Klarreich, "Bookish Math: Statistical Tests Are Unraveling Knotty Literary Mysteries," *Science News* 164, no. 26 (2003), https://www.sciencenews.org/article/bookish-math.

12. Martin Gardner, *Visitors from Oz: The Wild Adventures of Dorothy, the Scarecrow, and the Tin Woodman* (New York: St. Martin's Press, 1998), xv.

13. José N. G. Binongo, "Who Wrote the 15th Book of Oz? An Application of Multivariate Analysis to Authorship Attribution," *Chance* 16, no. 2 (2003): 9–17.

14. Martin Gardner, *Undiluted Hocus-Pocus: The Autobiography of Martin Gardner* (Princeton, NJ: Princeton University Press, 2014), 6.

15. Binongo, "Who Wrote the 15th Book of Oz?"

16. Hervey Allen and Thomas O. Mabbot, eds., *Poe's Brother: The Poems of William Henry Leonard Poe* (New York: George H. Dorian Co., 1926).

17. Paul Collins, "Poe's Debut, Hidden in Plain Sight?," *The New Yorker*, October 4, 2013.

18. Patrick Juola, "The Rowling Case: A Proposed Standard Analytic Protocol for Authorship Questions," *Digital Scholarship in the Humanities* 30, suppl. 1 (2015): 100–113.

19. Terence Whalen, "Poe and the American Publishing Industry," in *A Historical Guide to Edgar Allan Poe*, ed. J. Gerald Kennedy (Oxford: Oxford University Press, 2001), 63–93.

20. Terence Whalen, "Average Racism: Poe, Slavery, and the Wages of Literary Nationalism," in *Romancing the Shadow: Poe and Race*, ed. J. Gerald Kennedy and Liliane Weissberg (Oxford: Oxford University Press, 2001), 3–40.

21. Edgar Allen Poe Society of Baltimore, "Where Poe Lived, Worked, and Visited," January 2014, https://www.eapoe.org/places/phindx.htm.

22. Lesley Ginsberg, "Slavery and the Gothic Horror of Poe's 'The Black Cat,'" in *American Gothic: New Interventions in a National Narrative*, ed. Robert K. Martin and Eric Savoy (Iowa City: University of Iowa Press, 1998), 99–128.

23. Toni Morrison, *Playing in the Dark: Whiteness and the Literary Imagination* (Cambridge, MA: Harvard University Press, 1992).

24. William Doyle Hull II, "A Canon of the Critical Works of Edgar Allen Poe: With a Study of Poe as Editor and Reviewer," unpublished doctoral dissertation, University of Virginia, Charlottesville, 1941.

25. James Southall Wilson, "Unpublished Letters of Edgar Allan Poe," *The Century Magazine* 107 (March 1924): 652–56.

26. Hull, "A Canon of the Critical Works of Edgar Allen Poe."

27. Bernard Rosenthal, "Poe, Slavery, and the 'Southern Literary Messenger': A Reexamination," *Poe Studies* 7, no. 2 (1974): 29–38.

28. J. V. Ridgely, "Review: The Authorship of the 'Paulding-Drayton Review,'" *PSA Newsletter* 20, no. 3 (Fall 1992): 1–3, 6.

29. Stefan Schöberlein, "Poe or Not Poe? A Stylometric Analysis of Edgar Allan Poe's Disputed Writings," *Digital Scholarship in the Humanities* 32, no. 3 (2017): 656.

30. Whalen, "Average Racism."

31. Walter Hooper, "Preface; A Note on 'The Dark Tower,'" in C. S. Lewis, *The Dark Tower and Other Stories* (New York: Harcourt Brace Jovanovich, 1977).

32. Barbara Reynolds, "Review of 'Sleuthing C.S. Lewis: More Light in the Shadowlands,'" *VII: Journal of the Marion E. Wade Center* 18 (2001): 102–7.

33. Kathryn Lindskoog, "Some Problems in C. S. Lewis Scholarship," *Christianity and Literature* 27, no. 4 (1978): 43–61.

34. Kathryn A. Lindskoog, *The C. S. Lewis Hoax* (Portland, OR: Multnomah Books, 1988).

35. Kathryn Lindskoog, *Light in the Shadowlands: Protecting the Real C. S. Lewis.* (Portland, OR: Multnomah Books, 1994).

36. Kathryn A. Lindskoog, *Sleuthing C. S. Lewis: More Light in the Shadowlands* (Macon, GA: Mercer University Press, 2001).

37. Scott McLemee, "Holy War in the Shadowlands," *The Chronicle of Higher Education*, July 20, 2001, https://www.chronicle.com/article/holy-war-in-the-shadow lands.

38. Nicolas Barker, "C. S. Lewis, Darkly," *Essays in Criticism* 40 (1990): 367.

39. Hooper, "Preface."

40. Alastair Fowler, "C. S. Lewis: Supervisor," *The Yale Review* 91, no. 4 (2003): 71.

41. James Tankard, "The Literary Detective," *Byte*, February 1986, 231–38.

42. Carla F. Jones, "The Literary Detective Computer Analysis of Stylistic Differences between 'The Dark Tower' and C. S. Lewis' Deep Space Trilogy," *Mythlore: A Journal of J. R. R. Tolkien, C. S. Lewis, Charles Williams, and Mythopoeic Literature* 15, no. 2 (1989): 11–15.

43. Lindskoog, *Sleuthing C. S. Lewis.*

44. Jeffrey R. Thompson and John Rasp, "Did C. S. Lewis Write the 'The Dark Tower'? An Examination of the Small-Sample Properties of the Thisted-Efron Test of Authorship," *Austrian Journal of Statistics* 38, no. 2 (2009): 71–82.

45. Michael P. Oakes, "Computer Stylometry of C. S. Lewis's 'The Dark Tower' and Related Texts," *Digital Scholarship in the Humanities* 33, no. 3 (2018): 637–50.

46. Erin Nyborg, "Elena Ferrante, Charlotte Brontë and How Anonymity Protects against Female Writing Stereotypes," *The Conversation*, October 5, 2016, https:// theconversation.com/elena-ferrante-charlotte-bronte-and-how-anonymity-protects -against-female-writing-stereotypes-66500.

47. Carol Ohmann, "Emily Brontë in the Hands of Male Critics," *College English* 32, no. 8 (1971): 906–13.

48. Irene Wiltshire, "Speech in 'Wuthering Heights': Joseph's Dialect and Charlotte's Emendations," *Brontë Studies* 30, no. 1 (2005):19–29.

49. Christine Alexander and Margaret Smith, *The Oxford Companion to the Brontës: Anniversary Edition* (Oxford: Oxford University Press, 2018).

50. None, "Patrick Branwell Brontë and 'Wuthering Heights,'" *Brontë Society Transactions* 7, no. 2 (1927): 99.

51. Irene Cooper Willis, "The Authorship of 'Wuthering Heights,'" *The Trollopian* 2, no. 3 (1947): 157–68.

52. Chris Firth, *Branwell Brontë's Tale: Who Wrote "Wuthering Heights"?* (Electraglade Press, 2014).

53. John Malham-Dembleby, *The Key to the Brontë Works* (London: Walter Scott, 1911), 90.

54. Melvin R. Watson, "'Wuthering Heights' and the Critics," *The Trollopian* 3, no. 4 (1949): 243–63.

55. *New York Times*, "The Three Sisters of the Moors," August 7, 1932, 4.

56. Edward Frederic Benson, *Charlotte Bronte: A Biography* (New York: Longman, Green and Co., 1932), 176.

57. Michele Carter, *Charlotte Brontë's Thunder: The Truth behind the Bronte Sisters' Genius* (Lincoln, NE: Boomer Publications, 2011).

58. Michele Carter, "Author Attribution Analysis of the Brontë Novels," *The McScribble Salon*, May 18, 2017, http://www.michelecartersblog.com/2017/05/author -attribution-analysis-of-bronte.html.

59. Victor A. Neufeldt, ed., *A Bibliography of the Manuscripts of Patrick Branwell Brontë* (London: Routledge, 2015).

60. Rachel McCarthy and James O'Sullivan, "Who Wrote 'Wuthering Heights'?," *Digital Scholarship in the Humanities* 36, no. 2 (2021): 383–91.

61. The Brontës, *Tales of Glass Town, Angria, and Gondal: Selected Early Writings* (Oxford: Oxford University Press, 2010).

62. Alexandra Alter, "Harper Lee and Truman Capote: A Collaboration in Mischief," *New York Times*, August 9, 2015; William Grimes, "Harper Lee, Author of 'To Kill a Mockingbird,' Dies at 89," *New York Times*, February 19, 2016.

63. Michał Choiński, Maciej Eder, and Jan Rybicki, "Harper Lee and Other People: A Stylometric Analysis," *Mississippi Quarterly* 70/71, no. 3 (2017/2018): 355–74.

64. Lawrence Van Gelder, "Harper Lee Writes Again," *New York Times*, June 28, 2006.

65. Tom Leonard, "Jealousy, Lies and Troubling Questions about a Book That Inspired the World," *Daily Mail*, February 5, 2015.

66. Ellen Gamerman, "Data Miners Dig Into 'Watchman,'" *Wall Street Journal*, July 17, 2015, D5.

67. Mike Marshall, "To Kill a Myth, Museum Has Letter to Disprove It," *Chicago Tribune*, March 4, 2006.

68. Casey Cep, "Harper Lee's Abandoned True-Crime Novel," *The New Yorker*, March 17, 2015.

69. Mark Seal, "To Steal* a Mockingbird*?," *Vanity Fair*, August 2013.

70. Allan Kozinn, "Harper Lee Says New Book Not Authorized." *New York Times*, July 15, 2014.

71. Jonathan Mahler, "The Invisible Hand behind Harper Lee's 'To Kill a Mockingbird,'" *New York Times*, July 12, 2015.

72. Serge F. Kovaleski and Alexandra Alter, "Harper Lee's 'Go Set a Watchman' May Have Been Found Earlier Than Thought." *New York Times,* July 2, 2015.

73. Randall Kennedy, "Harper Lee's 'Go Set a Watchman,'" *New York Times*, July 14, 2015.

74. Serge F. Kovaleski, "Alabama Officials Find Harper Lee in Control of Decision to Publish Second Novel," *New York Times*, April 3, 2015.

75. Jennifer Crossley Howard, "In Harper Lee's Letters: Books, Fame and a 'Lying' Capote," *New York Times*, April 28, 2017.

76. M. Eder and J. Rybicki, "Go Set a Watchman while We Kill the Mockingbird in Cold Blood, with Cats and Other People," in *Digital Humanities 2016: Conference Abstracts* (Kraków: Jagiellonian University and Pedagogical University, 2016), 185.

77. Avi Selk, "The Ironic, Enduring Legacy of Banning 'To Kill a Mockingbird' for Racist Language," *Washington Post*, October 17, 2017.

78. Jim Milliot, "BookScan: Patterson Was Decade's Bestselling Author," *Publishers Weekly*, November 13, 2020.

79. Dave Itzkoff, "Yes, James Patterson Signs a 17-Book Deal," *New York Times*, September 8, 2009.

80. Anthony Lane, "Bill Clinton and James Patterson's Concussive Collaboration," *The New Yorker*, June 5, 2018.

81. Sarah Lyall, "In Bill Clinton and James Patterson's Second Novel, an Ex-President Goes Rogue," *New York Times*, June 8, 2021.

82. National Public Radio, "'Dreams Do Still Come True,' in a New Novel by Dolly Parton and James Patterson," *Morning Edition*, April 29, 2022.

83. Jonathan Mahler, "James Patterson Inc.," *New York Times Magazine*, January 20, 2010.

84. Troy Patterson, "James Patterson Would Like You to Read," *The New Yorker*, June 9, 2016.

85. Karen Heller, "James Patterson Mostly Doesn't Write His Books. And His New Readers Mostly Don't Read—Yet," *Washington Post*, June 6, 2016.

86. Nicholas Wroe, "James Patterson: A Life in Writing," *The Guardian*, May 11, 2013.

87. Wroe, "James Patterson."

88. Simon Fuller and James O'Sullivan, "Structure over Style: Collaborative Authorship and the Revival of Literary Capitalism," *Digital Humanities Quarterly* 11, no. 1 (2017): 1–12.

89. James O'Sullivan, "Why You Don't Need to Write Much to Be the World's Bestselling Author," *The Conversation*, April 3, 2017, https://theconversation.com/why-you-dont-need-to-write-much-to-be-the-worlds-bestselling-author-75261.

90. James O'Sullivan, "Bill Clinton and James Patterson are Co-Authors—But Who Did the Writing?," *The Guardian*, June 7, 2018.

CHAPTER FIVE

1. Ludovic Kennedy, *Ten Rillington Place* (New York: Simon and Schuster, 1961).

2. UCL Survey of English Usage, "Jan Svartvik," https://www.ucl.ac.uk/english-usage/about/svartvik.htm.

3. Jan Svartvik, "The Evans Statements: A Case for Forensic Linguistics, Part 1," in *Gothenburg Studies in English*, ed. Alvar Ellengård (Göteborg: University of Göteborg Press, 1968).

4. William B. Hollmann, "Forensic Linguistics," in *Knowing about Language: Linguistics and the Secondary English Classroom*, ed. Marcello Giovanelli and Dan Clayton (London: Routledge, 2016), 137–48.

5. Svartvik, "The Evans Statements."

6. John Olsson, "Forensic Linguistics," in *Linguistics*, ed. Vesna Muhvic-Dimanovski and Lelija Socanac (Oxford: Eolss Publishers, 2009), 378–93.

7. Sanja Ćetković, "Position of Temporal Adverbs in Police Reports in English," *Mediterranean Journal of Social Sciences* 5, no. 13 (2014): 217–21.

8. Frank Dawtry, "The Abolition of the Death Penalty in Britain," *British Journal of Criminology* 6, no. 2 (1966): 183–92.

9. Malcolm Coulthard and Alison Johnson, *An Introduction to Forensic Linguistics: Language in Evidence* (London: Routledge, 2007).

10. Phil Drake, "Unabomber's Legacy Resonates 25 Years after Arrest in Montana," *Helena Independent Record*, April 2, 2021.

11. Dave Davies, "FBI Profiler Says Linguistic Work Was Pivotal in Capture of Unabomber, *Fresh Air*, National Public Radio, August 22, 2017.

12. Frank Bruni, "On the Unabomber's Track: The Hunters; With a Family Discovery, a Manhunt Comes to an End. *New York Times*, April 4, 1996, B13.

13. Daniel McDermon, "F.B.I. Listed Author as Unabomber Suspect," *New York Times*, August 22, 2013, C3.

14. David Johnston, "A Device in Cabin Is Said to Match the Unabomber's," *New York Times*, April 9, 1996, A1.

15. William Glaberson, "Publication of Unabomber's Tract Draws Mixed Response," *New York Times*, September 20, 1995, A16.

16. David Kaczynski, *Every Last Tie: The Story of the Unabomber and His Family* (Durham, NC: Duke University Press, 2016).

17. Rudolf Flesch, "A New Readability Yardstick," *Journal of Applied Psychology* 32 (1948): 221–33.

18. Theodore J. Kaczynski, *Industrial Society and Its Future*, *Washington Post* supplement, September 22, 1995, para. 1.

19. Jack Hitt, "Words on Trial: Can Linguists Solve Crimes That Stump the Police?," *The New Yorker*, July 16, 2012.

20. Roger W. Shuy, *The Language of Murder Cases: Intentionality, Predisposition, and Voluntariness* (Oxford: Oxford University Press, 2014).

21. Kaczynski, *Industrial Society and Its Future*, para. 185.

22. James R. Fitzgerald, "Using a Forensic Linguistic Approach to Track the Unabomber," in *Profilers: Leading Investigators Take You inside the Criminal Mind*, ed. John H. Campbell and Don DeNevi (Amherst, NY: Prometheus, 2004), 193–222.

23. Phil Ryan. *Multicultiphobia* (Toronto: University of Toronto Press, 2010).

24. David Johnston, "On the Unabomber Track: The Overview; Ex-Professor Is Seized in Montana as Suspect in the Unabom Attacks," *New York Times*, April 4, 1996, A1.

25. B. Drummond Ayres, "Man Held as Unabomber Is Indicted in 2 Slayings," *New York Times*, June 19, 1996, A12.

26. True Crime Detectives Guild, *Listen Carefully! Truth and Evidence in the JonBenet Ramsey Case* (ALLFORONE, 2016), 158.

27. Michelle Dresbold, *Sex, Lies and Handwriting: A Top Expert Reveals the Secrets Hidden in Your Handwriting* (New York: Free Press, 2017).

28. John Ramsey and Patsy Ramsey, *The Death of Innocence: The Untold Story of JonBenét's Murder and How Its Exploitation Compromised the Pursuit of Truth* (Nashville, TN: Thomas Nelson, 2000).

29. Andy Geller, "Ex-Jonbenet Prober Says Mom Wrote Ransom Note," *New York Post*, April 9, 2000.

30. Hillary E. Crawford, "The JohnBenet Ransom Note Was Signed 'S.B.T.C.,'" *Bustle*, September 18, 2016, https://www.bustle.com/articles/184633-what-does-sbtc-stand-for-the-jonbenet-ramsey-ransom-note-had-a-mysterious-signature.

31. True Crime Detectives Guild, *Listen Carefully!*

32. Jim Fisher, *Forensics under Fire: Are Bad Science and Dueling Experts Corrupting Criminal Justice?* (New Brunswick, NJ: Rutgers University Press, 2008).

33. John Ingold and Kirk Mitchell, "JonBenét Ramsey Grand Jury Indictment Accused Parents of Child Abuse Resulting in Death," *Denver Post*, October 25, 2013.

34. BBC News, "Life Term for Man Who Shot Lover," November 8, 2005, news.bbc.co.uk/2/hi/uk_news/england/south_yorkshire/4418518.stm.

35. John Olsson, *Wordcrime: Solving Crime through Forensic Linguistics* (London: Continuum, 2009).

36. Elizabeth Svoboda, "Speech Patterns in Messages Betray a Killer," *New York Times*, May 11, 2009.

37. BBC News, "Murder Probe Police Discover Body," July 21, 2005, news.bbc.co.uk/2/hi/uk_news/england/south_yorkshire/4703689.stm.

38. *The Mirror*, "Shot by Lover and Left in an Oil Drum," November 1, 2005, mirror.co.uk/news/uk-news/shot-by-lover-and-left-in-an-oil-drum-563593.

39. Nathan Bevan, "Welsh Expert Key Witness in Da Vinci Battle," *WalesOnline*, June 11, 2006, https://www.walesonline.co.uk/news/wales-news/welsh-expert-key-witness-da-2332668

40. Sally Williams, "Da Vinci Code Expert Needs Your Text Messages," *Wales Online*, May 9, 2009, https://www.walesonline.co.uk/news/wales-news/da-vinici-code-expert-needs-2104536.

41. Gavin Fernando, "How a Murderer Was Brought to Justice by His Texting Style," news.com.au, August 8, 2018, https://www.news.com.au/lifestyle/real-life/true-stories/how-a-murderer-was-brought-to-justice-by-his-texting-style/news-story/34934b3177ab070ea6cce510059a574e.

42. John Olsson, *More Wordcrime: Solving Crime with Linguistics* (New York: Bloomsbury, 2018).

CHAPTER SIX

1. Eusebius, *Life of Constantine*, trans. Averil Cameron and Stuart G. Hall (Oxford: Clarendon Press, 1999).

2. Jacobus de Voragine, *The Golden Legend: Readings on the Saints*, trans. William G. Ryan (Princeton, NJ: Princeton University Press, 1993).

3. Christopher Coleman, *The Treatise of Lorenzo Valla on the Donation of Constantine: Text and Translation into English* (New Haven, CT: Yale University Press, 1922).

4. Dabney G. Park, "Dante and the Donation of Constantine," *Dante Studies, with the Annual Report of the Dante Society*, no. 130 (2012): 67–161.

5. Nicholas of Cusa, *The Catholic Concordance*, ed. and trans. Paul E. Sigmund (Cambridge: Cambridge University Press, 1991).

6. Eusebius, *Life of Constantine*.

7. de Voragine, *The Golden Legend*.

8. Joseph M. Levine, "Reginald Pecock and Lorenzo Valla on the Donation of Constantine," *Studies in the Renaissance* 20 (1973): 118–43.

9. Salvatore I. Camproreale, "Lorenzo Valla's 'Oratio' on the Pseudo-Donation of Constantine: Dissent and Innovation in Early Renaissance Humanism," *Journal of the History of Ideas* 57, no. 1 (1996): 9–26.

10. Coleman, *The Treatise of Lorenzo Valla on the Donation of Constantine*, 95.

11. Wolfram Brandes, "The Satraps of Constantine," in *Donation of Constantine and Constitum Constantini*, by James Fried (Berlin: de Gruyter, 2007), 115–27.

12. Coleman, *The Treatise of Lorenzo Valla on the Donation of Constantine*, 85–87.

13. Levine, "Reginald Pecock and Lorenzo Valla on the Donation of Constantine."

14. Coleman, *The Treatise of Lorenzo Valla on the Donation of Constantine*, 29.

15. Lorenzo Valla, *On the Donation of Constantine*, trans. G. W. Bowersock (Cambridge, MA: Harvard University Press, 2008).

16. Paul Richard Blum, *Philosophers of the Renaissance*, trans. Brian McNeil (Washington, DC: Catholic University of America Press, 2010).

17. Preserved Smith, *The Age of the Reformation* (New York: Henry Holt & Co., 1920).

18. Daniel Mendelsohn, "God's Librarians: The Vatican Library Enters the Twenty-First Century," *The New Yorker*, January 3, 2011.

19. Timothy R. Levine, *Encyclopedia of Deception*, vol. 2 (Los Angeles: Sage Reference, 2014).

20. Johann Peter Kirsch, "Donation of Constantine," *The Catholic Encyclopedia*, vol. 5 (New York: Robert Appleton Co., 1909).

21. Barry Wood, *Invented History, Fabricated Power: The Narrative Shaping of Civilization and Culture* (London: Anthem Press, 2020).

22. P. R. Coleman-Norton, "The Fragmentary Philosophical Treatises of Cicero," *The Classical Journal* 34, no. 4 (1939): 213–28.

23. Han Baltussen, "Cicero's 'Consolatio ad se': Character, Purpose and Impact of a Curious Treatise," in *Greek and Roman Consolations: Eight Studies of a Tradition and Its Afterlife*, ed. Hans Baltussen (Swansea: The Classical Press of Wales, 2013), 67–91.

24. Robinson Ellis, "On the Pseudo-Ciceronian 'Consolatio,'" *The Classical Review* 7, no. 5 (1893): 197.

25. William McCuaig, *Carlo Sigonio: The Changing World of the Late Renaissance* (Princeton, NJ: Princeton University Press, 1989), 291.

26. Ellis, "On the Pseudo-Ciceronian 'Consolatio.'"

27. J. A. Farrer, *Literary Forgeries* (New York: Longman Green & Co., 1907), 8.

28. Ellis, "On the Pseudo-Ciceronian 'Consolatio,'" 197.

29. Evan T. Sage, "The Pseudo-Ciceronian 'Consolatio,'" unpublished doctoral dissertation, University of Chicago, 1910.

30. Thomas G. Hendrickson, "Spurious Manuscripts of Genuine Works: The Cases of Cicero and Virgil," in *Animo Decipiendi? Rethinking Fakes and Authorship in Classical, Late Antique and Early Christian Works*, ed. Antonio Guzmán and Javier Martínez (Groningen: Barkhuis, 2018), 125–38.

31. W. S. Watt, "The Text of the Pseudo-Ciceronian Epistula ad Octavianum," *The Classical Quarterly* 8, no. 1/2 (1958): 25–31.

32. Irene O'Daly, "Managing Knowledge: Diagrammatic Glosses to Medieval Copies of the 'Rhetorica ad Herennium,'" *International Journal of the Classical Tradition* 23, no. 1 (2016): 1–28.

33. Richard S. Forsyth, David I. Holmes, and Emily K. Tse, "Cicero, Sigonio, and Burrows: Investigating the Authenticity of the 'Consolatio,'" *Literary and Linguistic Computing* 14, no. 3 (1999): 1–26.

34. Jack Lynch, "William Henry Ireland's Forgeries, Unique and Otherwise," *Princeton University Library Chronicle* 72, no. 2 (2011): 465–70.

35. Samuel Ireland, *Miscellaneous Papers and Legal Instruments under the Hand and Seal of William Shakspeare* (London: Egerton, 1796).

36. James Boaden, *A Letter to George Stevens, Esq. Containing a Critical Examination of the Papers of Shakspeare* (London: Martin and Bain, 1796).

37. Doug Stewart, *The Boy Who Would Be Shakespeare: A Tale of Forgery and Folly* (Cambridge, MA: Da Capo Press, 2010).

38. Edmond Malone, *An Inquiry into the Authenticity of Certain Miscellaneous Papers and Legal Instruments* (London: T. Cadell and W. Davies, 1796).

39. William-Henry Ireland, *The Confessions of William-Henry Ireland* (London: Ellerton and Byworth, 1805), 158.

40. Camdram, "Vortigern," https://www.camdram.net/shows/2008-vortigern.

41. William-Henry Ireland, *An Authentic Account of the Shaksperian Manuscripts* (London: J. Debrett, 1796).

42. Stephen Greenblatt, "Shakespeare and the Will to Deceive," *New York Times*, April 28, 2011.

43. Robert Miles, "Forging a Romantic Identity: Herbert Croft's 'Love and Madness' and W. H. Ireland's Shakespeare MS," *Eighteenth-Century Fiction* 17, no. 4 (2005): 599–627.

44. Zachary Turpin, "Thomas Jefferson Snodgrass Goes to England," *American Literary Realism* 49, no. 2 (2017): 176.

45. J. R. LeMaster and James D. Wilson, *The Mark Twain Encyclopedia* (New York: Garland Publishing, 1993).

46. Samuel L. Clemens, *The Adventures of Thomas Jefferson Snodgrass*, ed. Charles Honce (Chicago: Pascal Covici, 1928).

47. Minnie M. Brashear, *Mark Twain: Son of Missouri* (Chapel Hill: University of North Carolina Press, 1934).

48. Ernest E. Leisy, ed., *The Letters of Quintus Curtius Snodgrass* (Dallas, TX: Southern Methodist University, 1946).

49. Leisy, *The Letters of Quintus Curtius Snodgrass*, 59.

50. Mark Twain, "The Private History of a Campaign That Failed," *The Century Illustrated Monthly Magazine* 31, no. 2 (1885): 193–204, https://archive.org/details /centuryillustratv31newy/page/n205/mode/2up.

51. Edwin C. Bearss, "The Seizure of the Forts and Public Property in Louisiana," *Louisiana History: The Journal of the Louisiana Historical Association* 2, no. 4 (1961): 401–9.

52. Brashear, *Mark Twain*, 191.

53. Joseph Jones, "Review of 'The Letters of Quintus Curtius Snodgrass,'" *The Southwestern Historical Quarterly* 50, no. 4 (1947): 525.

54. Dixon Wecter, "Mark Twain: 'The Letters of Quintus Curtius Snodgrass,'" *New England Quarterly* 20, no. 2 (1947): 269.

55. Brashear, *Mark Twain*, 174.

56. Brashear, *Mark Twain*, 193.

57. Adam Goodheart, "Mark Twain and the Fortune-Teller," *New York Times*, February 5, 2011.

58. Claude S. Brinegar, "Mark Twain and the Quintus Curtius Snodgrass Letters: A Statistical Test of Authorship," *Journal of the American Statistical Association* 58, no. 301 (1963): 85–96.

59. Allan Bates, "The Quintus Curtius Snodgrass Letters: A Clarification of the Mark Twain Canon," *American Literature* 36, no. 1 (1964): 31–7.

60. Brashear, *Mark Twain*.

61. Howard G. Baetzhold, "Mark Twain and Dickens: Why the Denial?," *Dickens Studies Annual* 16 (1987): 189–219.

62. Caroline E. Janney, "'One of the Best Loved, North and South': The Appropriation of National Reconciliation by LaSalle Corbell Pickett," *Virginia Magazine of History and Biography* 116, no. 4 (2008): 371–406.

63. LaSalle Corbell Pickett, *The Heart of a Soldier, as Revealed in the Intimate Letters of Gen'l George E. Pickett, C.S.A.* (New York: Seth Moyle, 1913).

64. Corbell Pickett, *The Heart of a Soldier*, 75.

65. Gary W. Gallagher, "A Widow and Her Soldier: LaSalle Corbell Pickett as Author of the George E. Pickett Letters," *Virginia Magazine of History and Biography* 94, no. 3 (1986): 329–44.

66. Gallagher, "A Widow and Her Soldier,"

67. Gallagher, "A Widow and Her Soldier," 335.

68. Lesley J. Gordon, "Let the People See the Old Life as It Was," in *The Myth of the Lost Cause and Civil War History*, ed. Gary W. Gallagher and Alan T. Nolan (Bloomington: Indiana University Press, 2000), 170–84.

69. David I. Holmes, "Stylometry and the Civil War: The Case of the Pickett Letters," *Chance* 16, no. 2 (2003): 18–25.

70. David I. Holmes, Lesley J. Gordon, and Christine Wilson, "A Widow and Her Soldier: Stylometry and the Civil War," *Literary and Linguistic Computing* 16, no. 4 (2001): 403–20.

CHAPTER SEVEN

1. Donald W. Foster, *Author Unknown: On the Trail of Anonymous* (New York: Henry Holt, 2000).

2. Donald W. Foster, *Elegy by W.S.: A Study in Attribution* (Newark: University of Delaware Press, 1989).

3. Donald W. Foster, "SHAXICON 1995," *The Shakespeare Newsletter* 45, no. 2 (1995): 1, 30, 32.

4. Richard Dawson, "Author of Verse Was Not Bard," *Swissinfo.ch*, August 19, 2002, https://www.swissinfo.ch/eng/author-of-verse-was-not-bard/2839898.

5. Donald W. Foster, "A Funeral Elegy: W[illiam] S[hakespeare]'s 'Best-Speaking Witnesses,'" *PMLA* 111, no. 5 (1996): 1080–1105.

6. Stephen Wigler, "Requiem for an Elegy Essay: Attributing the 1612 'A Funeral Elegy' to Shakespeare Is Folly for a Very Good Reason: It's Too Bad," *Baltimore Sun*, April 8, 1996.

7. William H. Honan, "A Sleuth Gets His Suspect: Shakespeare," *New York Times*, January 14, 1996, A1.

8. G. D. Monsarrat, "'A Funeral Elegy': Ford, W.S., and Shakespeare," *The Review of English Studies* 53, no. 210 (2002): 192.

9. Ward E. Y. Elliott and Robert J. Valenza, "Smoking Guns and Silver Bullets: Could John Ford Have Written the 'Funeral Elegy'?," *Literary and Linguistic Computing* 16, no. 3, (2001): 205–32.

10. William S. Niederkorn, "A Scholar Recants on His 'Shakespeare' Discovery," *New York Times*, June 20, 2002, E1.

11. Brian Vickers, *"Counterfeiting" Shakespeare: Evidence, Authorship, and John Ford's "Funerall Elegye"* (Cambridge: Cambridge University Press, 2002).

12. William S. Niederkorn, "Beyond the Briefly Inflated Canon: Legacy of the Mysterious 'W.S.,'" *New York Times*, June 26, 2002.

13. Ron Rosenbaum, "Shakespeare's Ghostwriter: The Elegy Mystery Solved?," *The Observer*, January 19, 1998, https://observer.com/1998/01/shakespeares-ghostwriter-the-Elegy-mystery-solved.

14. Anonymous, "I Am Part of the Resistance inside the Trump Administration," *New York Times*, September 5, 2018.

15. Peter Baker and Maggie Haberman, "Trump Seethes as a 'Resistance' Spills into View," *New York Times*, September 6, 2018, A1.

16. Peter Baker, Maggie Haberman, and Eileen Sullivan, "Fingers Point, Denials Spread and Fury Rises," *New York Times*, September 7, 2018, A1.

17. Christal Hayes, "Whodunit? Social Media Users Search for Anonymous Trump Official Who Penned Scathing NYT Essay," *USA Today*, September 5, 2018.

18. *Inside Edition*, "New York Times Op-Ed Shrouded in Mystery as President Trump Desperately Tries to Find Writer," September 6, 2018.

19. Mahita Gajanan, "Vice President Pence Denies He's the 'Lodestar' behind Anonymous New York *Times* Op-Ed," *Time*, September 6, 2018.

20. *Inside Edition*, "New York Times Op-Ed Shrouded in Mystery as President Trump Desperately Tries to Find Writer."

21. Anonymous, *A Warning* (New York City: Twelve, 2019).

22. Tina Jordan, "'A Warning,' by Anonymous, Cracks the Best-Seller List," *New York Times*, November 27, 2019.

23. David Kusnet, "Could This Be the Guy Who Wrote Anonymous's Warning?," *The New Republic*, November 25, 2019.

24. Daniel Lippman, "Navarro Penned 15-Page Memo Falsely Accusing Coates of Being Anonymous," *Politico*, March 2, 2021.

25. Peter Navarro, *Memorandum. Subject: Identity of Anonymous*, December 2, 2019, https://www.politico.com/f/?id=00000177-ef37-d750-a77f-ffb703c00000.

26. Navarro, *Memorandum*, 3.

27. Meridith McGraw, "White House Transfers Top National Security Aide after Whisper Campaign," *Politico*, February 20, 2020.

28. Miles Taylor, "Why I'm No Longer 'Anonymous,'" https://milestaylor.medium.com/a-statement-a13bc5173ee9.

29. Janet Ainsworth and Patrick Juola, "Who Wrote This: Modern Forensic Authorship Analysis as a Model for Valid Forensic Science," *Washington University Law Review* 96, no. 5 (2019): 1159–88.

30. Carrie Tuhy, "Elena Ferrante's Publishers Discuss Her New Novel," *Publishers Weekly*, April 17, 2020.

31. James Wood, "Women on the Verge," *The New Yorker*, January 13, 2013.

32. Luigi Galella, "Ferrante è Starnone. Parola di computer," *l'Unita*, November 23, 2006, https://www.orphanalytics.com/fr/news/unita-ferrante-e-starnone.

33. Rachel Donadio, "Is Mystery Author Elena Ferrante Actually a History Professor?," *Sydney Morning Herald*, March 14, 2016.

34. E. Ce Miller, "Who Is Elena Ferrante? 9 Theories on the Author," *Bustle*, March 28, 2016, https://www.bustle.com/articles/150054-who-is-elena-ferrante-9-theories-on-the-identity-of-the-italian-author.

35. Claudio Gatti, "Elena Ferrante: An Answer? The Story behind a Name," *New York Review*, October 6, 2016.

36. Arjuna Tuzzi and Michele A. Cortelazzo, "It Takes Many Hands to Draw Elena Ferrante's Profile," in *Drawing Elena Ferrante's Profile: Workshop Proceedings*, ed. Arjuna Tuzzi and Michele A. Corelazzo (Padua: Padova University Press, 2018), 9–29.

37. Jacques Savoy, "Elena Ferrante Unmasked," in Tuzzi and Cortelazzo, *Drawing Elena Ferrante's Profile*, 123–41.

38. Arjuna Tuzzi and Michele A. Cortelazzo, "What Is Elena Ferrante? A Comparative Analysis of a Secretive Bestselling Italian Writer," *Digital Scholarship in the Humanities* 33, no. 3 (2018): 685–702.

39. Karen Bojar, *In Search of Elena Ferrante: The Novels and the Question of Authorship* (Jefferson, NC: McFarland, 2018).

40. Jan Rybicki, "Partners in Life, Partners in Crime?," in Tuzzi and Cortelazzo, *Drawing Elena Ferrante's Profile*, 111–22.

41. Elisa Sotgiu, "Have Italian Scholars Figured Out the Identity of Elena Ferrante?," *Literary Hub*, March 31, 2021, https://lithub.com/have-italian-scholars-figured-out-the-identity-of-elena-ferrante.

42. Alexandra Schwartz, "The 'Unmasking' of Elena Ferrante," *The New Yorker*, October 3, 2016.

43. Jeanette Winterson, "The Malice and Sexism behind the 'Unmasking' of Elena Ferrante," *The Guardian*, October 16, 2016.

44. Rachel Donadio, "My Search for Elena Ferrante." *The New Yorker*, December 2018.

45. Rybicki, "Partners in Life, Partners in Crime?"

46. Andrew Q. Morton, *Literary Detection: How to Prove Authorship and Fraud in Literature and Documents* (New York: Charles Scribner, 1978).

47. M. W. A. Smith, "An Investigation of the Basis of Morton's Method for the Determination of Authorship," *Style* 19, no. 3 (1985): 355.

48. Thomas Merriam, "The Strange Case of Sir Thomas More," *Moreana* 18, no. 71/72 (1981): 113.

49. M. W. A. Smith, "Pseudoscience: A Comedy of Statistical Errors," *Style* 22, no. 4 (1988): 650–53.

50. Thomas Merriam, "A Reply to 'An Investigation of the Basis of Morton's Method for the Determination of Authorship,'" *Style* 22, no. 4 (1988): 646–49.

51. Trevor Howard Howard-Hill, ed., *Shakespeare and Sir Thomas More: Essays on the Play and Its Shakespearian Interest* (Cambridge: Cambridge University Press, 1989).

52. Jill M. Farringdon, *Analysing for Authorship: A Guide to the Cusum Technique* (Cardiff: University of Wales Press, 1996).

53. Michael L. Hilton and David I. Holmes, "An Assessment of Cumulative Sum Charts for Authorship Attribution," *Literary and Linguistic Computing* 8, no. 2 (1993): 73–80.

54. David Canter and Joanne Chester, "Investigation into the Claim of Weighted Cusum in Authorship Attribution Studies," *Forensic Linguistics* 4 (1997): 252–61.

55. David Canter, "An Evaluation of the 'CUSUM' Stylistic Analysis of Confessions," *Expert Evidence* 1, no. 2 (1992): 93–99.

56. Malcolm Coulthard and Alison Johnson, *An Introduction to Forensic Linguistics* (London: Routledge, 2007), 168.

57. Michael P. Oakes, "Computer Stylometry of CS Lewis's The Dark Tower and Related Texts," *Digital Scholarship in the Humanities* 33, no. 3 (2018): 637–50.

58. Anthony J. Sanford, Joy P. Aked, Linda M. Moxey, and James Mullin, "A Critical Examination of Assumptions Underlying the Cusum Technique of Forensic Linguistics," *International Journal of Speech, Language and the Law* 1, no. 2 (1994): 151–67.

59. David I. Holmes, "The Evolution of Stylometry in Humanities Scholarship," *Literary and Linguistic Computing* 13, no. 3 (1998): 111–17.

60. Russell Blackstock, "'We Need More Like Him, People Unafraid to Stand Up to the System, and for Justice': One of the Birmingham Six Hails Scots Minister Who Helped Clear Them," *Sunday Post*, February 12, 2019.

61. Robert Matthews, "Linguistics on Trial: Forensic Scientists Have Fiercely Condemned a Technique Used in Court to Show That Confessions Have Been Tampered With," *New Scientist*, August 21, 1993.

62. Alan Q. Morton, "The Rev Andrew Q Morton Obituary," *The Guardian*, February 5, 2019.

63. Stephen Engelberg, Greg Gordon, Jim Gilmore, and Mike Wiser, "Did Bruce Ivins Hide Attack Anthrax from the FBI?," *Frontline*, October 10, 2011, https://www.pbs.org/wgbh/frontline/article/did-bruce-ivins-hide-attack-anthrax-from-the-fbi.

64. Steve Thomas, *JonBenét: Inside the Ramsey Murder Investigation* (New York: St. Martin's Press, 2000).

65. Jane Musgrave, "Signs of Madness Boost Anthrax Suit," *Palm Beach Post*, August 17, 2008, C1.

66. Don Foster, "The Message in the Anthrax," *Vanity Fair*, October 2003, 180–200.

67. *Hatfill, Steven J. v. Donald Foster et al.*, USDC-EDVA, 04-cv-1001 (LMB).

68. Josh Gerstein, "Hatfill Settles $10M Libel Lawsuit," *New York Sun*, February 27, 2007.

69. Scott Shane and Eric Lichtblau, "Scientist Is Paid Millions by U.S. in Anthrax Suit," *New York Times*, June 28, 2008.

70. *New York Times*, "Man Suspected in Anthrax Attacks Said to Commit Suicide," August 1, 2008.

71. Engelberg et al., "Did Bruce Ivins Hide Attack Anthrax from the FBI?"

72. U.S. Department of Justice, *Amerithrax Investigative Summary*, February 19, 2010, https://www.justice.gov/archive/amerithrax/docs/amx-investigative-summary.pdf.

73. David Willman, *The Mirage Man: Bruce Ivins, the Anthrax Attacks, and America's Rush to War* (New York: Random House, 2011).

74. Yudhijit Bhattacharjee, "Science in Ivins Case Not Ironclad, NRC Say," *Science* 331, no. 6019 (2011): 835.

75. U.S. Government Accountability Office, "Anthrax: Agency Approaches to Validation and Statistical Analyses Could Be Improved," December 2014, https://www.gao.gov/products/gao-15-80.

76. David Freed, "The Wrong Man," *The Atlantic*, May 2010, 46–56, https://www.theatlantic.com/magazine/archive/2010/05/the-wrong-man/308019.

CHAPTER EIGHT

1. John M. Jones and Robert C. Rowland, "The Weekly Radio Addresses of President Ronald Reagan," *Journal of Radio Studies* 7, no. 2 (2000): 257–81.

2. Russell D. Buhite and David W. Levy, *FDR's Fireside Chats* (Norman: University of Oklahoma Press, 1992).

3. Ronald Reagan, *Ronald Reagan: An American Life* (New York: Simon and Schuster, 1990), 169.

4. David Brooks, "Reagan Was a Reaganite," *New York Times*, January 28, 2001, sec. 7, p. 5.

5. Kiron K. Skinner, Annelise Anderson, and Martin Anderson, eds., *Reagan's Path to Victory: The Shaping of Ronald Reagan's Vision: Selected Writings* (New York: Free Press, 2004).

6. Kiron K. Skinner, Annelise Anderson, and Martin Anderson, eds., *Reagan in His Own Hand: The Writings of Ronald Reagan That Reveal His Revolutionary Vision for America* (New York: Touchstone, 2001).

7. Edoardo M. Airoldi, *Who Wrote Ronald Reagan's Radio Addresses?* (Technical Report CMU-STAT-03-789, Carnegie Mellon University, 2003).

8. Steven F. Hayward, *The Age of Reagan: The Fall of the Old Liberal Order, 1964–1980* (New York: Three Rivers Press, 2001).

9. Stephen F. Knott and Russell L. Riley, *Ronald Reagan Oral History Project Interview with Peter Hannaford* (Charlottesville: University of Virginia, The Miller

Center Foundation, 2005), http://web1.millercenter.org/poh/transcripts/ohp_2003 _0110_hannaford.pdf.

10. Edoardo M. Airoldi, Stephen E. Fienberg, and Kiron K. Skinner, "Whose Ideas? Whose Words? Authorship of Ronald Reagan's Radio Addresses," *PS: Political Science and Politics* 40, no. 3 (2007): 501–6.

11. Edoardo M. Airoldi, Annelise G. Anderson, Stephen E. Fienberg, and Kiron K. Skinner, "Who Wrote Ronald Reagan's Radio Addresses?," *Bayesian Analysis* 1, no. 2 (2006): 289–319.

12. William Safire, "Bugging Each Other," *New York Times*, October 11, 1981, sec. 4, p. 21.

13. Robert C. Rowland and John M. Jones. "'Until Next Week': The Saturday Radio Addresses of Ronald Reagan," *Presidential Studies Quarterly* 32, no. 1 (2002): 84–110.

14. Lori Cox Han, "New Strategies for an Old Medium: The Weekly Radio Addresses of Reagan and Clinton," *Congress and the Presidency: A Journal of Capital Studies* 33, no. 1 (2006): 25–45.

15. Jason Slotkin, "Biden Revives Presidential Tradition, Releasing First Weekly Address," National Public Radio, February 6, 2021.

16. Christopher Hitchens, *Thomas Paine's Rights of Man: A Biography* (New York: Grove Press, 2006).

17. Jill Lepore, "The Sharpened Quill: Was Thomas Paine Too Much of a Freethinker for the Country He Helped Free?," *The New Yorker*, October 16, 2006.

18. Thomas Paine, *The American Crisis No. 1* (Fishkill, NY: Samuel Loudon, 1776).

19. Thomas Paine, *Rights of Man: Being an Answer to Mr. Burke's Attack on the French Revolution* (Dublin, 1791).

20. Paul Collins, *The Trouble with Tom: The Strange Afterlife and Times of Thomas Paine* (New York: Bloomsbury Publishing, 2005).

21. Gary Berton, Smiljana Petrovic, Lubomir Ivanov, and Robert Schiaffino, "Examining the Thomas Paine Corpus: Automated Computer Authorship Attribution Methodology Applied to Thomas Paine's Writings," in *New Directions in Thomas Paine Studies*, ed. Scott Cleary and Ivy L. Stabell (New York: Palgrave Macmillan, 2016), 31–47.

22. Lee Sigelman, Colin Martindale, and Dean McKenzie, "The Common Style of 'Common Sense,'" *Computers and the Humanities* 30, no. 5 (1996): 373.

23. J. C. D. Clark, "Monuments to Liberty," *The Times Literary Supplement*, September 18, 2015, 15.

24. Richard Forsyth and David Holmes. "The Writeprints of Man: A Stylometric Study of Lafayette's Hand in Paine's 'Rights of Man,'" *Digital Humanities Quarterly* 12, no. 1 (2018), http://www.digitalhumanities.org/dhq/vol/12/1/000371/000371.html.

25. Mike Duncan, *Hero of Two Worlds: The Marquis de Lafayette in the Age of Revolution* (New York: PublicAffairs, 2021).

26. Israel Shenker, "Thomas Paine, Radical of 1776, Honored Belatedly by City Fathers," *New York Times*, January 10, 1976, 55.

27. *New York Times*, "Thomas Paine's Old House: Place Where the Writer Labored Is in the Hands of the Wreckers," March 9, 1930, 148.

28. Olivia B. Waxman, "Fact-Checking 'The Ballad of Davy Crockett,'" *Time*, August 17, 2016.

29. Thomas Lawrence Connelly, "Did David Crockett Surrender at the Alamo? A Contemporary Letter," *Journal of Southern History* 26, no. 3 (1960): 368–76.

30. Melvin Rosser Mason, "'The Lion of the West': Satire on Davy Crockett and Frances Trollope," *The South Central Bulletin* 29, no. 4 (1969): 143–45.

31. Joseph Leach, "Crockett's Almanacs and the Typical Texan," *Southwest Review* 35, no. 2 (1950): 88–95.

32. James French, *Sketches and Eccentricities of Col. David Crockett, of West Tennessee* (New York: J & J Harper, 1833).

33. James Atkins Shackford, "The Author of David Crockett's Autobiography," *Boston Library Quarterly*, October 1951, 294–304.

34. David Crockett, *A Narrative of the Life of David Crockett of the State of Tennessee, Written by Himself* (Philadelphia: E. L. Carey and A. Hart, 1834).

35. James Atkins Shackford, *David Crockett: The Man and the Legend* (Lincoln: University of Nebraska Press, 1956).

36. David Crockett, *An Account of Col. Crockett's Tour to the North and Down East* (Philadelphia: E. L. Carey and A. Hart, 1835).

37. Michael Wallis, *David Crockett: The Lion of the West* (New York: Norton, 2011).

38. David Crockett, *The Life of Martin van Buren, Heir-Apparent to the "Government" and the Appointed Successor of General Andrew Jackson* (Philadelphia: Robert Wright, 1837).

39. John Donald Wade, "The Authorship of David Crockett's 'Autobiography,'" *Georgia Historical Quarterly* 6, no. 3 (1922): 265–68.

40. Richard Penn Smith, *Col. Crockett's Exploits and Adventures in Texas* (Philadelphia: T. K. and P. G. Collins, 1836).

41. J. C. Derby, *Fifty Years among Authors, Books and Publishers* (New York: G. W. Carleton, 1884).

42. David Salsburg and Dena Salsburg, "Searching for the 'Real' Davy Crockett," *Chance* 12, no. 2 (1999): 29–34.

43. David Holmes and Ferris Samara, "Was the Wild Frontiersman a Prolific Penman? A Stylometric Investigation into the Works of Davy Crockett," *Chance* 33, no. 2 (2020): 7–18.

44. Wallis, *David Crockett*.

45. Graham Seal and Kennedy White, eds., *Folk Heroes and Heroines around the World*, 2nd ed. (Santa Barbara, CA: ABC-CLIO).

46. John F. Kennedy, *Profiles in Courage: Decisive Moments in the Lives of Celebrated Americans* (New York: Harper & Brothers, 1956).

47. James Piereson, *Shattered Consensus: The Rise and Decline of America's Postwar Political Order* (New York: Encounter Books, 2015).

48. John F. Kennedy, *Why England Slept* (New York: Wilfred Funk, 1940).

49. Craig Fehrman, *Author in Chief: The Untold Story of Our Presidents and the Books They Wrote* (New York: Avid Reader Press, 2020), 266.

50. Robert Mcg. Thomas Jr., "Jules Davids Dies at 75; Helped Kennedy with 'Profiles' Book," *New York Times*, December 12, 1996, B24.

51. Patricia Cohen, "An Old Letter Backs a Claim of Helping Kennedy Write 'Profiles,'" *New York Times*, October 18, 1997, B7.

52. David R. Stokes, *JFK's Ghost: Kennedy, Sorensen and the Making of "Profiles in Courage"* (Lanham, MD: Lyons Press, 2021).

53. Mike Wallace and Gary P. Gates, *Between You and Me: A Memoir* (New York: Hyperion, 2005).

54. Richard Reeves, *President Kennedy: Profile of Power* (New York: Simon and Schuster, 1993).

55. Herbert S. Parmet, *Jack: The Struggles of John F. Kennedy* (New York: Dial Press, 1980).

56. Jeffrey Toobin, "Amanuensis," *The New Yorker*, May 5, 2008.

57. Ted Sorensen, *Counselor: A Life at the Edge of History* (New York: HarperCollins, 2008), 151.

58. Sorensen, *Counselor*, 146.

59. Donald J. Trump and Tony Schwartz, *Trump: The Art of the Deal* (New York: Random House, 1987).

60. Jane Mayer, "Donald Trump's Ghostwriter Tells All," *The New Yorker*, July 18, 2016.

61. Peter Osnos, "Editing Donald Trump," *The New Yorker*, November 3, 2019.

62. Alan Rappeport, "'I Feel a Deep Sense of Remorse,' Donald Trump's Ghostwriter Says," *New York Times*, July 18, 2016.

63. Time Staff, "Here's Donald Trump's Presidential Announcement Speech," June 16, 2015, https://time.com/3923128/donald-trump-announcement-speech.

64. Mayer, "Donald Trump's Ghostwriter Tells All."

65. Nicholas Fandos, "Trump Lawyer Sends 'Art of the Deal' Ghostwriter a Cease-and-Desist Letter," *New York Times*, July 21, 2016.

EPILOGUE

1. Efstathios Stamatatos, "A Survey of Modern Authorship Attribution Methods," *Journal of the American Society for Information Science and Technology* 60, no. 3 (2009): 538–56.

2. James Somers, "How the Artificial-Intelligence Program AlphaZero Mastered Its Games, *The New Yorker*, December 28, 2018.

3. Davide Castelvecchi, "Can We Open the Black Box of AI?," *Nature News* 538, no. 7623 (October 6, 2016): 20–23.

4. Mudit Bhargava, Pulkit Mehndiratta, and Krishna Asawa, "Stylometric Analysis for Authorship Attribution on Twitter," in *International Conference on Big Data Analytics* (Cham: Springer, 2013), 37–47.

5. Annie Linskey, "Inside the Trump Tweet Machine: Staff-Written Posts, Bad Grammar (on Purpose), and Delight in the Chaos," *Boston Globe*, May 22, 2018.

6. Andrew W. E. McDonald, Sadia Afroz, Aylin Caliskan, Ariel Stolerman, and Rachel Greenstadt, "Use Fewer Instances of the Letter 'i': Toward Writing Style Anonymization," in *Privacy Enhancing Technologies. PETS 2012. Lecture Notes in Computer Science*, vol. 7384, ed. S. Fischer-Hübner and M. Wright (Berlin: Springer, 2012), 299–318.

7. Asad Mahmood, Zubair Shafiq, and Padmini Srinivasan, "A Girl Has a Name: Detecting Authorship Obfuscation," in *Proceedings of the 58th Annual Meeting of the Association for Computational Linguistics* (Stroudsburg, PA: Association for Computational Linguistics, 2020), 2235–45.

8. Antonios Patergianakis and Konstantinos Limniotis, "Privacy Issues in Stylometric Methods," *Cryptography* 6, no. 2 (2022): 17.

Bibliography

Adair, Douglass. "The Authorship of the Disputed Federalist Papers." *William and Mary Quarterly* 1, no. 2 (April 1944a): 97–122.

———. "The Authorship of the Disputed Federalist Papers: Part II." *William and Mary Quarterly* 1, no. 3 (July 1944b): 235–64.

Ainsworth, Janet, and Patrick Juola. "Who Wrote This: Modern Forensic Authorship Analysis as a Model for Valid Forensic Science." *Washington University Law Review* 96, no. 5 (2019): 1159–88.

Airoldi, Edoardo M. *Who Wrote Ronald Reagan's Radio Addresses?* Technical Report CMU-STAT-03-789, Carnegie Mellon University, 2003.

Airoldi, Edoardo M., Annelise G. Anderson, Stephen E. Fienberg, and Kiron K. Skinner. "Who Wrote Ronald Reagan's Radio Addresses?" *Bayesian Analysis* 1, no. 2 (2006): 289–319.

Airoldi, Edoardo M., Stephen E. Fienberg, and Kiron K. Skinner. "Whose Ideas? Whose Words? Authorship of Ronald Reagan's Radio Addresses." *PS: Political Science & Politics* 40, no. 3 (2007): 501–6.

Alexander, Christine, and Margaret Smith. *The Oxford Companion to the Brontës: Anniversary Edition.* Oxford: Oxford University Press, 2018.

Allen, Hervey, and Thomas O. Mabbot, eds. *Poe's Brother: The Poems of William Henry Leonard Poe.* New York: George H. Dorian Co., 1926.

Alter, Alexandra. "Harper Lee and Truman Capote: A Collaboration in Mischief." *New York Times*, August 9, 2015.

Anderson, Frank Maloy. *The Mystery of "A Public Man": A Historical Detective Story.* Minneapolis: University of Minnesota Press, 1948.

Anderson, R. C., C. A. Klofstad, W. J. Mayew, and M. Venkatachalam. "Vocal Fry May Undermine the Success of Young Women in the Labor Market." *PLoS One* 9, no. 5 (2014): e97506.

Anonymous. "I Am Part of the Resistance inside the Trump Administration." *New York Times*, September 5, 2018.

———. *A Warning.* New York: Twelve, 2019.

Anonymous/Joe Klein. *Primary Colors: A Novel of Politics.* New York: Random House, 1996.

————. "No, Really, I Am Anonymous." *New York Times*, May 19, 1996, sec. 7, p. 43.

Ayres, B. Drummond. "Man Held as Unabomber is Indicted in 2 Slayings." *New York Times*, June 19, 1996, A12.

Baetzhold, Howard G. "Mark Twain and Dickens: Why the Denial?" *Dickens Studies Annual* 16, 1987: 189–219.

Bailey, S. A. "Notes on Authorship of Disputed Numbers of the Federalist." *Case and Content* 22 no. 8 (1916): 674–75.

Baker, Peter, and Maggie Haberman. "Trump Seethes as a 'Resistance' Spills into View." *New York Times*, September 6, 2018, A1.

Baker, Peter, Maggie Haberman, and Eileen Sullivan. "Fingers Point, Denials Spread and Fury Rises." *New York Times*, September 7, 2018, A1.

Baltussen, Han. "Cicero's 'Consolatio ad se': Character, Purpose and Impact of a Curious Treatise." In *Greek and Roman Consolations: Eight Studies of a Tradition and Its Afterlife*, edited by Hans Baltussen, 67–91. Swansea: The Classical Press of Wales, 2013.

Barker, Nicolas. "C. S. Lewis, Darkly." *Essays in Criticism* 40 (1990): 358–67.

Bates, Allan. "The Quintus Curtius Snodgrass Letters: A Clarification of the Mark Twain Canon." *American Literature* 36, no. 1 (1964): 31–37.

Baum, L. Frank, and Ruth Plumly Thompson. *The Royal Book of Oz*. Chicago: Reilly & Lee Co., 1921.

BBC News. "Murder Probe Police Discover Body," July 21, 2005. news.bbc.co.uk/2 /hi/uk_news/england/south_yorkshire/4703689.stm.

————. "Life Term for Man Who Shot Lover," November 8, 2005. news.bbc.co.uk/2 /hi/uk_news/england/south_yorkshire/4418518.stm.

Bearss, Edwin C. "The Seizure of the Forts and Public Property in Louisiana." *Louisiana History* 2, no. 4 (1961): 401–9.

Benson, Edward Frederic. *Charlotte Bronte: A Biography*. New York: Longman, Green and Co., 1932.

Berton, Gary, Smiljana Petrovic, Lubomir Ivanov, and Robert Schiaffino. "Examining the Thomas Paine Corpus: Automated Computer Authorship Attribution Methodology Applied to Thomas Paine's Writings." In *New Directions in Thomas Paine Studies*, edited by Scott Cleary and Ivy L. Stabell, 31–47. New York: Palgrave Macmillan, 2016.

Bevan, Nathan. "Welsh Expert Key Witness in Da Vinci Battle." *WalesOnline*, June 11, 2006. https://www.walesonline.co.uk/news/wales-news/welsh-expert-key-witness -da-2332668.

Bhargava, Mudit, Pulkit Mehndiratta, and Krishna Asawa. "Stylometric Analysis for Authorship Attribution on Twitter." In *International Conference on Big Data Analytics*, 37–47. Cham: Springer, 2013.

Bhattacharjee, Yudhijit. "Science in Ivins Case Not Ironclad, NRC Say." *Science* 331, no. 6019 (February 18, 2011): 835.

Binongo, José N. G. "Who Wrote the 15th Book of Oz? An Application of Multivariate Analysis to Authorship Attribution." *Chance* 16, no. 2 (2003): 9–17.

Binongo, José N. G., and D'arcy P. Mays III. "A Study of the Authorship of the Books of Oz Using Nested Linear Models." *Computations in Statistics—Simulation and Computation* 34 (2005): 293–308.

Blackstock, Russell. "'We Need More Like Him, People Unafraid to Stand Up to the System, and for Justice': One of the Birmingham Six Hails Scots Minister Who Helped Clear Them." *The Sunday Post*, February 12, 2019.

Bloch, Bernard. "A Set of Postulates for Phonemic Analysis." *Language* 24, no. 1 (1948): 3–46.

Blum, Paul Richard, ed. *Philosophers of the Renaissance*, translated by Brian McNeil. Washington, DC: Catholic University of America Press, 2010.

Boaden, James. *A Letter to George Stevens, Esq. Containing a Critical Examination of the Papers of Shakspeare*. London: Martin and Bain, 1796.

Bojar, Karen. *In Search of Elena Ferrante: The Novels and the Question of Authorship*. Jefferson, NC: McFarland, 2018.

Books, Richard, and Cal Flyn. "JK Rowling, the Cuckoo in Crime Novel Nest." *Sunday Times*, July 14, 2013.

Bosman, Julie. "Rowling Book Skyrockets to Instant Hit." *New York Times*, July 16, 2013.

———. "Rowling Leak Mystery: The Lawyer Did It." *New York Times*, July 18, 2013, C3.

Boyd, Ryan L., and James W. Pennebaker. "Did Shakespeare Write 'Double Falsehood'? Identifying Individuals by Creating Psychological Signatures with Text Analysis." *Psychological Science* 26, no. 5 (2015): 570–82.

Brandes, Wolfram. "The Satraps of Constantine." In James Fried, *Donation of Constantine and Constitum Constantini*, 115–27. Berlin: de Gruyter, 2007.

Brandwood, Leonard. *The Chronology of Plato's Dialogues*. Cambridge: Cambridge University Press, 1990.

Brashear, Minnie M. *Mark Twain: Son of Missouri*. Chapel Hill: University of North Carolina Press, 1934.

Brinegar, Claude S. "Mark Twain and the Quintus Curtius Snodgrass Letters: A Statistical Test of Authorship." *Journal of the American Statistical Association* 58, no. 301 (1963): 85–96.

Brontës, The. *Tales of Glass Town, Angria, and Gondal: Selected Early Writings*. Oxford: Oxford University Press, 2010.

Brooks, David. "Reagan Was a Reaganite." *New York Times*, January 28, 2001, sec. 7, p. 5.

Bruni, Frank. "On the Unabomber's Track: The Hunters; With a Family Discovery, a Manhunt Comes to an End." *New York Times*, April 4, 1996, B13.

Buhite, Russell D., and David W. Levy. *FDR's Fireside Chats*. Norman: University of Oklahoma Press, 1992.

Burrows, John F. *Computation into Criticism: A Study of Jane Austen's Novels and an Experiment in Method*. Oxford: Clarendon Press, 1987.

———. "Not unless You Ask Nicely: The Interpretative Nexus between Analysis and Information." *Literary and Linguistic Computing* 7, no. 2 (1992): 91–109.

———. "Computers and the Study of Literature." In *Computers and Written Texts*, edited by Christopher S. Butler, 167–204. Oxford: Blackwell, 1992.

———. "'Delta': A Measure of Stylistic Difference and a Guide to Likely Authorship." *Literary and Linguistic Computing* 17, no. 3 (2002): 267–87.

———. "Questions of Authorship: Attribution and Beyond." *Computers and the Humanities* 37, no. 1 (2003): 5–32.

———. "All the Way Through: Testing for Authorship in Different Frequency Strata." *Literary and Linguistic Computing* 22, no. 1 (2007): 27–47.

Burrows, John F., and Anthony J. Hassall. "'Anna Boleyn' and the Authenticity of Fielding's Feminine Narratives." *Eighteenth-Century Studies* 21, no. 4 (1988): 427–53.

Busa, Roberto. "The Annals of Computing: The Index Thomisticus." *Computers and the Humanities* 14, no. 2 (1980): 83–90.

Camdram. "Vortigern." https://www.camdram.net/shows/2008-vortigern.

Camproreale, Salvatore I. "Lorenzo Valla's 'Oratio' on the Pseudo-Donation of Constantine: Dissent and Innovation in Early Renaissance Humanism." *Journal of the History of Ideas* 57, no. 1 (1996): 9–26.

Canter, David. "An Evaluation of the 'CUSUM' Stylistic Analysis of Confessions." *Expert Evidence* 1, no. 2 (1992): 93–99.

Canter, David, and Joanne Chester. "Investigation into the Claim of Weighted Cusum in Authorship Attribution Studies." *Forensic Linguistics* 4 (1997): 252–61.

Carnegie, David, and Gary Taylor. *The Quest for Cardenio: Shakespeare, Fletcher, Cervantes, and the Lost Play*. Oxford: Oxford University Press, 2012.

Carter, Michele. *Charlotte Brontë's Thunder: The Truth behind the Bronte Sisters' Genius*. Lincoln, NE: Boomer Publications, 2011.

———. "Author Attribution Analysis of the Brontë Novels." *The McScribble Salon*, May 18, 2017. http://www.michelecartersblog.com/2017/05/author-attribution -analysis-of-bronte.html.

Castelvecchi, Davide. "Can We Open the Black Box of AI?" *Nature News* 538, no. 7623 (October 6, 2016): 20–23.

Ce Miller, E. "Who Is Elena Ferrante? Theories on the Author." *Bustle*, March 28, 2016. https://www.bustle.com/articles/150054-who-is-elena-ferrante-9-theories-on-the -identity-of-the-italian-author.

Cep, Casey. "Harper Lee's Abandoned True-Crime Novel." *The New Yorker*, March 17, 2015.

Ćetković, Sanja. "Position of Temporal Adverbs in Police Reports in English." *Mediterranean Journal of Social Sciences* 5, no. 13 (2014): 217–21.

Chicago Tribune. "Handwriting Gives Clues to 'Primary' Author, Paper Says." July 17, 1996.

Choiński, Michał, Maciej Eder, and Jan Rybicki. "Harper Lee and Other People: A Stylometric Analysis." *Mississippi Quarterly* 70/71, no. 3 (2017/2018): 355–74.

Clark, J. C. D. "Monuments to Liberty." *Times Literary Supplement*, September 18, 2015, 14–15.

Clemens, Samuel L. *The Adventures of Thomas Jefferson Snodgrass*, edited by Charles Honce. Chicago: Pascal Covici, 1928.

Cohen, Patricia. "An Old Letter Backs a Claim of Helping Kennedy Write 'Profiles.'" *New York Times*, October 18, 1997, sec. B, p. 7.

Coleman, Christopher. *The Treatise of Lorenzo Valla on the Donation of Constantine: Text and Translation into English*. New Haven, CT: Yale University Press, 1922.

Coleman-Norton, P. R. "The Fragmentary Philosophical Treatises of Cicero." *The Classical Journal* 34, no. 4 (1939): 213–28.

Collins, Paul. *The Trouble with Tom: The Strange Afterlife and Times of Thomas Paine*. New York: Bloomsbury Publishing, 2005.

———. "Poe's Debut, Hidden in Plain Sight?" *The New Yorker*, October 4, 2013.

Connelly, Thomas Lawrence. "Did David Crockett Surrender at the Alamo? A Contemporary Letter." *Journal of Southern History* 26, no. 3 (1960): 368–76.

Cook, Erik C., Jessica L. Schleider, and Leah H. Somerville. "A Linguistic Signature of Psychological Distancing in Emotion Regulation." *Journal of Experimental Psychology: General* 46, no. 3 (2017): 337–46.

Cooper Willis, Irene. "The Authorship of 'Wuthering Heights.'" *The Trollopian* 2, no. 3 (1947): 157–68.

Corbell Pickett, LaSalle. *The Heart of a Soldier, as Revealed in the Intimate Letters of Gen'l George E. Pickett, C.S.A.* New York: Seth Moyle, 1913.

Corley, Pamela C., J. D. Robert, M. Howard, and David C. Nixon. "The Supreme Court and Opinion Content: The Use of the Federalist Papers." *Political Research Quarterly* 58, no. 2 (2005): 329–40.

Corrigan, Maureen. "The Only Surprise in Rowling's 'Cuckoo's Calling' Is the Author." National Public Radio, July 18, 2013.

Coulthard, Malcolm. "Explorations in Applied Linguistics 3: Forensic Stylistics." In *Principle and Practice in Applied Linguistics: Studies in Honour of H. G. Widdowson*, edited by Guy Cook and Barbara Seidlhofer, 229–43. Oxford: Oxford University Press, 1995.

———. "Author Identification, Idiolect, and Linguistic Uniqueness." *Applied Linguistics* 25, no. 4 (2004): 431–47.

Coulthard, Malcolm, and Alison Johnson. *An Introduction to Forensic Linguistics.* London: Routledge, 2007.

Cowart, David. *Thomas Pynchon and the Dark Passages of History.* Athens: University of Georgia Press, 2011.

Craig, Hugh. "John Burrows, AM, FAHA." *Australian Academy of the Humanities, Obituaries 2019–2020.* https://www.humanities.org.au/wp-content/uploads/2020/12/BURROWS-Final-2.pdf.

Crawford, Hillary E. "The JonBenet Ransom Note Was Signed 'S.B.T.C.'" *Bustle*, September 18, 2016. https://www.bustle.com/articles/184633-what-does-sbtc-stand-for-the-jonbenet-ramsey-ransom-note-had-a-mysterious-signature.

Creasy, William C. *The Imitation of Christ: A New Reading of the 1441 Latin Autograph Manuscript.* Macon, GA: Mercer University Press, 2007.

Crockett, David. *A Narrative of the Life of David Crockett of the State of Tennessee, Written by Himself.* Philadelphia: E. L. Carey and A. Hart, 1834.

———. *An Account of Col. Crockett's Tour to the North and Down East.* Philadelphia: E. L. Carey and A. Hart, 1835.

———. *The Life of Martin van Buren, Heir-Apparent to the "Government" and the Appointed Successor of General Andrew Jackson.* Philadelphia: Robert Wright, 1837.

Crofts, Daniel W. *A Secession Crisis Enigma: William Henry Hurlbert and 'The Diary of a Public Man.'* Baton Rouge: Louisiana State University Press, 2010.

Cruise, Francis Richard. *Who Was the Author of "The Imitation of Christ"?* London: Catholic Truth Society, 1898

Crystal, Ben, and David Crystal. *You Say Potato: A Book about Accents.* New York: Macmillan, 2015.

Da, Nan Z. "The Computational Case against Computational Literary Studies." *Critical Inquiry* 45 (Spring 2019): 601–39.

Davies, Dave. "FBI Profiler Says Linguistic Work Was Pivotal in Capture of Unabomber." *Fresh Air*, National Public Radio, August 22, 2017.

Dawson, Richard. "Author of Verse Was Not Bard," August 19, 2002. https://www.swissinfo.ch/eng/author-of-verse-was-not-bard/2839898.

Dawtry, Frank. "The Abolition of the Death Penalty in Britain." *British Journal of Criminology* 6, no. 2 (1966): 183–92.

Dempsey, David. "The Wizard of Baum." *New York Times*, May 13, 1956, 255.

Derby, J. C. *Fifty Years among Authors, Books and Publishers.* New York: G. W. Carleton, 1884.

DiLollo, Anthony, Julie Scherz, and Robert A. Neimeyer. "Psychosocial Implications of Foreign Accent Syndrome: Two Case Examples." *Journal of Constructivist Psychology* 27, no. 1 (2014): 14–30.

Donadio, Rachel. "Is Mystery Author Elena Ferrante Actually a History Professor?" *Sydney Morning Herald*, March 14, 2016.

———. "My Search for Elena Ferrante." *The New Yorker*, December 2018.

Drake, Phil. "Unabomber's Legacy Resonates 25 Years after Arrest in Montana." *Helena Independent Record*, April 2, 2021.

Dresbold, Michelle. *Sex, Lies and Handwriting: A Top Expert Reveals the Secrets Hidden in Your Handwriting*. New York: Free Press, 2017.

Drew, Sybil. *Self Styled Genius: The Life of Thomas Corwin Mendenhall*. Jan & Brooklyn, 2016.

Duncan, Mike. *Hero of Two Worlds: The Marquis de Lafayette in the Age of Revolution*. New York: PublicAffairs, 2021.

Eder, M., and J. Rybicki. "Go Set a Watchman while We Kill the Mockingbird in Cold Blood, with Cats and Other People." In *Digital Humanities 2016: Conference Abstracts*, 184–6. Kraków: Jagiellonian University and Pedagogical University, 2016.

Edgar Allen Poe Society of Baltimore. "Where Poe Lived, Worked, and Visited," January 2014. https://www.eapoe.org/places/phindx.htm.

Elliott, Ward E. Y., and Robert J. Valenza. "Smoking Guns and Silver Bullets: Could John Ford Have Written the 'Funeral Elegy'?" *Literary and Linguistic Computing* 16, no. 3 (2001): 205–32.

Ellis, E. Earle. "The Authorship of the Pastorals: A Résumé and Assessment of Current Trends." *Evangelical Quarterly* 32 (1960): 151–61.

Ellis, Robinson. "On the Pseudo-Ciceronian 'Consolatio.'" *The Classical Review* 7, no. 5 (1893): 197.

Elster, Charles Harrington. *The Big Book of Beastly Mispronunciations: The Complete Guide for the Careful Speaker*. Boston: Houghton Mifflin, 2005.

Engelberg, Stephen, Greg Gordon, Jim Gilmore, and Mike Wiser. "Did Bruce Ivins Hide Attack Anthrax from the FBI?" *Frontline*, October 10, 2011. https://www.pbs.org/wgbh/frontline/article/did-bruce-ivins-hide-attack-anthrax-from-the-fbi.

Eusebius. *Life of Constantine*. Translated by Averil Cameron and Stuart G. Hall. Oxford: Clarendon Press, 1999.

Evert, Stefan, Thomas Proisl, Fotis Jannidis, Isabella Reger, Steffen Pielström, Christof Schöch, and Thorsten Vitt. "Understanding and Explaining Delta Measures for Authorship Attribution." *Digital Scholarship in the Humanities* 32, suppl. 2 (2017): ii4–16.

Fandos, Nicholas. "Trump Lawyer Sends 'Art of the Deal' Ghostwriter a Cease-and-Desist Letter." *New York Times*, July 21, 2016.

Farey, Peter. "Playing Dead: An Updated Review of the Case for Christopher Marlowe." *Journal of Marlovian Research* 3 (2011): 1–13.

Farley-Winer, Charlotte A. "Henry Lee Smith Jr. (1913–1972): A *Nachruf* Twenty Years After." *Historiographia Linguistica* 19, no. 1 (1992): 187–98.

Farrer, J. A. *Literary Forgeries*. New York: Longman Green & Co., 1907.

Farringdon, Jill M. *Analysing for Authorship: A Guide to the Cusum Technique.* Cardiff: University of Wales Press, 1996.

Fasold, Ralph W. "The Relation between Black and White Speech in the South." *American Speech* 56, no. 3 (1981): 163–89.

Fehrman, Craig. *Author in Chief: The Untold Story of Our Presidents and the Books They Wrote.* New York: Avid Reader Press, 2020.

Fernando, Gavin. "How a Murderer Was Brought to Justice by His Texting Style." August 8, 2018. https://www.news.com.au/lifestyle/real-life/true-stories/how-a -murderer-was-brought-to-justice-by-his-texting-style/news-story/34934b3177 ab070ea6cce510059a574e.

Fienberg, Stephen E. "Review of 'Inference and Disputed Authorship: The Federalist.'" *Journal of Interdisciplinary History* 1, no. 3 (1971): 557–60.

Fienberg, Stephen E., David C. Hoaglin, and Judith M. Tanur, eds. *The Pleasures of Statistics: An Autobiography of Frederick Mosteller.* New York: Springer, 2010.

Firth, Chris. *Branwell Brontë's Tale: Who Wrote "Wuthering Heights"?* Electraglade Press, 2014.

Fisher, Jim. *Forensics under Fire: Are Bad Science and Dueling Experts Corrupting Criminal Justice?* New Brunswick, NJ: Rutgers University Press, 2008.

Fitzgerald, James R. "Using a Forensic Linguistic Approach to Track the Unabomber." In *Profilers: Leading Investigators Take You inside the Criminal Mind*, edited by John H. Campbell and Don DeNevi, 193–222. Amherst, NY: Prometheus, 2004.

Flesch, Rudolf. "A New Readability Yardstick." *Journal of Applied Psychology* 32 (1948): 221–33.

Floccia, Caroline, Claire Delle Luche, Samantha Durrant, Joseph Butler, and Jeremy Goslin. "Parent or Community: Where Do 20-Month-Olds Exposed to Two Accents Acquire Their Representation of Words?" *Cognition* 124, no. 1 (2012): 95–100.

Folkenflik, Robert. "'Shakespearesque': The Arden 'Double Falsehood.'" *Huntington Library Quarterly* 75, no. 1 (2012): 131–43.

Forsyth, Richard, and David Holmes. "The Writeprints of Man: A Stylometric Study of Lafayette's Hand in Paine's 'Rights of Man.'" *Digital Humanities Quarterly* 12, no. 1 (2018).

Forsyth, Richard S., David I. Holmes, and Emily K. Tse. "Cicero, Sigonio, and Burrows: Investigating the Authenticity of the 'Consolatio.'" *Literary and Linguistic Computing* 14, no. 3 (1999): 1–26.

Foster, Donald W. *Elegy by W.S.: A Study in Attribution.* Newark: University of Delaware Press, 1989.

———. "SHAXICON 1995." *The Shakespeare Newsletter* 45, no. 2 (1995): 1, 30, 32.

———. "A Funeral Elegy: W[illiam] S[hakespeare]'s 'Best-Speaking Witnesses.'" *PMLA* 111, no. 5 (1996): 1080–1105.

Foster, Donald. "Who Is Anonymous?" *New York Magazine*, February 26, 1996, 50–57.

———. *Author Unknown: On the Trail of Anonymous.* New York: Henry Holt, 2000.

Foster, Don. "The Message in the Anthrax." *Vanity Fair*, October 2003, 180–200.

Foster, Paul. "Who Wrote 2 Thessalonians? A Fresh Look at an Old Problem." *Journal for the Study of the New Testament* 35, no. 2 (2012): 150–75.

Fowler, Alastair. "C. S. Lewis: Supervisor." *Yale Review* 91, no. 4 (2003): 64–80.

Frazier, Harriet C. "Theobald's 'The Double Falsehood': A Revision of Shakespeare's 'Cardenio'?" *Comparative Drama* 1, no. 3 (1967): 219–33.

Freed, David. "The Wrong Man." *The Atlantic*, May 2010, 46–56. https://www.the atlantic.com/magazine/archive/2010/05/the-wrong-man/308019.

Freehafer, John. "'Cardenio,' by Shakespeare and Fletcher." *Publications of the Modern Language Association of America* 84, no. 3 (1969): 501–13.

French, James. *Sketches and Eccentricities of Col. David Crockett, of West Tennessee.* New York: J & J Harper, 1833.

Frumkin, Lara A., and Anna Stone. "Not All Eyewitnesses Are Equal: Accent Status, Race and Age Interact to Influence Evaluations of Testimony." *Journal of Ethnicity in Criminal Justice* 18, no. 2 (2020): 123–45.

Fuller, Simon, and James O'Sullivan. "Structure over Style: Collaborative Authorship and the Revival of Literary Capitalism." *Digital Humanities Quarterly* 11, no. 1 (2017): 1–12.

Gajanan, Mahita. "Vice President Pence Denies He's the 'Lodestar' behind Anonymous New York *Times* Op-Ed." *Time*, September 6, 2018.

Galella, Luigi. "Ferrante è Starnone: Parola di computer." *L'Unita*, November 23, 2006. https://www.orphanalytics.com/fr/news/unita-ferrante-e-starnone.

Gallagher, Gary W. "A Widow and Her Soldier: LaSalle Corbell Pickett as Author of the George E. Pickett Letters." *Virginia Magazine of History and Biography* 94, no. 3 (1986): 329–44.

Gamerman, Ellen. "Data Miners Dig into 'Watchman.'" *Wall Street Journal*, July 17, 2015, D5.

Gardner, Martin. *Visitors From Oz: The Wild Adventures of Dorothy, the Scarecrow, and the Tin Woodman.* New York: St. Martin's Press, 1998.

———. *Undiluted Hocus-Pocus: The Autobiography of Martin Gardner.* Princeton, NJ: Princeton University Press, 2014.

Gardner-Chloros, Penelope. *Code-Switching.* Cambridge: Cambridge University Press, 2009.

Garreau, Joel, and Linton Weeks. "'Anonymous' Sleuths Get a Byte Fishing by Computer: Is the Author About to Be Reeled In?" *Washington Post*, February 16, 1996.

Gatti, Claudio. "Elena Ferrante: An Answer? The Story behind a Name." *New York Review,* October 6, 2016.

Geller, Andy. "Ex-Jonbenet Prober Says Mom Wrote Ransom Note." *New York Post,* April 9, 2000.

Georgy, Jason. "What Kind of Accent Is That, Anyway?" *Chicago Tribune,* September 18, 2008.

Gerstein, Josh. "Hatfill Settles $10M Libel Lawsuit." *New York Sun,* February 27, 2007.

Ginsberg, Lesley. "Slavery and the Gothic Horror of Poe's 'The Black Cat.'" In *American Gothic: New Interventions in a National Narrative,* edited by Robert K. Martin and Eric Savoy, 99–128. Iowa City: University of Iowa Press, 1998.

Glaberson, William. "Publication of Unabomber's Tract Draws Mixed Response." *New York Times,* September 20, 1995, A16.

Goodheart, Adam. "Mark Twain and the Fortune-Teller." *New York Times,* February 5, 2011.

Goodman, Leah McGrath. "The Face behind Bitcoin." *Newsweek,* March 6, 2014.

Gordon, Lesley J. "Let the People See the Old Life as It Was." In *The Myth of the Lost Cause and Civil War History,* edited by Gary W. Gallagher and Alan T. Nolan, 170–84. Bloomington: Indiana University Press, 2000.

Gramling, Oliver. *Free Men Are Fighting: The Story of World War II.* New York: Farrar and Rinehart, 1942.

Greenblatt, Stephen. "Shakespeare and the Will to Deceive." *New York Times,* April 28, 2011.

Greenwood, H. H. "St. Paul Revisited—A Computational Result." *Literary and Linguistic Computing* 7, no. 1 (1992): 43–47.

Grimes, William. "Harper Lee, Author of 'To Kill a Mockingbird,' Dies at 89." *New York Times,* February 19, 2016.

Grzybek, Peter. "History and Methodology of Word Length Studies: The State of the Art." In *Contributions to the Science of Language: Word Length Studies and Related Issues,* edited by Peter Grzybek, 15–90. Dordrecht: Springer, 2007.

Hammond, Brean, ed. *Double Falsehood or The Distressed Lovers.* London: Methuen Drama, 2010.

Han, Lori Cox. "New Strategies for an Old Medium: The Weekly Radio Addresses of Reagan and Clinton." *Congress and the Presidency: A Journal of Capital Studies* 33, no. 1 (2006): 25–45.

Harrison, P. N. *The Problem of the Pastoral Epistles.* Oxford: Oxford University Press, 1921.

Hart, Joseph C. *The Romance of Yachting: Voyage the First.* New York: Harper and Brothers, 1848.

Hatfill, Steven J. v. Donald Foster et al., USDC-EDVA, 04-cv-1001 (LMB).

Hayes, Christal. "Whodunit? Social Media Users Search for Anonymous Trump Official Who Penned Scathing NYT Essay." *USA Today*, September 5, 2018.

Hayward, Steven F. *The Age of Reagan: The Fall of the Old Liberal Order, 1964–1980.* New York: Three Rivers Press, 2001.

Heller, Karen. "James Patterson Mostly Doesn't Write His Books. And His New Readers Mostly Don't Read—Yet." *Washington Post*, June 6, 2016.

Hendrickson, Thomas G. "Spurious Manuscripts of Genuine Works: The Cases of Cicero and Virgil." In *Animo Decipiendi? Rethinking Fakes and Authorship in Classical, Late Antique and Early Christian Works*, edited by Antonio Guzmán and Javier Martínez, 125–38. Groningen: Barkhuis, 2018.

Herman, Peter. "'Is This Winning?' Prince Henry's Death and the Problem of Chivalry in 'The Two Noble Kinsmen.'" *South Atlantic Review* 62, no. 1 (1997): 1–31.

Herper, Matthew. "Linguistic Analysis Says Newsweek Named the Wrong Man as Bitcoin's Creator." *Forbes*, March 10, 2014.

Hesse, Monica. "Elizabeth Holmes's Weird Possibly Fake Baritone Is Actually Her Least Baffling Quality." *Washington Post*, March 21, 2019.

Higdon, David Leon. "The Concordance: Mere Index or Needful Census?" *Text* 15 (2003): 51–68.

Hilton, Michael L., and David I. Holmes. "An Assessment of Cumulative Sum Charts for Authorship Attribution." *Literary and Linguistic Computing* 8, no. 2 (1993): 73–80.

Hitchens, Christopher. *Thomas Paine's Rights of Man: A Biography.* New York: Grove Press, 2006.

Hitt, Jack. "Words on Trial: Can Linguists Solve Crimes That Stump the Police?" *The New Yorker*, July 16, 2012.

Hollmann, William B. "Forensic Linguistics." In *Knowing about Language: Linguistics and the Secondary English Classroom*, edited by Marcello Giovanelli and Dan Clayton, 137–48. London: Routledge, 2016.

Holmes, David I. "The Evolution of Stylometry in Humanities Scholarship." *Literary and Linguistic Computing* 13, no. 3 (1998): 111–17.

———. "Stylometry and the Civil War: The Case of the Pickett Letters." *Chance* 16, no. 2 (2003): 18–25.

Holmes, David I., and Daniel W. Crofts. "The Diary of a Public Man: A Case Study in Traditional and Non-Traditional Authorship Attribution." *Literary and Linguistic Computing* 25 (2010): 179–97.

Holmes, D. I., and R. S. Forsyth. "'The Federalist' Revisited: New Directions in Authorship Attribution." *Literary and Linguistic Computing* 10, no. 2 (2010): 111–27.

Holmes, David I., Lesley J. Gordon, and Christine Wilson. "A Widow and Her Soldier: Stylometry and the Civil War." *Literary and Linguistic Computing* 16, no. 4 (2001): 403–20.

Holmes, David I., and Judit Kardos. "Who Was the Author? An Introduction to Stylometry." *Chance* 16, no. 2 (2003): 5–8.

Holmes, David, and Ferris Samara. "Was the Wild Frontiersman a Prolific Penman? A Stylometric Investigation into the Works of Davy Crockett." *Chance* 33, no. 2 (2020): 7–18.

Holtzmann, Heinrich J. *Die Pastoralbriefe: Kritisch und Exgentisch Behandelt.* Leipzig: Wilhelm Engelmann, 1880.

Honan, William H. "A Sleuth Gets His Suspect: Shakespeare." *New York Times*, January 14, 1996, A1.

Hooper, Walter. "Preface; A Note on 'The Dark Tower.'" In C. S. Lewis, *The Dark Tower and Other Stories.* New York: Harcourt Brace Jovanovich, 1977.

Howard, Jennifer Crossley. "In Harper Lee's Letters: Books, Fame and a 'Lying' Capote." *New York Times*, April 28, 2017.

Howard-Hill, Trevor Howard, ed. *Shakespeare and Sir Thomas More: Essays on the Play and Its Shakespearian Interest.* Cambridge: Cambridge University Press, 1989.

Howe, Lawrence. "Property and Dialect Narrative in 'Huckleberry Finn': The 'Jim Dilemma' Revisited." *The Mark Twain Annual* 7 (2009): 5–21.

Hughes, Virginia. "How Forensic Linguistics Outed J.K. Rowling (Not to Mention James Madison, Barack Obama, and the Rest of Us)." *National Geographic*, July 19, 2013.

Hull, William Doyle II. "A Canon of the Critical Works of Edgar Allen Poe: With a Study of Poe as Editor and Reviewer." Unpublished doctoral dissertation, University of Virginia, 1941.

Ingold, John, and Kirk Mitchell. "JonBenét Ramsey Grand Jury Indictment Accused Parents of Child Abuse Resulting in Death." *Denver Post*, October 25, 2013.

Inside Edition Staff. "New York Times Op-Ed Shrouded in Mystery as President Trump Desperately Tries to Find Writer." *Inside Edition*, September 6, 2018.

Ireland, Samuel. *Miscellaneous Papers and Legal Instruments under the Hand and Seal of William Shakspeare.* London: Egerton, 1796.

Ireland, William-Henry. *An Authentic Account of the Shaksperian Manuscripts.* London: J. Debrett, 1796.

———. *The Confessions of William-Henry Ireland.* London: Ellerton and Byworth, 1805.

Itzkoff, Dave. "Yes, James Patterson Signs a 17-Book Deal." *New York Times*, September 8, 2009.

Jacewicz, Ewa, and Robert A. Fox. "Acoustics of Regionally Accented Speech." *Acoustics Today* 12, no. 2 (2016): 31–38.

Jamaluddin. "The Cuckoo's Calling: Good under Robert Galbraith, Excellent under JK Rowling." *The Express Tribune*, September 5, 2013.

James, Caryn. "July 14–20; Anonymous Shows His Colors." *New York Times*, July 21, 1996, sec. 4, p. 2.

Janney, Caroline E. "'One of the Best Loved, North and South': The Appropriation of National Reconciliation by LaSalle Corbell Pickett." *Virginia Magazine of History and Biography* 116, no. 4 (2008): 371–406.

Johnston, David. "On the Unabomber Track: The Overview; Ex-Professor Is Seized in Montana as Suspect in the Unabom Attacks." *New York Times*, April 4, 1996, A1.

———. "A Device in Cabin Is Said to Match the Unabomber's." *New York Times*, April 9, 1996, A1.

Jones, Carla F. "The Literary Detective Computer Analysis of Stylistic Differences between 'The Dark Tower' and C. S. Lewis' Deep Space Trilogy." *Mythlore: A Journal of J. R. R. Tolkien, C. S. Lewis, Charles Williams, and Mythopoeic Literature* 15, no. 2 (1989): 11–15.

Jones, John M., and Robert C. Rowland. "The Weekly Radio Addresses of President Ronald Reagan." *Journal of Radio Studies* 7, no. 2 (2000): 257–81.

Jones, Joseph. "Review of 'The Letters of Quintus Curtius Snodgrass.'" *Southwestern Historical Quarterly* 50, no. 4 (1947): 524–26.

Jordan, Tina. "'A Warning,' by Anonymous, Cracks the Best-Seller List." *New York Times*, November 27, 2019.

Juola, Patrick. "How a Computer Program Helped Show J.K. Rowling Write a Cuckoo's Calling." *Scientific American*, August 20, 2013.

———. "The Rowling Case: A Proposed Standard Analytic Protocol for Authorship Questions." *Digital Scholarship in the Humanities* 30, suppl. 1 (2015): 100–113.

Juola, Patrick, John Noecker, Mike Ryan, and Mengjia Zhao. "JGAAP3.0—Authorship Attribution for the Rest of Us." *Digital Humanities 2008* (2008): 250–51.

Kaczynski, David. *Every Last Tie: The Story of the Unabomber and His Family*. Durham, NC: Duke University Press, 2016.

Kaczynski, Theodore J. *Industrial Society and Its Future*. Supplement to the *Washington Post*, September 22, 1995.

Kakutani, Michiko. "Light Out Huck, They Still Want to Sivilize You." *New York Times*, January 6, 2011.

Katz, Josh. *Speaking American: How Y'all, Youse, and You Guys Talk: A Visual Guide*. New York: Houghton Mifflin Harcourt, 2016.

Katz, Josh, and Wilson Andrews. "How Y'all, Youse and You Guys Talk." *New York Times*, December 21, 2013.

Kendall, M. G. "George Udny Yule C.B.E, F.R.S." *Journal of the Royal Statistical Society: Series A (General)* 115, no. 1 (1952): 156–61.

Kennedy, John F. *Why England Slept*. New York: Wilfred Funk, 1940.

———. *Profiles in Courage: Decisive Moments in the Lives of Celebrated Americans*. New York: Harper & Brothers, 1956.

Kennedy, Ludovic. *Ten Rillington Place*. New York: Simon and Schuster, 1961.

Kennedy, Maev. "Lawyer Who Uncovered JK Rowling's Robert Galbraith Alter Ego Fined £1,000." *The Guardian*, December 10, 2013.

Kennedy, Randall. "Harper Lee's 'Go Set a Watchman.'" *New York Times*, July 14, 2015.

Kinkead, Eugene, and Russell Maloney. "Dr. Smith." *The New Yorker*, November 30, 1940, 12.

Kinzler, Katherine D. *How You Say It: Why We Judge Others by the Way They Talk—And the Costs of This Hidden Bias*. New York: Houghton Mifflin Harcourt, 2020.

Kirkpatrick, David D. "Who Is behind QAnon? Linguistic Detectives Find Fingerprints." *New York Times*, February 19, 2022.

Kirsch, Johann Peter. "Donation of Constantine." In *The Catholic Encyclopedia*. Vol. 5. New York: Robert Appleton Co., 1909.

Klarreich, Erica. "Bookish Math: Statistical Tests Are Unraveling Knotty Literary Mysteries." *Science News* 164, no. 26 (2003). https://www.sciencenews.org/article/bookish-math.

Knott, Stephen F., and Russell L. Riley. "Ronald Reagan Oral History Project Interview with Peter Hannaford." The Miller Center Foundation, University of Virginia, 2005. http://web1.millercenter.org/poh/transcripts/ohp_2003_0110_hannaford.pdf.

Konnikova, Maria. "When Authors Disown Their Work, Should Readers Care?" *The Atlantic*, August 28, 2012.

Kovaleski, Serge F. "Alabama Officials Find Harper Lee in Control of Decision to Publish Second Novel." *New York Times*, April 3, 2015.

Kovaleski, Serge F., and Alexandra Alter. "Harper Lee's 'Go Set a Watchman' May Have Been Found Earlier Than Thought." *New York Times*, July 2, 2015.

Kozinn, Allan. "Harper Lee Says New Book Not Authorized." *New York Times*, July 15, 2014.

Kurath, Hans, Bernard Bloch, Marcus Lee Hansen, and Julia Bloch. *Linguistic Atlas of New England: Handbook of the Linguistic Geography of New England*. Providence, RI: Brown University Press, 1939.

Kusnet, David. "'Primary Colors'—Outside the White House beyond the Beltway; Unmasking 'Anonymous': A Suspect Lays the Book at Joe Klein's Doorstep." *Baltimore Sun*, February 11, 1996.

———. "Could This Be the Guy Who Wrote Anonymous's Warning?" *New Republic*, November 25, 2019.

Labov, William. *A Study of Non-Standard English*. Washington, DC: Center for Applied Linguistics, 1969.

Labov, William, Sharon Ash, and Charles Boberg. *The Atlas of North American English: Phonetics, Phonology and Sound Change*. Berlin: Mouton de Gruyter, 2006.

Lane, Anthony. "Bill Clinton and James Patterson's Concussive Collaboration." *The New Yorker*, June 5, 2018.

Leach, Joseph. "Crockett's Almanacs and the Typical Texan." *Southwest Review* 35, no. 2 (1950): 88–95.

Leisy, Ernest E., ed. *The Letters of Quintus Curtius Snodgrass*. Dallas, TX: Southern Methodist University Press, 1946.

Leithauser, Brad. "Pet Words." *The New Yorker*, September 11, 2013.

LeMaster, J. R., and James D. Wilson. *The Mark Twain Encyclopedia*. New York: Garland Publishing, 1993.

Leonard, Tom. "Jealousy, Lies and Troubling Questions about a Book That Inspired the World." *Daily Mail*, February 5, 2015.

Lepore, Jill. "The Sharpened Quill: Was Thomas Paine Too Much of a Freethinker for the Country He Helped Free?" *The New Yorker*, October 16, 2006.

Lev-Ari, Shiri, and Boaz Keysar. "Why Don't We Believe Non-Native Speakers? The Influence of Accent on Credibility." *Journal of Experimental Social Psychology* 46, no. 6 (2010): 1093–96.

Levine, Joseph M. "Reginald Pecock and Lorenzo Valla on the Donation of Constantine." *Studies in the Renaissance* 20 (1973): 118–43.

Levine, Timothy R. *Encyclopedia of Deception*. Vol. 2. Los Angeles: Sage Reference, 2014.

Libby, James A. "The Pauline Canon Sung in a Linguistic Key: Visualizing New Testament Text Proximity by Linguistic Structure, System, and Strata." *Biblical and Ancient Greek Linguistics* 5 (2016): 122–201.

Lindskoog, Kathryn. "Some Problems in C. S. Lewis Scholarship." *Christianity and Literature* 27, no. 4 (1978): 43–61.

———. *The C. S. Lewis Hoax*. Portland, OR: Multnomah Books, 1988.

———. *Light in the Shadowlands: Protecting the Real C. S. Lewis*. Portland, OR: Multnomah Books, 1994.

———. *Sleuthing C. S. Lewis: More Light in the Shadowlands*. Macon, GA: Mercer University Press, 2001.

Linskey, Annie. "Inside the Trump Tweet Machine: Staff-Written Posts, Bad Grammar (on Purpose), and Delight in the Chaos." *Boston Globe*, May 22, 2018.

Lippman, Daniel. "Navarro Penned 15-Page Memo Falsely Accusing Coates of Being Anonymous." *Politico*, March 2, 2021.

Lokken, Roy N. "Has the Mystery of 'A Public Man' Been Solved?" *Mississippi Valley Historical Review* 40, no. 3 (1953): 419–40.

Loncraine, Rebecca. *The Real Wizard of Oz: The Life and Times of L. Frank Baum*. New York: Gotham Books, 2009.

Lord, R. D. "Studies in the History of Probability and Statistics. VIII: De Morgan and the Statistical Study of Literary Style." *Biometrika* 48 (1958): 282.

Lutosławski, Wincenty. *The Origin and Growth of Plato's Logic, with an Account of Plato's Style and of the Chronology of His Writings*. London: Longman, Green and Co., 1897.

Lyall, Sarah. "The Detective Novel's Story Doesn't Add Up." *New York Times*, July 14, 2013.

———. "In Bill Clinton and James Patterson's Second Novel, an Ex-President Goes Rogue." *New York Times*, June 8, 2021.

Lynch, Jack. "William Henry Ireland's Forgeries, Unique and Otherwise." *Princeton University Library Chronicle* 72, no. 2 (2011): 465–70.

Maguire, Gregory. *Wicked: The Life and Times of the Wicked Witch of the West*. New York: ReganBooks, 1995.

Mahler, Jonathan. "James Patterson Inc." *New York Times Magazine*, January 20, 2010.

———. "The Invisible Hand behind Harper Lee's 'To Kill a Mockingbird.'" *New York Times*, July 12, 2015.

Mahmood, Asad, Zubair Shafiq, and Padmini Srinivasan. "A Girl Has a Name: Detecting Authorship Obfuscation." In *Proceedings of the 58th Annual Meeting of the Association for Computational Linguistics*, 2235–45 (Stroudsburg, PA: Association for Computational Linguistics, 2020).

Malady, Matthew J. X. "Fingerprint Words: The Verbal Tics That Make Up Who We Are—And How They Spread to Others." *Slate*, September 11, 2014. https://slate.com/human-interest/2014/09/fingerprint-words-verbal-tics-that-define-us-and-how-they-spread-to-others.html.

Malham-Dembleby, John. *The Key to the Brontë Works*. London: Walter Scott, 1911.

Malone, Edmond. *An Inquiry into the Authenticity of Certain Miscellaneous Papers and Legal Instruments*. London: T. Cadell and W. Davies, 1796.

Marshall, Mike. "To Kill a Myth, Museum Has Letter to Disprove It." *Chicago Tribune*, March 4, 2006.

Mason, Melvin Rosser. "'The Lion of the West': Satire on Davy Crockett and Frances Trollope." *South Central Bulletin* 29, no. 4 (1969): 143–45.

Matthews, Robert. "Linguistics on Trial: Forensic Scientists Have Fiercely Condemned a Technique Used in Court to Show That Confessions Have Been Tampered With." *NewScientist*, August 21, 1993.

Mayer, Jane. "Donald Trump's Ghostwriter Tells All." *The New Yorker*, July 18, 2016.

McCarthy, Rachel, and James O'Sullivan. "Who Wrote 'Wuthering Heights'?" *Digital Scholarship in the Humanities* 36, no. 2 (2021): 383–91.

McCuaig, William. *Carlo Sigonio: The Changing World of the Late Renaissance*. Princeton, NJ: Princeton University Press, 1989.

McDermon, Daniel. "F.B.I. Listed Author as Unabomber Suspect." *New York Times*, August 22, 2013, C3.

McDonald, Andrew W. E., Sadia Afroz, Aylin Caliskan, Ariel Stolerman, and Rachel Greenstadt. "Use Fewer Instances of the Letter 'i': Toward Writing Style Anonymization." In *Privacy Enhancing Technologies. PETS 2012. Lecture Notes in Computer Science*, edited by S. Fischer-Hübner and M. Wright, 299–318. Berlin: Springer, 2012.

McGraw, Meridith. "White House Transfers Top National Security Aide after Whisper Campaign." *Politico*, February 20, 2020.

McGrayne, Sharon Bertsch. *The Theory That Would Not Die*. New Haven, CT: Yale University Press, 2011.

McLemee, Scott. "Holy War in the Shadowlands." *Chronicle of Higher Education*, July 20, 2001. https://www.chronicle.com/article/holy-war-in-the-shadowlands.

Mearns, David C. "'Diary of a Public Man'—Whodunit?" *New York Times*, January 16, 1949, 104.

Mendelsohn, Daniel. "God's Librarians: The Vatican Library Enters the Twenty-First Century." *The New Yorker*, January 3, 2011.

Mendenhall, T. C. "The Characteristic Curves of Composition." *Science* 9, no. 214 (March 11, 1887): 237–46.

———. "A Mechanical Solution of a Literary Problem." *Popular Science Monthly* 60 (December 1901): 97–105.

Merriam, Thomas. "The Strange Case of Sir Thomas More." *Moreana* 18, no. 71/72 (1981): 113–14.

———. "A Reply to 'An Investigation of the Basis of Morton's Method for the Determination of Authorship.'" *Style* 22, no. 4 (1988): 646–49.

Michaelson, Sidney, and Andrew Q. Morton. "The New Stylometry: A One-Word Test of Authorship for Greek Writers." *The Classical Quarterly* 22, no. 1 (1972): 89–102.

Mifflin, Lawrie. "Primary Colors' Author Resigns as Commentator at CBS News." *New York Times*, July 26, 1996, sec. A, p. 17.

Miles, Robert. "Forging a Romantic Identity: Herbert Croft's 'Love and Madness' and W. H. Ireland's Shakespeare MS." *Eighteenth-Century Fiction* 17, no. 4 (2005): 599–627.

Milliot, Jim. "BookScan: Patterson Was Decade's Bestselling Author. *Publisher's Weekly*, November 13, 2020.

Mills, Terence C. *A Statistical Biography of George Udny Yule: A Loafer of the World*. Newcastle upon Tyne: Cambridge Scholars Publishing, 2017.

The Mirror. "Shot by Lover and Left in an Oil Drum." November 1, 2005. https://www.mirror.co.uk/news/uk-news/shot-by-lover-and-left-in-an-oil-drum-563593.

Monsarrat, G. D. "'A Funeral Elegy': Ford, W.S., and Shakespeare." *Review of English Studies* 53, no. 210 (2002): 186–203.

Morrison, Toni. *Playing in the Dark: Whiteness and the Literary Imagination*. Cambridge, MA: Harvard University Press, 1992.

Morton, Alan Q. "The Rev Andrew Q Morton Obituary." *The Guardian*, February 5, 2019.

Morton, Andrew Q. "The Authorship of Greek Prose." *Journal of the Royal Statistical Society. Series A (General)* 128, no. 2 (1965): 169–233.

———. *Literary Detection: How to Prove Authorship and Fraud in Literature and Documents*. New York: Charles Scribner, 1978.

Mosteller, Frederick, and David L. Wallace. "Inference in an Authorship Problem." *Journal of the American Statistical Association* 58, no. 302 (1963): 275–309.

———. *Inference and Disputed Authorship: The Federalist*. Reading, MA: Addison-Wesley, 1964.

Musgrave, Jane. "Signs of Madness Boost Anthrax Suit." *Palm Beach Post*, August 17, 2008, C1.

Muth, Katie. "The Grammars of the System: Thomas Pynchon at Boeing." *Textual Practice* 33, no. 3 (2019): 473–93.

Nance, John V. "Shakespeare, Theobald, and the Prose Problem in 'Double Falsehood.'" In *The Creation and Re-Creation of Cardenio: Performing Shakespeare, Transforming Cervantes*, edited by Terri Bourus and Gary Talor, 109–23. New York: Palgrave Macmillan.

National Public Radio. "'Dreams Do Still Come True,' in a New Novel by Dolly Parton and James Patterson." *Morning Edition*, April 29, 2022.

Navarro, Peter. *Memorandum. Subject: Identity of Anonymous*, December 2, 2019. https://www.politico.com/f/?id=00000177-ef37-d750-a77f-ffb703c00000.

Neufeldt, Victor A., ed. *A Bibliography of the Manuscripts of Patrick Branwell Brontë*. London: Routledge.

New York Times. "Denies A-Kempis Is Author." December 19, 1925, 3.

———. "Thomas Paine's Old House: Place Where the Writer Labored Is in the Hands of the Wreckers." March 9, 1930, 148.

———. "The Three Sisters of the Moors." August 7, 1932, 4, 12.

———. "New Bomarc Contract." March 22, 1959, 40.

———. "Faulkner Novel Award Given." February 3, 1964, 25.

———. "Man Suspected in Anthrax Attacks Said to Commit Suicide." August 1, 2008.

Nicholas of Cusa. *The Catholic Concordance*. Edited and translated by Paul E. Sigmund. Cambridge: Cambridge University Press, 1991.

Niederkorn, William S. "A Scholar Recants on His 'Shakespeare' Discovery." *New York Times*, June 20, 2002, E1.

———. "Beyond the Briefly Inflated Canon: Legacy of the Mysterious 'W.S.'" *New York Times*, June 26, 2002.

None. "Patrick Branwell Brontë and 'Wuthering Heights.'" *Brontë Society Transactions* 7, no. 2 (1927): 97–102.

Noonan, Peggy. "Out of Many, Two?" *Wall Street Journal*, July 31, 2014.

Nunberg, Geoff. "For Candidates, an Accent on Authenticity." *Fresh Air*, WHYY-FM, Philadelphia, October 15, 2008.

Nyborg, Erin. "Elena Ferrante, Charlotte Brontë and How Anonymity Protects against Female Writing Stereotypes." *The Conversation*, October 5, 2016. https://

theconversation.com/elena-ferrante-charlotte-bronte-and-how-anonymity-pro
tects-against-female-writing-stereotypes-66500.

Nye, Russel B. "The Wizardess of Oz." *The Baum Bugle*, Autumn 1965, 119–22.

Nyhan, Julianne, and Andrew Flinn. *Computation and the Humanities: Towards an Oral History of Digital Humanities*. Cham: Springer, 2016.

Oakes, Michael P. "Computer Stylometry of C. S. Lewis's 'The Dark Tower' and Related Texts." *Digital Scholarship in the Humanities* 33, no. 3 (2018): 637–50.

O'Daly, Irene. "Managing Knowledge: Diagrammatic Glosses to Medieval Copies of the 'Rhetorica ad Herennium.'" *International Journal of the Classical Tradition* 23, no. 1 (2016): 1–28.

Ohmann, Carol. "Emily Brontë in the Hands of Male Critics." *College English* 32, no. 8 (1971): 906–13.

Oliveira, G., A. Davidson, R. Holcezer, S. Kaplan, and A. Paretzky. "A Comparison of the Use of Glottal Fry in the Spontaneous Speech of Young and Middle-Aged American Women." *Journal of Voice* 30, no. 6 (2016): 684–87.

Olsson, John. *Forensic Linguistics: An Introduction to Language, Crime, and the Law*. London: Continuum, 2004.

———. "Forensic Linguistics." In *Linguistics*, edited by Vesna Muhvic-Dimanovski and Lelija Socanac, 378–93. Oxford: Eolss Publishers, 2009.

———. *Wordcrime: Solving Crime Through Forensic Linguistics*. London: Continuum, 2009.

———. *More Wordcrime: Solving Crime with Linguistics*. New York: Bloomsbury, 2018.

Osnos, Peter. "Editing Donald Trump." *The New Yorker*, November 3, 2019.

Ostrowski, Donald. *Who Wrote That? Authorship Controversies from Moses to Sholokhov*. Ithaca, NY: Cornell University Press, 2020.

O'Sullivan, James. "Why You Don't Need to Write Much to Be the World's Bestselling Author." *The Conversation*, April 3, 2017. https://theconversation.com/why-you-dont-need-to-write-much-to-be-the-worlds-bestselling-author-75261.

———. "Bill Clinton and James Patterson are Co-Authors—But Who Did the Writing?" *The Guardian*, June 7, 2018.

Page, Evelyn. "The Diary and the Public Man." *New England Quarterly* 22, no. 2 (1949): 147–92.

Paine, Thomas. *The American Crisis No. 1*. Fishkill, NY: Samuel Loudon, 1776.

———. *Rights of Man: Being an Answer to Mr. Burke's Attack on the French Revolution*. Dublin, 1791.

Pantos, Andrew J., and Andrew W. Perkins. "Measuring Implicit and Explicit Attitudes toward Foreign Accented Speech." *Journal of Language and Social Psychology* 32, no. 1 (2013): 3–20.

Park, Dabney G. "Dante and the Donation of Constantine." *Dante Studies, with the Annual Report of the Dante Society*, no. 130 (2012): 67–161.

Parmet, Herbert S. *Jack: The Struggles of John F. Kennedy*. New York: Dial Press, 1980.

Patergianakis, Antonios, and Konstantinos Limniotis. "Privacy Issues in Stylometric Methods." *Cryptography* 6, no. 2 (2022): 17.

Patterson, Troy. "James Patterson Would Like You to Read." *The New Yorker*, June 9, 2016.

Pennebaker, James W. *The Secret Life of Pronouns: What Our Words Say about Us*. New York: Bloomsbury Press, 2011.

Piereson, James. *Shattered Consensus: The Rise and Decline of America's Postwar Political Order*. New York: Encounter Books, 2015.

Price, Benjamin M. "Who Wrote 'The Diary of a Public Man'? A Seventy-Two-Year-Old Mystery." *American Bar Association Journal* 37, no. 8 (1951): 579–81.

Publishers Weekly. "Review of 'Primary Colors: A Novel of Politics.'" January 1, 1996.

Pynchon, Thomas. "Togetherness." *Aerospace Safety* 16, no. 12 (1960): 6–8.

———. *V.* New York: J. B. Lippincott, 1963.

———. *Slow Learner: Early Stories*. Boston: Little, Brown, 1984.

Ramsey, John, and Patsy Ramsey. *The Death of Innocence: The Untold Story of JonBenét's Murder and How Its Exploitation Compromised the Pursuit of Truth*. Nashville, TN: Thomas Nelson, 2000.

Rappeport, Alan. "'I Feel a Deep Sense of Remorse,' Donald Trump's Ghostwriter Says." *New York Times*, July 18, 2016.

Reagan, Ronald. *Ronald Reagan: An American Life*. New York: Simon and Schuster, 1990.

Reeves, Richard. *President Kennedy: Profile of Power*. New York: Simon & Schuster, 1993.

Reuters. "Lawyer Fined for Revealing JK Rowling as Secret Author." *The Irish Times*, January 2, 2014.

Reynolds, Barbara. "Review of 'Sleuthing C.S. Lewis: More Light in the Shadowlands.'" *VII: Journal of the Marion E. Wade Center* 18 (2001): 102–7.

Rickford, John R., and Sharese King. "Language and Linguistics on Trial: Hearing Rachel Jeantel (and Other Vernacular Speakers) in the Courtroom and Beyond." *Language* 92, no. 4 (2016): 948–88.

Ridgely, J. V. "Review: The Authorship of the 'Paulding-Drayton Review.'" *PSA Newsletter* 20, no. 3 (Fall 1992): 1–3, 6.

Rosenbaum, Ron. "Shakespeare's Ghostwriter: The Elegy Mystery Solved?" *Observer*, January 19, 1998. https://observer.com/1998/01/shakespeares-ghostwriter-the-Elegy-mystery-solved.

———. "The Double Falsehood of Double Falsehood." *Slate*, May 13, 2010. https://slate.com/human-interest/2010/05/the-terrible-decision-to-include-a-bogus-play-double-falsehood-in-the-arden-shakespeare.html.

Rosenthal, Bernard. "Poe, Slavery, and the 'Southern Literary Messenger': A Reexamination." *Poe Studies* 7, no. 2 (1974): 29–38.

Rowland, Robert C., and John M. Jones. "'Until Next Week': The Saturday Radio Addresses of Ronald Reagan." *Presidential Studies Quarterly* 32, no. 1 (2002): 84–110.

Royster, Paul. "Thomas Pynchon: A Brief Chronology." Faculty Publications, University of Nebraska–Lincoln Libraries, 2005. https://digitalcommons.unl.edu/libraryscience/2.

Rudman, Joseph. "Cherry Picking in Nontraditional Authorship Attribution Studies." *Chance* 16, no. 2 (2003): 26–32.

Ryan, Phil. *Multicultiphobia.* Toronto: University of Toronto Press, 2010.

Rybicki, Jan. "Partners in Life, Partners in Crime?" In *Drawing Elena Ferrante's Profile: Workshop Proceedings*, edited by Arjuna Tuzzi and Michele A. Corelazzo, 111–22. Padua: Padova University Press, 2018.

Rybicki, Jan, and Maciej Eder. "Deeper Delta across Genres and Languages: Do We Really Need the Most Frequent Words?" *Literary and Linguistic Computing* 26, no. 3 (2011): 315–21.

Safire, William. "Bugging Each Other." *New York Times*, October 11, 1981, sec. 4, p. 21.

Sage, Evan T. The Pseudo-Ciceronian "Consolatio." Unpublished doctoral dissertation, University of Chicago, 1910.

Salsburg, David, and Dena Salsburg. "Searching for the 'Real' Davy Crockett." *Chance* 12, no. 2 (1999): 29–34.

Sanford, Anthony J., Joy P. Aked, Linda M. Moxey, and James Mullin. "A Critical Examination of Assumptions Underlying the Cusum Technique of Forensic Linguistics." *International Journal of Speech, Language and the Law* 1, no. 2 (1994): 151–67.

Savoy, Jacques. "Elena Ferrante Unmasked." In *Drawing Elena Ferrante's Profile: Workshop Proceedings*, edited by Arjuna Tuzzi and Michele A. Cortelazzo, 123–41. Padua: Padova University Press, 2018.

———. "Authorship of Pauline Epistles Revisited." *Journal of the Association for Information Science and Technology* 70, no. 10 (2019): 1089–97.

Schechter, Stephen L., ed. *The Reluctant Pillar: New York and the Adoption of the Federal Constitution.* New York: New York State Commission on the Bicentennial of the United States Constitution, 1985.

Schöberlein, Stefan. "Poe or Not Poe? A Stylometric Analysis of Edgar Allan Poe's Disputed Writings." *Digital Scholarship in the Humanities* 32, no. 3 (2017): 643–59.

Schwartz, Alexandra. "The 'Unmasking' of Elena Ferrante." *The New Yorker*, October 3, 2016.

Seal, Graham, and Kennedy White, eds. *Folk Heroes and Heroines around the World.* 2nd ed. Santa Barbara, CA: ABC-CLIO.

Seal, Mark. "To Steal* a Mockingbird*?" *Vanity Fair*, August 2013.

Selk, Avi. "The Ironic, Enduring Legacy of Banning 'To Kill a Mockingbird' for Racist Language." *Washington Post*, October 17, 2017.

Shackford, James Atkins. "The Author of David Crockett's Autobiography." *The Boston Library Quarterly* 3 (October 1951): 294–304.

———. *David Crockett: The Man and the Legend.* Lincoln: University of Nebraska Press, 1956.

Shaffi, Sarah. "Rowling's Galbraith Sales Reach 1.5m." *The Bookseller*, October 12, 2015.

Shane, Scott, and Eric Lichtblau. "Scientist Is Paid Millions by U.S. in Anthrax Suit." *New York Times*, June 28, 2008.

Shaw, George Bernard. *Pygmalion.* New York: Dover, 1994.

Shenker, Israel. "Thomas Paine, Radical of 1776, Honored Belatedly by City Fathers." *New York Times*, January 10, 1976, 55.

Shuy, Roger W. *The Language of Murder Cases: Intentionality, Predisposition, and Voluntariness.* Oxford: Oxford University Press, 2014.

Sigelman, Lee, Colin Martindale, and Dean McKenzie. "The Common Style of 'Common Sense.'" *Computers and the Humanities* 30, no. 5 (1996): 373–79.

Skinner, Kiron K., Annelise Anderson, and Martin Anderson, eds. *Reagan, in His Own Hand: The Writings of Ronald Reagan That Reveal His Revolutionary Vision for America.* New York: Touchstone, 2001.

———. eds. *Reagan's Path to Victory, The Shaping of Ronald Reagan's Vision: Selected Writings.* New York: Free Press, 2004.

Slotkin, Jason. "Biden Revives Presidential Tradition, Releasing First Weekly Address." National Public Radio, February 6, 2021.

Smith, M. W. A. "An Investigation of the Basis of Morton's Method for the Determination of Authorship." *Style* 19, no. 3 (1985): 341–68.

———. "Pseudoscience: A Comedy of Statistical Errors." *Style* 22, no. 4 (1988): 650–53.

Smith, Preserved. *The Age of the Reformation.* New York: Henry Holt & Co., 1920.

Smith, Richard Penn. *Col. Crockett's Exploits and Adventures in Texas.* Philadelphia: T. K. and P. G. Collins, 1836.

Snow, J., *Who's Who in Oz.* Chicago: Reilly & Lee, 1954.

Soloski, Alexis. "A Lost Shakespeare? It's a Mystery." *New York Times*, March 10, 2011, AR 4.

Somers, James. "How the Artificial-Intelligence Program AlphaZero Mastered Its Games." *The New Yorker*, December 28, 2018.

Sorensen, Ted. *Counselor: A Life at the Edge of History.* New York: HarperCollins, 2008.

Sostke, Anya. "Duquesne Professor Helps ID Rowling as Author of 'The Cuckoo's Calling.'" *Pittsburgh Post-Gazette*, July 16, 2013.

Sotgiu, Elisa. "Have Italian Scholars Figured Out the Identity of Elena Ferrante?" *Literary Hub*, March 31, 2021. https://lithub.com/have-italian-scholars-figured-out-the -identity-of-elena-ferrante.

Srihari, Sargur N., Harish Srinivasan, and Gang Fang. "Discriminability of Fingerprints of Twins." *Journal of Forensic Identification* 58, no. 1 (2008): 109–27.

Stamatatos, Efstathios. "A Survey of Modern Authorship Attribution Methods." *Journal of the American Society for Information Science and Technology* 60, no. 3 (2009): 538–56.

Stern, Tiffany. "'The Forgery of Some Modern Author?' Theobald's Shakespeare and Cadenio's Double Falsehood." *Shakespeare Quarterly* 62, no. 4 (2011): 555–93.

Stewart, Doug. *The Boy Who Would Be Shakespeare: A Tale of Forgery and Folly.* Cambridge, MA: Da Capo Press, 2010.

Stewart, James B. "Long Odds for Authors Newly Published." *New York Times*, August 30, 2013.

St. John, Warren. "Serif Sleuth." *The New Yorker*, July 28, 1996.

Stokes, David R. *JFK's Ghost: Kennedy, Sorensen and the Making of "Profiles in Courage."* Lanham, MD: Lyons Press, 2021.

Streitfeld, David. "'Anonymous' Undone by His Own Hand?" *Washington Post*, July 17, 1996.

Svartvik, Jan. "The Evans Statements: A Case for Forensic Linguistics, Part 1." In *Gothenburg Studies in English*, edited by Alvar Ellengård. Göteborg: University of Göteborg Press, 1968.

———. "The Evans Statements: A Case for Forensic Linguistics, Part 2." In *Gothenburg Studies in English*, edited by Alvar Ellengård. Göteborg: University of Göteborg Press, 1968.

Svoboda, Elizabeth. "Speech Patterns in Messages Betray a Killer." *New York Times*, May 11, 2009.

Swartz, Mark E. *Oz before the Rainbow: L. Frank Baum's The Wonderful Wizard of Oz on Stage and Screen to 1939*. Baltimore: Johns Hopkins University Press, 2000.

Tabor, Mary B. W. "'Anonymous' Gets $1 Million in a Film Deal." *New York Times*, February 9, 1996, sec. A, p. 18.

———. "Campaign '92; Author, Subject of Article, Denies He Wrote 'Colors.'" *New York Times*, February 21, 1996, sec. A, p. 14.

Tanaka-Ishii, Kumiko, and Shunsuke Aihara. "Computational Constancy Measures of Texts—Yule's K and Rényi's Entropy." *Computational Linguistics* 41, no. 3 (2015): 481–502.

Tankard, James. "The Literary Detective." *Byte*, February 1986, 231–38.

Taranto, James. "The Dialect Dialectic: Is It Racist to Translate a Black Speaker's Quote into Standard English—or Racist Not To?" *Wall Street Journal*, September 27, 2011.

Tausczik, Yla R., and James W. Pennebaker. "The Psychological Meaning of Words: LIWC and Computerized Text Analysis Methods." *Journal of Language and Social Psychology* 29, no. 1 (2010): 24–54.

Taylor, Gary. "Fake Shakespeare." *Journal of Early Modern Studies* 5 (2016): 353–79.

Taylor, John M. "The Diary of 'A Public Man.'" *North American Review* 261, no. 2 (1976): 78–80.

Taylor, Miles. "Why I'm No Longer 'Anonymous.'" October 28, 2020. https://milestaylor.medium.com/a-statement-a13bc5173ee9.

Theobald, Lewis. *Double Falsehood; or the Distrest Lovers*. London: J. Watts, 1728.

Thomas, Erik R. "Phonological and Phonetic Characteristics of African American Vernacular English." *Language and Linguistics Compass* 1, no. 5 (2007): 450–75.

Thomas, Robert Mcg., Jr. "Jules Davids Dies at 75; Helped Kennedy with 'Profiles' Book." *New York Times*, December 12, 1996, sec. B, p. 24.

Thomas, Steve. *JonBenét: Inside the Ramsey Murder Investigation*. New York: St. Martin's Press, 2000.

Thompson, Jeffrey R., and John Rasp. "Did C. S. Lewis Write the 'The Dark Tower'? An Examination of the Small-Sample Properties of the Thisted-Efron Test of Authorship." *Austrian Journal of Statistics* 38, no. 2 (2009): 71–82.

Thompson, Ruth Plumly. "How I Came to Write Nineteen of the Oz Books." *The Baum Bugle* 1, no. 2 (October 1957).

Time. "Radio: Where Are You From?" May 6, 1940.

———. "Education: Madison's Avenue." September 21, 1962.

Time Staff. "Here's Donald Trump's Presidential Announcement Speech." June 16, 2015. https://time.com/3923128/donald-trump-announcement-speech.

Toobin, Jeffrey. "Amanuensis." *The New Yorker*, May 5, 2008.

True Crime Detectives Guild. *Listen Carefully! Truth and Evidence in the JonBenet Ramsey Case*. ALLFORONE, 2016.

Trump, Donald J., and Tony Schwartz. *Trump: The Art of the Deal*. New York: Random House, 1987.

Tuhy, Carrie. "Elena Ferrante's Publishers Discuss Her New Novel." *Publishers Weekly*, April 17, 2020.

Turpin, Zachary. "Thomas Jefferson Snodgrass Goes to England." *American Literary Realism* 49, no. 2 (2017): 175–79.

Tuzzi, Arjuna, and Michele A. Cortelazzo. "It Takes Many Hands to Draw Elena Ferrante's Profile." In *Drawing Elena Ferrante's Profile: Workshop Proceedings*, edited by Arjuna Tuzzi and Michele A. Corelazzo, 9–29. Padua: Padova University Press, 2018.

———. "What Is Elena Ferrante? A Comparative Analysis of a Secretive Bestselling Italian Writer." *Digital Scholarship in the Humanities* 33, no. 3 (2018): 685–702.

Twain, Mark. *The Adventures of Huckleberry Finn.* New York: Harper & Brothers, 1884.

———. "The Private History of a Campaign That Failed." *The Century Illustrated Monthly Magazine* 31, no. 2 (1885): 193–204. https://archive.org/details/century illustratv31newy/page/n205/mode/2up.

UCL Survey of English Usage. "Jan Svartvik." https://www.ucl.ac.uk/english-usage /about/svartvik.htm.

United States Department of Justice. *Amerithrax Investigative Summary,* February 19, 2010. https://www.justice.gov/archive/amerithrax/docs/amx-investigative-sum mary.pdf.

United States Government Accountability Office. *Anthrax: Agency Approaches to Validation and Statistical Analyses Could Be Improved.* December 2014. https:// www.gao.gov/products/gao-15–80.

Valla, Lorenzo. *On the Donation of Constantine.* Translated by G. W. Bowersock. Cambridge, MA: Harvard University Press, 2008.

Van Gelder, Lawrence. "Harper Lee Writes Again." *New York Times,* June 28, 2006.

Van Nes, Jermo. "On the Origin of the Pastorals' Authenticity Criticism: A 'New' Perspective." *New Testament Studies* 62, no. 2 (2016): 315–20.

———. "Hapax Legomena in Disputed Pauline Letters: A Reassessment." *Zeitschrift für die Neutestamentliche Wissenschaft* 109, no. 1 (2018): 118–37.

Vaux, Bert, and Scott Golder. "How Do You Pronounce Mary / Merry / Marry?" *The Harvard Dialect Survey.* Cambridge, MA: Harvard University Linguistics Department, 2003.

Vickers, Brian. "'Counterfeiting' Shakespeare: Evidence, Authorship, and John Ford's 'Funerall Elegye.'" Cambridge: Cambridge University Press, 2002.

Voragine, Jacobus, de. *The Golden Legend: Readings on the Saints,* translated by William G. Ryan. Princeton, NJ: Princeton University Press, 2012.

Wade, John Donald. "The Authorship of David Crockett's 'Autobiography.'" *Georgia Historical Quarterly* 6, no. 3 (1922): 265–68.

Wallace, Mike, and Gary P. Gates. *Between You and Me: A Memoir.* New York: Hyperion, 2005.

Wallis, Michael. *David Crockett: The Lion of the West.* New York: Norton, 2011.

Washington Post. "Wanted Anonymous: Sure, They Deny It. But if They Didn't Do It, Who Did?" February 2, 1996, B01.

Watson, Carly. "From Restorer to Editor: The Evolution of Lewis Theobald's Textual Critical Practice." *The Library* 20, no. 2 (2019): 147–71.

Watson, Melvin R. "'Wuthering Heights' and the Critics." *The Trollopian* 3, no. 4 (1949): 243–63.

Watt, W. S. "The Text of the Pseudo-Ciceronian Epistula ad Octavianum." *The Classical Quarterly* 8, no. 1/2 (1958): 25–31.

Waxman, Olivia B. "Fact-Checking 'The Ballad of Davy Crockett.'" *Time*, August 17, 2016.

Wecter, Dixon. "Mark Twain: 'The Letters of Quintus Curtius Snodgrass.'" *New England Quarterly* 20, no. 2 (1947): 269–71.

Whalen, Terence. "Poe and the American Publishing Industry." In *A Historical Guide to Edgar Allan Poe*, edited by J. Gerald Kennedy, 69–93. Oxford: Oxford University Press, 2001.

———. "Average Racism: Poe, Slavery, and the Wages of Literary Nationalism." In *Romancing the Shadow: Poe and Race*, edited by J. Gerald Kennedy and Liliane Weissberg, 3–40. Oxford: Oxford University Press, 2001.

Wiesman, Aly. "Samuel L. Jackson Slams Obama: 'Stop Trying to Relate and Be More Presidential.'" *Insider*, September 24, 2013.

Wigler, Stephen. "Requiem for an Elegy Essay: Attributing the 1612 'A Funeral Elegy' to Shakespeare Is Folly for a Very good Reason: It's Too Bad." *Baltimore Sun*, April 8, 1996.

Williams, Angie, Peter Garrett, and Nikolas Coupland. "Dialect Recognition." In *Handbook of Perceptual Dialectology, Volume 1*, edited by Dennis R. Preston, 345–58. Amsterdam: John Benjamins, 1999.

Williams, C. B. "Studies in the History of Probability and Statistics: IV. A Note on an Early Statistical Study of Literary Style." *Biometrika* 43 (1956): 248–56.

———. "Mendenhall's Studies of Word-Length Distribution in the Works of Shakespeare and Bacon." *Biometrika* 62 (1975): 207–12.

Williams, Sally. "Da Vinci Code Expert Needs Your Text Messages." *WalesOnline*, May 9, 2009. https://www.walesonline.co.uk/news/wales-news/da-vinici-code-expert -needs-2104536.

Willman, David. *The Mirage Man: Bruce Ivins, the Anthrax Attacks, and America's Rush to War*. New York: Random House, 2011.

Wilpon, Jay G., and Claus N. Jacobsen. "A Study of Speech Recognition for Children and the Elderly." In *1996 IEEE International Conference on Acoustics, Speech, and Signal Processing Conference Proceedings*. Vol. 1, 349–52. New York: IEEE, 1996.

Wilson, James Southall. "Unpublished Letters of Edgar Allan Poe." *The Century Magazine* 107 (March 1924): 652–56.

Wiltshire, Irene. "Speech in 'Wuthering Heights': Joseph's Dialect and Charlotte's Emendations." *Brontë Studies* 30, no. 1 (2005):19–29.

Wiltshire, John. "Jane Austen: Computation or Criticism?" *Cambridge Quarterly* 17, no. 4 (1988): 369–81.

Winterson, Jeanette. "The Malice and Sexism behind the 'Unmasking' of Elena Ferrante." *The Guardian*, October 16, 2016.

Wisnicki, Adrian. "A Trove of New Works by Thomas Pynchon? 'Bomarc Service News' Rediscovered." *Pynchon Notes* 46 (2001): 9–34.

Wolfram, Walt, and Natale Schilling. *American English: Dialects and Variation*. 3rd ed. New York: Wiley, 2016.

Wood, Barry. *Invented History, Fabricated Power: The Narrative Shaping of Civilization and Culture*. London: Anthem Press, 2020.

Wood, James. "Women on the Verge." *The New Yorker*, January 13, 2013.

Woods, Laura. "25 of the Highest-Grossing Broadway Shows Ever." April 1, 2021. https://www.yahoo.com/lifestyle/25-highest-grossing-broadway-shows-2300 20553.html.

Workman, W. P. "The Hapax Legomena of St. Paul." *The Expository Times* (1896): 418–19.

Wroe, Nicholas. "James Patterson: A Life in Writing." *The Guardian*, May 11, 2013.

Wyler, Grace. "CREEPY: Mitt Romney Is Asking for Hugs from Southern Girls." *Insider*, March 13, 2012. https://www.businessinsider.com/mitt-romney-asks-for -hugs-from-southern-girls-2012-3.

Yates, F. "George Udny Yule 1871–1951." *Obituary Notices of the Fellows of the Royal Society* 8, no. 21 (1952): 308–23.

Yule, G. Udny. "On Sentence-Length as a Statistical Characteristic of Style in Prose: With Application to Two Cases of Disputed Authorship." *Biometrika* 30, no. 3/4 (1939): 363–90.

———. *The Statistical Study of Literary Vocabulary*. Cambridge: Cambridge University Press, 1944.

Zettle, Jennifer. "UW Linguists Analyze Palin's Accent." *The Badger Herald*, November 17, 2009.

Index

Abrams, Richard, 133
accents, 10–13
Adair, Douglass, 34
Adams, Charles, 51
Adams, Henry, 51–53
Adams, John, 157
African American Vernacular English, 13
age: and language use, 13; and voice, 2
Agen, Jarrod, 136
Ainsworth, Janet, 139
Airoldi, Edoardo, 155
à Kempis, Thomas, 24–27
Akers, Darren, 103–5
Alfonso V, king of Aragon, 111
Ambrose, saint, 110
anachronisms, analysis of, 111–12, 115, 127
Anderson, Annelise, 155
Anderson, Frank Maloy, 51
Anderson, Martin, 155
anonymous authorship, 41–62, 135–39
anthrax attacks, 95, 147–51
artificial intelligence, 171. *See also* machine learning
Assad, Ayaad, 149
Atkinson, Edward, 22
Atticus, Titus Pomponius, 113
attribution, 38, 171

Austen, Jane, 36–40, 77
authenticity, speech and, 14–18
Ayers, Nick, 137

Bacon, Francis, 22, 25
Bailey, S. A., 33
Barker, Nicolas, 72
Barlow, Samuel, 53
Baronchelli, Andrea, 140
Baronius, Caesar, cardinal, 112
Bates, Allan, 125
Baum, Lyman Frank, 63–67
Bayesian approach, 35, 156
Belle, Pearl, 80
Benson, Edward Frederic, 76
Bernard, saint, 24
Biden, Joe, 157
Binongo, José, 64–66
Bird, Robert Montgomery, 69
Birmingham Six, 146–47
Bitcoin, ix
black-box problem, 171–72
Bloch, Bernard, 5
Bloom, Harold, 60
Boaden, James, 119
Bolton, John, 136
Bomarc, 54–55
BookShots, 85

bootstrap consensus tree, 86, 164
Boswell, James, 118
Boyd, Ryan, 60–62
Brashear, Minnie, 122–24
Bremberg, Andrew, 137
Brinegar, Claude, 124
Brokaw, Tom, 148
Brontë family works, 75–79
Brooks, Richard, 46
Brown, Dan, 106–7
bucket/pail, 8–10
Burke, Edmund, 158
Burns, Ken, 128
Burr, Aaron, 32
Burrows, John, 36–40
Busa, Roberto, 39
Bush, George H. W., 157
Bush, George W., 15–16, 157

Caesar, Julius, 115–16
Callegari, Judith, 46
Capote, Truman, 79–83
Cardenno, 58–62
Carter, Mary Ida, 81
Carter, Michele, 76–77
Carter, Tonja, 81
Chase, Salmon, 52–53
Child, Lydia Maria, 69
Chilton, Thomas, 162–64
Christie, Ethel, 90
Christie, John, 89–93
Churchill, Winston, 166
Cicero, Marcus Tullius, 113–17
Clark, Jonathan, 159–61
Clark, William, 162–65
Clayton, Augustin, 163–64
Clemens, Orion, 125
Clemens, Samuel, 121–25
Clifford, Clark, 156
Clinton, Bill, 23, 41, 84, 87, 157

Clinton, Hillary, 41
cluster analysis, 164
Coates, Victoria, 138
Coats, Dan, 136
code-switching, 17
Coleridge, Samuel Taylor, 25
collaborations, Patterson and, 83–87
Collins, Paul, 67–71
collocations, 143
Common Sense (Paine), 157–58
computational stylistics, 37–38
computerization, 34, 36–37
concealed authorship, 41–62
concordances: of Aquinas, 39; of Austen,
    36; Biblical, 28–29; Federalist, 34
confessions, analysis of, 89–93
Conrad, Joseph, 61
Consolatio, 113–17
Constantine the Great, 109–13
Cooper, Anderson, 138
Cooper, James Fenimore, 68, 163–64
Corbin, Richard, 129
corpus, 31; Baum, 65; Crockett, 163–64;
    Latin/Neo-Latin, 115; Padova Italian,
    140–41; Paine, 159; Poe, 70; Reagan,
    155–56
corpus linguistics, 91
correlation matrices, 37
Cortelazzo, Michele, 140
Coulthard, Malcolm, 146
Crantor, philosopher, 113
criminal cases, 89–107
Crockett, Davy, 161–65
Crofts, Daniel, 52
The Cuckoo's Calling, 45–49
Cuomo, Mario, 41
cusum technique, 73, 144–47

Da, Nan, 39–40
Dabney, Thomas, 122

Dante Alighieri, 110
The Dark Tower, 71–75, 146
Daschle, Tom, 147
Daubert standard, 147
Davids, Julie, 166
Dearden, William, 76
Deep Throat, 135
degli Uberti, Bernard, 24
de Jonge, Peter, 84, 86
Delta, 39–40, 47, 52; versus cusum, 146
De Luctu, 113
de Morgan, Augustus, 20–21
Denslow, W. W., 63
de Scudéry, Madeleine, 41
DeStefano, Johnny, 137
de Vere, Edward, 132
Diary of a Public Man, 49–53
Dickens, Charles, 21, 125
discriminant analysis, 130
disputed authorship, 22, 63–87; *The Federalist Papers,* 32–36; *The Imitation of Christ,* 23–27; letters of Paul, 27–31
Donation of Constantine, 109–13
Double Falsehood, 58–62
Douglas, Stephen, 50
Drayton, William, 70
Drew, Edward, 132
Dudley, Henry Bate, 119
Dumas, Alexandre, 85

Eder, Maciej, 39, 81–82
Elliott, Ward, 134
Ellis, Robinson, 114–15
errors, in stylometry, 131–51
ethics, and unmasking authors, 143
Eugenius IV, pope, 111
Eusebius, 109–11
Evans, Beryl, 89

Evans, Geraldine, 90
Evans, Timothy John, 89–93
experimental psychology, 60–62
expert evidence, 146–47

false positives, 131–51
Faulkner, William, 82
Feder, Ned, 44
The Federalist Papers, 32–36
Felt, Mark, 135
Ferrante, Elena, 139–40
Fielding, Henry, 38
Fielding, Sarah, 38
Fienberg, Stephen, 35
fingerprints, linguistic, 3–4. *See also* linguistic identity
Firth, Chris, 76
Fitzgerald, James, 5, 96–97
Fletcher, John, 59–62
Flowers, Gennifer, 41
Flyn, Cal, 47–48
Ford, John, 134
foreign accent syndrome, 11
forensic linguistics, 89–107, 146–47
forgeries, 109–30
Forney, John, 52
Forsyth, Richard, 115, 159
Foster, Donald, 42–43, 131–34, 148–49
4-grams, 74
Fowler, Alastair, 73
Fowles, John, 143
Francis of Assisi, saint, 24
Franklin, Ben, 159
frequency counts, Google and, 105
Frye standard, 147
Fuller, Simon, 85–86
function words, common, 30, 34, 65, 164
A Funerall Elegye, 131–35

Galbraith, Robert, 45–49
Galella, Luigi, 139
Gallagher, Gary, 128, 130
Gardner, Martin, 66
Gaskell, Elizabeth, 77, 79
Gatti, Claudio, 140
"g"-dropping, 15–18
gender: and Brontë authorship, 76; and
    Ferrante authorship, 142–43; and
    speech, 12–13
genre: and comparisons, 77–78; and
    linguistic identity, 53
geography: and accents, 12;
    and speech, 5–10; and status, 12
Gersen, John, 24
Gerson, Jean Charlier de, 25–26
ghost writers, 153–69
Giuliani, Rudy, 136
Golden Legend, 110–11
Goldstein, Ann, 140
Goodfellow, John, 77
Google, 105
Go Set a Watchman, 79–83
Gossage, Christopher, 46
Grabenstein, Chris, 84
Grisham, John, 84
Gross, Andrew, 86
Grunwald, Lisa, 43

Haley, Nikki, 138
Hamilton, Alexander, 32–36, 159
Hammond, Brean, 60
Hannaford, Peter, 155–56
hapax legomenon, term, 29
Harrison, James, 69
Harrison, Percival, 29
Harrison, Walter, 128–30
Hart, Joseph, 22
Harvard Dialect Survey, 8
Harvey, James E., 52–53

Hassall, Anthony, 38
Hatfill, Steven, 149–50
Hawthorne, Nathaniel, 68, 163–64
Hayes, Chris, 14
The Heart of a Soldier, 126–30
hendiadys, 134
Herper, Matthew, ix–x
The History of Cardenio, 58–62
Hobbes, Chuck, 155
Hoffman, Charles Fenno, 69
Hohoff, Tay, 81–82
Holcomb, Arthur, 166
Holmes, David, 52–53, 115, 128–30,
    159–60, 164
Holmes, Elizabeth, 17
Holtzmann, Heinrich, 28
Honce, Charles, 122
Hooper, Walter, 71–75
Hoosier apex, 12
Hull, William Doyle, 70
Hunter, Karen, 14
Hurlbert, William Henry, 52–53

idiolects, 4–5
The Imitation of Christ, 23–27
in-group bias, 10–11
initial vowel words, 145
insecurity, linguistic, 11–12
Ireland, Samuel, 117–21
Ireland, William-Henry, 117–21
Irving, Washington, 68
isoglosses, 7–10
Ivins, Bruce, 150–51

Jackson, Samuel L., 15
Java Graphical Authorship Attribution
    Program (JGAAP), 47, 68
Jay, John, 32, 159
Jeantel, Rachel, 13
Jefferson, Thomas, 159

Jerome, saint, 110
Johnson, Alison, 146
Johnson, Walter, 166
Jones, Carla Faust, 73
Jonson, Ben, 133
Juola, Patrick, 47–49, 139

Kaczynski, David, 95
Kaczynski, Theodore John, 93–97
Kaczynski, Wanda, 97
K characteristic, 26
Kelly, John, 136
Kemble, John Philip, 120–21
Kendall, Amos, 51
Kennedy, John F., 165–69
Kennedy, John Pendleton, 69
Kennedy, Joseph P., 167
Kennedy, Richard, 134
Kim, Peter, 84
King, Horatio, 50
King, Stephen, 85
Kissinger, Henry, 136
Klein, Joe, 43–45
Knight, India, 46
Krock, Arthur, 166–67
Kurath, Hans, 9
Kushner, Jared, 136
Kusnet, David, 44, 137

Labov, William, 15
Lactantius, 114
Lafayette, marquis de, 159–61
Lamb, Charles, 25
language acquisition, 10
Lauredanus (Giovanni Loredan), 115–16
Leahy, Pat, 147
Ledwidge, Michael, 84
Lee, Alice Finch, 80–81
Lee, Diana, 107
Lee, Harper, 79–83

Lee, Robert E., 126, 129
Leisy, Ernest, 122
lemma, 30
L'Engle, Madeleine, 72, 74
Lewis, C. S., 71–75
Lewis, Warren, 71
lexical diversity, 26
Lincoln, Abraham, 50, 122
Lindskoog, Kathryn, 72, 74–75, 146
Linguistic Atlas of New England (LANE), 9
linguistic identity, 1–18, 171–72
Linguistic Inquiry and Word Count (LIWC), 60–61
Lippard, George, 68
Literary Detective program, 73
Longstreet, Augustus, 69
Longstreet, James, 126
Loreto, Vittorio, 140
low-base-rate tells, 61
Lozada, Carlos, 137
Luce, Henry, 166
Luther, Martin, 112
Lutosławski, Wincenty, x

MacAleenan, Kevin, 138
Macaulay, Thomas Babington, 25
machine learning, 56, 141, 171; drawbacks of, 171–72; supervised, 56–57, 61
Madison, James, 32–36, 159
Maguire, Gregory, 64
Malham-Dembleby, John, 76
Malone, Edmond, 120
Manhunt (TV show), 5
Marchington, Tony, 72, 74–75
Marklund, Liza, 84
Marlowe, Christopher, 23
Marmo, Marcella, 140
Martin, Trayvon, 13

Martineau, Harriet, 77
Mary/marry/merry, 6, 8
Matthew, Gervase, 72–73
Mattis, Jim, 136–37
Mays, D'Arcy, 64–66
McCain, John, 136
McCarthy, Rachel, 78
McClaughry, John, 155
McMaster, H. R., 137
McNamara, Robert, 167
McWhorter, John, 14
Melville, Herman, 164
Mendenhall, Thomas Corwin, 19–23
Merriam, Thomas, 144
Merton, Thomas, 23
metaphors for linguistic identity, 1–5
Michaelson, Sidney, 30, 144
Michelson, Albert, 20
Mill, John Stuart, 22
Millican, Peter, 48
Mills, Marja, 81
misattributions, 109–30
Monroe, James, 158
Monsarrat, Gilles, 134
Morrison, Toni, 70
Morton, Andrew, 30, 73, 143–47
Moseley, Humphrey, 59
Mosteller, Fred, 33–36
multivariate analyses, 27, 31, 37, 141
Muretus (Marc-Antoine Muret), 115–17
Muth, Katie, 56–58

Nakamoto, Satoshi, ix–x
Nance, John, 60
Napoleon Bonaparte, 158
Navarro, Peter, 137–38
Neal, John, 68
Nepos, 116
Newhouse, Si, 168
Newman, Omarosa Manigault, 137

New York Times regional dialect quiz, 6–7
n-gams, 47
Nicholas of Cusa, 110
Nicholas V, pope, 112
Nichols, Mike, 42, 45
Nielsen, Kirstjen, 138
Nofzinger, Lynn, 155
Noonan, Peggy, 15
Northern Cities Vowel Shift, 12

Oakes, Michael, 74–75
Obama, Barack, 14, 16–17, 157
O'Connor, Flannery, 82
Olsson, John, 3–4, 104–7
1-grams, 73
O'Sullivan, James, 78, 85–87
Owens, Maureen Casey, 44–45

Padova Italian Corpus, 140–41
Paetro, Maxine, 84, 86
Page, Evelyn, 51
Paine, Thomas, 157–61
Palin, Sarah, 15–16
Parmet, Herbert, 167
Parton, Dolly, 84
Patrick, Bill, 149
Patrik, Linda, 95
Patterson, James, 83–87
Paulding, James, 162
Paulding-Drayton Review, 69–71
Paul the Apostle, letters of, 27–31
Pearson, Drew, 167
Pearson, Karl, 25
Peck, Gregory, 80
Pecock, Reginald, 110–11
peculiarities, Lutosławski on, x
Pence, Mike, 136
Pender, Dorsey, 129
Pennebaker, James, 13, 60–62
Perdue, Lewis, 106–7

Persons, Archulus, 80
Peter, William, 131–34
Petrarch, 113
Pickett, George Edward, 126–30
Pickett, LaSalle Corbell, 126–30
Pierce, Edward L., 51
plagiarism, 44, 128
Plato, x
Poe, Edgar Allen, 67–71
Poe, William Henry Leonard, 68–69
police register, 93
politicians: and collaboration, 84–87; and speech, 14–18
Pope, Alexander, 59
Price, Benjamin, 51
Primary Colors, 41–45
principal component analysis (PCA), 37–38
privacy, and unmasking authors, 142
Profiles in Courage, 165–69
proportionate word pairs, 143
Pynchon, Thomas, 54–58

Q, ix
Quinn, Sally, 44

race: Lee and, 79, 81, 83; Poe and, 70–71; and speech, 13
radio addresses, analysis of, 154–57
Raja, Anita, 140, 142–43
Ramsey, John, 98, 102–3
Ramsey, JonBenét, 97–103, 148–49
Ramsey, Patsy, 98, 102–3
ransom notes, analysis of, 98–103
Rasp, John, 73–74
Reagan, Ronald, 153–57
regional speech, 5–10, 102
register shifts, 3–4
Research Triangle, North Carolina, 12
Resistance editorial, 135–39

Riccobonus, Antonius, 114–227
Rice, Allen, 50
Ridgely, J. V., 70
Rights of Man, 158–61
Ritter, Conrad, x
Robespierre, Maximilien, 158
roman à clef, 41
Romney, Mitt, 15–16
Roosevelt, Franklin, 154
Rosenbaum, Rod, 60
Rosenthal, Bernard, 70
Rowling, J. K., 45–49, 142
Ryan, David, 107
Rybicki, Jan, 39, 81–82, 142–43

Sage, Evan, 115
Sallust, 115–16
Salsburg, David and Dena, 163
Samara, Ferris, 164
Santagata, Marco, 140
Savoy, Jacques, 31, 141
Schleiermacher, Friedrich, 28
Schlesinger, Arthur, 166
Schmidt, Johann, 28
Schöberlein, Stefan, 70–71
Schwarz, Tony, 168–69
Sedgwick, Catherine Maria, 69
Seneca, 115–16
sentence length, average, 25–27, 33, 145
settlement patterns, 7–9
Seward, William, 50–51
Shaara, Michael, 128
Shackford, James, 162
Shakespeare, William, 2, 4, 107; alleged lost works of, 58–62, 117–21, 131–35, 144; debate on authorship, 22–23, 132; hapaxes in, 29
Shaw, George Bernard, 6
Shaxicon, 132–33
Shelton, Thomas, 58

Sheridan, Richard, 118
shibboleths, 8
Shuy, Roger, 96–97
signatures, 4–5
Signature Stylometric System, 48
Sigonio, Carlo, 114–17
Simmerson, Howard, 103–7
Simms, William Gilmore, 68
Skinner, Kiron, 154–55
Smith, Henry Lee, Jr., 6
Smith, Mark, 14
Smith, Richard Penn, 163–64
Smith, Wilfred, 143–44
Snodgrass, Guy, 137
Snodgrass, Quintus Curtius, 122–25
Snodgrass, Thomas Jefferson, 122
Sorenson, Ted, 166–69
Southern dialect, 11–12
Starnone, Domenico, 139–43
status, accents and, 11
Stepien, Bill, 137
Stern, Tiffany, 60
Stewart, Charles E., 50
Stewart, Walter, 44
Streidfeld, David, 44
Strong, George Templeton, 52–53
style, 2
stylistic affinities, x
stylometry, ix–xi, 171–72; beginnings of, 19–40, 109–13; challenges in, 172; errors in, 131–51; term, x
Styron, William, 82
Sumner, Charles, 51
supervised machine learning, 56–57, 61
Svartvik, Jan, 91–93
Sylvester I, pope, 109–11
Szalai, Jennifer, 137

Tacitus, 115–16
Taft, Robert, 165

Tankard, Jim, 73
Taylor, Gary, 60
Taylor, John M., 52
Taylor, Miles, 138–39
technical writing, Pynchon and, 54–58
texts, analysis of, 103–7
Thackeray, William Makepeace, 22
Theobald, Lewis, 58, 61
Thomas, Evan, 166
Thomas Aquinas, 39
Thompson, Jeffrey, 73–74
Thompson, Ruth Plumly, 64–67
Tiraboschi, Girolamo, 114
tokens, 26
Tolkien, J. R. R., 73–74
tone, 2
Traversari, Ambrose, 114
Trump, Donald, 157, 168–69, 172
Trump, Ivanka, 136
Tse, Emily, 115
Tucker, Glenn, 127–28
Tucker, Nathaniel Beverly, 70
Turner, Julie, 103–7
Tuzzi, Arjuna, 140
Twain, Mark, 14–15, 121–25
tweets, analysis of, 172
2-grams, 73
types, 26

Unabomber, 5, 93–97
univariate analysis, 27
upspeak, 12
USAMRIID, 148–50

Valenza, Robert, 134
Valla, Lorenzo, 111–12
Van Buren, Martin, 162
van Nes, Jermo, 29
Vettori, 116–17

Vianello, Francesco, 114
Vickers, Brian, 134
vocabulary richness, 26
vocal fry, 12–13
voice, 1–3; Austen and, 37; shifts in, 3–4
Vollman, William T., 95
Vortigern and Rowena, 117–21

Wallace, David, 34–36
Wallace, David Foster, 83
Wallace, Mike, 167
Ward, Samuel, 51–53
Warton, Joseph, 118
Washington, George, 158–59
Wayne, John, 165
Weed, Thurlow, 51
Welles, Gideon, 52–53
Welty, Eudora, 82
"Where Are You From?" (radio show), 5–6

Wicked, 64
Wigler, Stephen, 133
Williams, Frederick, 33
Williams, Tennessee, 2
Willis, Irene Cooper, 76
Willis, N. P., 69
Willman, David, 151
Wisnicki, Adrian, 55
The Wizard of Oz, 63–67
Wolf, Christa, 142
word length, average, 20–21, 124
Workman, Walter, 29
Wyler, Grace, 15

Yule, George Udny, 25–27

Zeta, 39
Zimmerman, George, 13
z-scores, 39

About the Author

Roger Kreuz is an associate dean in the College of Arts and Sciences and professor of psychology at the University of Memphis. He earned his doctoral degree in cognitive psychology from Princeton University. Kreuz is the author of five other books on language and communication: *Becoming Fluent: How Cognitive Science Can Help Adults Learn a Foreign Language, Getting Through: The Pleasures and Perils of Cross-Cultural Communication, Changing Minds: How Aging Affects Language and How Language Affects Aging, Irony and Sarcasm,* and *Failure to Communicate: Why We Misunderstand What We Hear, Read, and See.* Translations of these books have appeared in Korean, Russian, Turkish, Japanese, Chinese, and Spanish.